SPECTRUM
Reading

Grade 5

School Specialty
Publishing

Copyright © 2007 School Specialty Publishing. Published by Spectrum, an imprint of
School Specialty Publishing, a member of the School Specialty Family.

Send all inquiries to:
School Specialty Publishing
8720 Orion Place
Columbus, OH 43240-2111

ISBN 0-7696-3875-9

3 4 5 6 7 8 9 10 POH 11 10 09 08 07

Index of Skills

Reading Grade 5

Numerals indicate the exercise pages on which these skills appear.

Vocabulary Skills

Abbreviations 15, 27, 59, 75, 81, 147, 151

Affixes 5, 9, 23, 41, 53, 61, 71, 83, 89, 93, 97, 101, 105, 117, 133, 137, 145

Antonyms 7, 19, 29, 43, 47, 53, 63, 71, 79, 95, 119, 131, 139, 145, 149

Classification 3, 9, 29, 57, 87, 99, 105, 127, 141

Complex Word Families 25, 41, 59, 137

Compound Words 3, 7, 13, 21, 37, 49, 55, 57, 67, 77, 87, 109, 111, 123, 129, 135

Homographs/Multiple Meaning 13, 23, 35, 39, 45, 61, 65, 81, 99, 101, 103, 107, 121, 129

Homophones 15, 31, 37, 41, 51, 69, 77, 89, 91, 99, 103, 107, 111, 117, 125, 131, 149

Idiomatic and Figurative Language 17, 19, 31, 33, 49, 61, 71, 77, 83, 109, 111, 119, 123, 147

Multisyllabic Words 11, 17, 43, 55, 57, 67, 73, 85, 129, 143

Possessives 3, 19, 27, 35, 51, 55, 63, 69, 79, 91, 95, 103, 115, 121, 139, 147

Sight Vocabulary *all activity pages*

Synonyms 5, 11, 25, 29, 49, 53, 71, 75, 97, 113, 119, 123, 133, 139, 149

Word Meaning from Context *all activity pages*

Reading Skills

Author's Purpose 19, 29, 39, 47, 63, 75, 85, 95, 101, 113, 123, 129, 141

Cause and Effect 5, 7, 9, 13, 21, 33, 35, 37, 45, 51, 63, 67, 81, 87, 91, 93, 99, 101, 105, 111, 113, 115, 117, 119, 123, 125, 129, 135, 141, 143, 147

Character Analysis 15, 27, 53, 71, 77, 89, 99, 111, 121, 127, 137, 143, 149

Comparing and Contrasting 17, 33, 37, 43, 45, 49, 51, 65, 69, 81, 85, 95, 99, 105, 117, 125, 131, 135, 137, 141

Context Clues 29, 37, 45, 65, 75, 95, 105, 125, 141, 151

Drawing Conclusions 7, 11, 17, 25, 31, 33, 37, 41, 43, 53, 57, 59, 61, 67, 73, 77, 79, 87, 89, 91, 93, 97, 99, 101, 105, 109, 111, 113, 115, 121, 123, 125, 133, 135, 143, 147, 149, 151

Fact and Opinion 3, 11, 25, 61, 73, 85, 97, 115, 129, 139, 145

Facts and Details *all activity pages*

Fantasy and Reality 49, 55, 71, 99, 103, 137

Main Idea 5, 35, 61, 73, 93, 109, 127

Mood and Tone 11, 17, 29, 53, 91, 111

Persuasive Text 21, 43, 75, 95, 103

Predicting Outcomes 5, 19, 21, 25, 37, 43, 55, 61, 65, 71, 91, 99, 109, 123, 137

Prior Knowledge 25, 43, 51, 53, 101, 115, 131, 135

Recognizes Features of Familiar Genres 19, 31, 39, 53, 57, 59, 63, 81, 93, 103, 107, 111, 115, 127, 151

Recognizes Story's Problem 11, 17, 33, 47, 51, 115, 129, 143

Sequence 27, 39, 53, 67, 79, 89, 109, 121, 123, 143

Shows Comprehension by Identifying Answers in Text *all activity pages*

Summarizing 21, 31, 41, 51, 59, 83, 95, 105, 125, 139,

Understand and Identify Simple Literary Terms 19, 27, 31, 55, 71, 77, 79, 91, 103, 119, 133, 149

Study Skills

Alphabetical Order 13, 105, 117, 137

Charts, Graphs, and Maps 9, 27, 31, 45, 47, 57, 65, 67, 75, 77, 101, 129, 135, 149

Dictionary Use 3, 17, 19, 49, 53, 63, 71, 79, 83, 85, 97, 99, 105, 109, 115, 125, 137, 143

Following Directions *all activity pages*

Life-Skills Materials 15, 23, 41, 51, 59, 91, 119, 129, 133, 147, 151

Outlines 21, 33, 69, 107

Parts of a Book 11, 39, 73, 95, 123, 145

Reference Materials 5, 7, 29, 37, 43, 55, 87, 93, 111, 113, 121, 139, 141

Table of Contents

A New Mate

What would it be like to live in Australia?

1 "I think most of you have already met our new student, Gemma," said Ms. Dimitri to her class. "As you know, she has recently moved here from Australia. I know you all have lots of questions about Australia, and Gemma has said she'd be happy to answer them. We can also try to give her an idea of what life is like here in Massachusetts."

2 Gemma was a tall girl with thick, dark brown hair. She had pale blue eyes, and there was a dusting of freckles across her nose. She smiled shyly at the class. "I'm very happy to be here," she said. "Everyone has been really nice to me. It feels like I've been here longer than a week already."

3 Ms. Dimitri smiled. "I'm glad to hear it. We're excited to have you here, Gemma. Before we get started, why don't you tell everyone where you lived in Australia."

4 "My family lived in Queensland," began Gemma. "It is one of Australia's six states, and it's located in the northeast part of the continent. Queensland is the second largest state in Australia. It's a bit more than twice as big as Texas."

5 "What is the weather like there?" asked Kayla. "Do you have cold, snowy winters like we do here?"

6 "Actually, because Australia is in the Southern Hemisphere, the seasons are the reverse of what they are in the United States," said Gemma. "Queensland is in a tropical part of Australia, so it doesn't get very cold. In January, which is summertime, it is in the 80s and 90s. In July, which is wintertime, it might be in the 60s. Queensland gets a lot of rain, and I won't miss that at all. I can't wait until it snows here this winter! I've never built a snowman or gone sledding before."

7 "Queensland is near Australia's Great Barrier Reef," Ms. Dimitri told the class. "Gemma, can you tell us a little about it?"

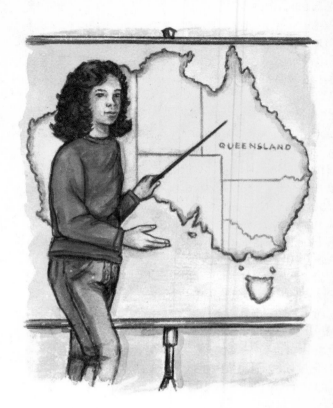

8 Gemma nodded. "The Great Barrier Reef is the largest coral reef in the world. It lies off the coast of Queensland and is more than 1,200 miles long. It is home to all kinds of animal and plant life. It is an amazing place to go scuba diving."

9 Vijay raised his hand. "Can you teach us how to say some words in Australian?" he asked.

10 "Most people in Australia speak English," said Gemma. "But we do have some different words and expressions than you do in America. For example, the word for *friend* is *mate*. *Bonza* means *very good*. *Umbrella* is *brolly*, and *honest* is *fair dinkum*."

11 "Is there another word or expression for *thank you*?" asked Ms. Dimitri.

12 "Yes, *ta* means *thank you*."

13 "Gemma, you have given us an excellent idea of what it is like to live in Australia. *Ta*, Gemma. We're so glad to have you in our class!"

Vocabulary Skills

Write the words from the story that have the meanings below.

1. just before the present time

   _____
   Par. 1

2. one half of Earth when divided by the equator

   _____
   Par. 6

3. opposite

   _____
   Par. 6

4. specific words or phrases

   _____
   Par. 10

In each row, circle the word that does not belong.

5. Australia   Texas   Massachusetts   Ohio

6. freezing   winter   sledding   tropical

7. brolly   bonza   idea   mate

Find the compound words from the selection that contain the words below.

8. north _____
   Par. 4

9. summer _____
   Par. 6

10. man _____
    Par. 6

When you add an apostrophe (') and the letter **s** to a singular noun, it shows that a person or thing owns something. Fill in the blanks below with the possessive form of the word in parentheses.

11. Ms. _____ class is interested in learning about Australia. (Dimitri)

12. _____ seasons are different than the seasons in the United States. (Australia)

13. _____ family lived in Queensland. (Gemma)

Reading Skills

A **fact** is something that is known to be true. An **opinion** is what a person believes. It may or may not be true. Write **F** before the sentences that are facts. Write **O** before the sentences that are opinions.

1. _____ Gemma moved to the United States from Australia.

2. _____ Queensland is more than twice as big as Texas.

3. _____ It would be exciting to visit Australia.

4. _____ The weather in Australia is more enjoyable than it is in Massachusetts.

5. _____ Australia is in the Southern Hemisphere.

6. What is the Great Barrier Reef?

   _____

7. What does *fair dinkum* mean?

   _____

Study Skills

Guide words are printed at the top of each page in a dictionary. The guide word at the left is the first word on the page. The guide word at the right is the last word on the page. Check each word that could be found on a page having the guide words shown in dark print.

1. **gown—grateful**

   _____ grape   _____ grasp   _____ going

2. **mallet—mansion**

   _____ manage   _____ mall   _____ maple

3. **reflect—relax**

   _____ reef   _____ reindeer   _____ rehearse

Australia's Giant Toads

How did cane toads get to Australia, and why do people see them as such a pest?

1   Think about toads that you may have seen in the woods, on a hike, or at a zoo. How large do you think they were? Even the largest toads probably were not as big as the cane toad. This toad, native to South America and the Caribbean, can weigh as much as four pounds!

2   In 1935, sugar cane farmers in Australia were having a problem with two types of beetles that were destroying their crops. About one hundred cane toads were shipped to Australia from Hawaii. People hoped the toads would be a solution to the problem. Unfortunately, things turned out very differently than they had anticipated. The cane toads quickly became a more annoying pest than the beetles had ever been.

3   There are several things that make the cane toad so unusual. First of all, the cane toad has almost no natural predators. If the cane toad feels threatened, it will secrete a poisonous liquid. This liquid can kill children and small animals. It can even blind an adult for several hours.

4   The cane toad is also poisonous in all stages of its life. Fish normally feed on the eggs of frogs and toads, but even the eggs of the cane toad are poisonous. Each pair of cane toads can produce more than 30,000 eggs each season. Because many of the eggs and tadpoles are able to mature, the cane toad population can grow very rapidly.

5   This is exactly what happened in Australia. Without any predators, there were suddenly thousands of cane toads in the Queensland area. People might have been more tolerant if the animals had been successful in getting rid of the sugar cane beetles. It turned out, however, that the cane toads did not have any effect on the beetles, which could easily fly out of harm's way.

6   The Australians are not quite sure how to get rid of cane toads. In fact, they continue to spread across the continent. Cane toads eat many types of Australian wildlife. They can also be dangerous to pets and children. Even so, not everyone in Australia hopes that the plans to rid the country of these animals will be successful. Some people even leave food in their backyards or adopt the giant toads as pets!

Vocabulary Skills

Write the words from the passage that have the meanings below.

1. originally from a particular place

   _____
   Par. 1

2. in danger

   _____
   Par. 3

3. to produce a liquid or other substance

   _____
   Par. 3

4. the number of people, plants, or animals in a specific place

   _____
   Par. 4

5. patient; accepting

   _____
   Par. 5

A **synonym** is a word that means the same, or almost the same, as another word. Find a synonym in the story for each of the words below.

6. irritating _____
   Par. 2

7. grow up _____
   Par. 4

8. quickly_____
   Par. 4

The suffix **-ist** means *someone who does something*. For example, a *biologist* is *someone who studies biology*. Add **ist** to each base word below. Then, use each new word in a sentence.

9. art _____

   _____

10. violin _____

    _____

11. novel _____

    _____

Reading Skills

1. Do you think cane toads will continue to be a problem in Australia? Explain your answer.

   _____

   _____

2. Why were cane toads first brought to Australia?

   _____

   _____

3. Why are there so many cane toads in Australia if only one hundred or so were originally released?

   _____

   _____

4. Check the sentence that best states the main idea of the selection.

   _____ Cane toads can weigh as much as four pounds.

   _____ Cane toads do not have any natural predators in Australia.

   _____ Cane toads were brought to Australia to eat sugar cane beetles, but they ended up becoming a dangerous pest.

Study Skills

1. If you wanted to learn more about the cane toads in Australia, check the subjects below you could use to find information in an encyclopedia.

   _____ amphibians   _____ Australia

   _____ sugar cane   _____ mammals

   _____ nonnative species   _____ toads

Aussie Animals

How are the animals in Australia different from those you might see where you live?

1   Gemma, Kayla, and Vijay were eating lunch on the small patio behind the school's cafeteria. Kayla and Vijay were asking Gemma questions about Australian animals. They couldn't believe that Gemma didn't think it was anything special to see a kangaroo hopping along the side of a road or grazing in a field.

2   "When you see something all the time," Gemma explained, "you hardly even notice it. Do you know how many times you've seen a squirrel, or a deer, or a raccoon in your life?"

3   "Of course not," said Vijay. "But seeing a kangaroo would be completely different."

4   Gemma laughed. "Not if you lived in Australia," she said.

5   "Is it true that a mother kangaroo carries her baby in her pouch?" asked Kayla.

6   "Sure," replied Gemma, pausing to take a bite of her sandwich. "Aussies call baby kangaroos *joeys*. They live in their mother's pouch until they grow a bit larger. Then, they can take care of themselves and keep up with the others in their group. Did you know that kangaroos can travel more than 30 miles per hour?"

7   "That's pretty fast!" exclaimed Vijay.

8   "Do any other animals carry their babies in a pouch?" wondered Kayla aloud.

9   "The koala and the wombat do," said Gemma. "They are marsupials like the kangaroo."

10   "I know what a koala bear is," said Vijay, "but what is a wombat?"

11   "Well, a koala isn't really a bear," Gemma explained. "People just call them that because they resemble a teddy bear. Koalas spend most of their lives sleeping. There is a type of tree called a *eucalyptus* (*yoo kah LIP tuss*) that grows in Australia. It's pretty much the only thing that koalas eat. They don't get much energy from the leaves, though, which is why they spend so much time sleeping."

12   "It sounds like they need a change in their diet," laughed Vijay. "Is the wombat similar to the koala and kangaroo?"

13   "The only real similarity is that it is a marsupial, too. Otherwise, the wombat looks like a beaver or a groundhog. It burrows underground and makes tunnels that are 10 to 15 feet long. Some people get wombats as babies and train them. I had a friend who had a very nice pet wombat named Gillian."

14   "Won't you miss the animals in Australia?" asked Kayla. "No one in Massachusetts has a wombat for a pet."

15   Gemma smiled. "I might miss them a little," she said, "but I've never seen snow. I never saw a real raccoon or a deer before I moved here. I also never saw a cardinal or a chickadee. I think Massachusetts is going to be a very interesting place to live."

16   "I guess it all depends on what you are used to," said Vijay. "But I'd take the animals of Australia over a deer any day of the week!"

Vocabulary Skills

Write the words from the story that have the meanings below.

1. an area next to a building that is often used for eating outdoors

   _____
   Par. 1

2. feeding on grass

   _____
   Par. 1

3. a type of mammal that carries its young in a pouch

   _____
   Par. 9

4. look like

   _____
   Par. 11

Words that are opposite in meaning are called **antonyms**. Read each word below. Then, write the letter of its antonym on the line beside the word.

5. _____ true   **a.** shrink

6. _____ grow   **b.** always

7. _____ similar   **c.** different

8. _____ never   **d.** false

Underline the compound word in each sentence. Then, write the two words that make up each compound.

9. The babies of marsupials live in their mothers' pouches until they can take care of themselves.

   _____   _____

10. The wombat makes its nest underground.

    _____   _____

11. The wombat looks like a groundhog or a beaver.

    _____   _____

Reading Skills

1. What are baby kangaroos called in Australia?

   _____

2. Why do koalas spend so much of their time sleeping?

   _____

   _____

3. What kind of pet is Gillian?

   _____

4. Why do you think a baby kangaroo lives in its mother's pouch for a while after it is born?

   _____

   _____

Study Skills

Write the name of the reference source you could use to find out the information in each question below.

| encyclopedia   dictionary |
| atlas |

1. Where could you look to find the location of a particular city in Australia?

   _____

2. Where could you look to find the meaning of the word *burrows*?

   _____

3. Where could you look to find information about what kangaroos eat?

   _____

The First Australians

Who are the Aboriginal people of Australia?

1   The Aboriginal people are the original inhabitants of Australia. Archaeologists believe that they have lived in Australia for about 50,000 to 60,000 years! Today, they make up a little more than two percent of the population of Australia.

2   In the past, Aboriginal people were hunters and gatherers. This means that they survived by hunting, fishing, and gathering plants. They did not settle permanently in one place. Instead, they moved around the continent when they needed to refresh their supply of food. The Aboriginal people had, and still have, a strong respect for and connection to the land and nature. It influences almost every part of their culture, from food and shelter, to art and religion.

3   Things quickly changed for the Aboriginal people when Europeans began arriving in Australia in 1788. They brought diseases that the Aboriginal people had never been exposed to before. The Aboriginal people also had to fight for the land that was theirs. There were many years of difficult times. The Aboriginal people had to learn to live in a society that was very different from their ancestors'. They had to fight to keep their culture alive.

4   The situation started to improve for the Aboriginal people in the 1960s. They were finally given the right to vote. Later, the Australian government also began trying to make up for some of the unfair treatment the people had suffered. They returned some of the land to the Aboriginal people that had been taken from them more than a century before.

5   The contributions of Aboriginal people to Australia can be seen in many areas. For example, they created the boomerang, a curved piece of wood that has been used both as a weapon and for sport. Aboriginal rock paintings can be found in many areas of Australia. Some are believed to be 30,000 years old. The didgeridoo (*didge er ee DOO*) is a well-known Australian wind instrument. It is a straight trumpet made from a hollow piece of wood or bamboo. Some people believe it may be one of the world's oldest wind instruments.

6   The Aboriginal people are an important and valuable part of Australian society. Today, many still live a traditional lifestyle in the bush, or Australian wilderness. Others have become a part of modern-day Australian culture and live in cities around the country. Their influences can be found in many aspects of Australian life.

Vocabulary Skills

Write the words from the passage that have the meanings below.

1. people who live in a particular place

   _____
   Par. 1

2. scientists who study past cultures

   _____
   Par. 1

3. for a long time

   _____
   Par. 2

4. has an effect on

   _____
   Par. 2

5. left open to harm without protection

   _____
   Par. 3

6. a period of 100 years

   _____
   Par. 4

In each row, circle the word that does not belong.

7. hunt   fish   settle   gather

8. fight   struggle   improve   conflict

9. hollow   trumpet   didgeridoo   instrument

10. Find the word with the suffix **-ist** in paragraph 1. Then, write the meaning of the word.

    _____

    _____

The suffix **-able** means *able to*. Add the suffix to the verbs below to form adjectives. Then, write a sentence with each adjective.

11. comfort _____

    _____

12. break _____

    _____

Reading Skills

1. Why did Aboriginal people move around instead of staying in one place?

   _____

   _____

2. What influences almost every part of the Aboriginal culture?

   _____

   _____

Study Skills

Use the map of Australia's six states and two territories to answer the questions that follow.

1. Which state is directly south of the Northern Territory?

   _____

2. Which state is east of the Northern Territory?

   _____

3. What is the name of the state that is the furthest south?

   _____

4. Which state is larger—Western Australia or New South Wales?

   _____

Shall We Dance?

Have you ever attended a dance performance?

1 "Gavin!" called Mr. Capshaw. "We're ready to go. Are you coming?"

2 Gavin shuffled slowly down the stairs and joined his parents at the front door. "I'm ready," he said with a sigh.

3 "This will be fun. I know you'll enjoy the performance," Mrs. Capshaw told her son. "Afterward, we might even get to go backstage and meet Dad's friend from college. Joseph has one of the lead roles in the show," she explained.

4 The Capshaws walked down the street toward the subway station. "I don't even like ballet," Gavin complained.

5 "Not all dance is ballet, Gavin," said Mr. Capshaw. "The show we're going to see tonight is modern dance. But there are many other kinds of dance, too—tap, jazz, break dancing, square dancing, the tango, the waltz. I'd like you to keep an open mind about this."

6 Gavin sighed again. "Okay, Dad. I'll do my best."

7 About 45 minutes later, the Capshaws arrived at the theater. A woman wearing a bright red vest and carrying a flashlight helped them find their seats in the mezzanine. Gavin looked around him while he waited for the performance to begin. He couldn't believe how many people there were in the theater. Gavin looked straight up at the ornate ceiling painted in gold, midnight blue, and maroon. Suddenly, the lights dimmed, and the audience began to clap.

8 Once the performance began, Gavin forgot all about the usher, his parents, the rest of the audience, and the ornate ceiling. He listened to the music and watched the dancers move. The performers made the moves look so easy, but he could tell it was much more difficult than it appeared. He leaned forward in his seat and tapped his toes in time to the rhythm of the music.

9 "Well, what did you think?" asked Gavin's parents when the lights came back on.

10 "That was amazing. I'm so glad we came," he replied.

11 "Come on, let's go see if we can find Joseph," said Mr. Capshaw, putting one arm around Gavin's shoulders. The Capshaws made their way to a small hallway at the front of the theater. A moment later, they were shaking hands with Joseph and complimenting him on his performance.

12 "Is it a lot of work to prepare the show?" Gavin asked Joseph.

13 Joseph chuckled. "I've never worked so hard in my life," he said, "but I've also never had so much fun. Are you a performer, Gavin?"

14 Gavin shook his head.

15 "Do you think dance is something you'd like to try?" asked Joseph. "You seem very enthusiastic about tonight's show. The performing arts center is only a few blocks from here, and they offer a beginner's class in modern dance. I know some of the teachers there. I'd be happy to introduce you if you're interested."

16 Gavin grinned. "When can I start?" he asked.

Vocabulary Skills

Write the words from the story that have the meanings below.

1. walked slowly, dragging the feet

    _____
    Par. 2

2. the main or most important part in a performance

    _____
    Par. 3

3. the lowest balcony in a theater

    _____
    Par. 7

4. decorated in a very detailed, complex way

    _____
    Par. 7

Words that have two middle consonants are divided into syllables between the consonants. For example, *pic/ture* or *bas/ket*. Divide the words below into syllables using a slash (/).

5. p e r f o r m   7. o r n a t e

6. t a n g o   8. c e n t e r

Read each word below. Then, write the letter of its synonym on the line beside the word.

9. _____ walked   a. beat

10. _____ began   b. strolled

11. _____ rhythm   c. started

12. _____ chuckle   d. laugh

Reading Skills

1. Find one sentence that shows Gavin was not looking forward to going to the dance performance. Write it on the lines below.

    _____

    _____

2. What problem did Gavin have at the beginning of the story?

    _____

3. How did Gavin feel about the performance once it began?

    _____

Write **F** before the sentences that are facts. Write **O** before the sentences that are opinions.

4. _____ Modern dance is interesting to watch.

5. _____ Joseph has one of the lead roles in the performance.

6. _____ The Capshaws took the subway to get to the theater.

7. _____ Gavin will be a good dancer.

Study Skills

A **table of contents** shows the chapters in a book and the page each chapter begins on. Use the table of contents below to answer the questions.

Table of Contents

Chapter 1 History of Dance in America........2
Chapter 2 Types of Dance.......................21
Chapter 3 Stars of the Stage...................39
Chapter 4 Most Popular Shows.................52

1. What is the title of Chapter 2?

    _____

2. Which chapter contains information about the history of dance?

    _____

3. What is the title of the chapter that begins on page 39?

    _____

STOMP!

What kind of everyday objects could you use to make music?

1   You might have used pencils to tap a rhythm on your desk or noticed that the ringing sound of basketballs was almost like the beat to a song. But did you know that these sounds could be taken seriously as music and even performed onstage?

2   The dance and percussion group STOMP has taken everyday objects and turned them into instruments. The performers strap oil drums to their feet and smash trash can lids together. This creates an exciting rhythmic music and dance that is a hit all over the world.

3   STOMP was formed by British musicians Luke Cresswell and Steve McNichols. They met in the early 1980s when they were both working as buskers, the British term for street performers. Busking has a long tradition in England and is still a popular way for musicians and actors to share their talents. The performers have to be extra creative and enticing to be able to capture the attention of people who are walking by. Cresswell and McNichols were part of a busking group called *Pookiesnackenburger* that became very popular throughout Britain. Eventually, they even had their own television show.

4   Cresswell was a drummer for the group. Because they performed on the street, he could not set up a traditional drum set. Instead, he wore one drum that hung around his shoulders. To be able to make a variety of sounds, Cresswell began beating on objects like lampposts and trash cans that were available wherever the group performed. This creative drumming formed the idea for STOMP.

5   STOMP made its debut at London's Bloomsbury Theater in 1991. The performers used one-of-a-kind instruments, such as brooms, empty water jugs, basketballs, and matchboxes to bang out rhythms. Wearing overalls and T-shirts, they danced around on a stage made to look like a closed warehouse. STOMP was an instant success, winning many theater awards and drawing huge crowds.

6   In 1994, STOMP came to the United States and played at the Orpheum Theater in New York City. A decade later it is still playing there! To honor its ten-year anniversary, New York City Mayor Michael Bloomberg renamed the street outside of the theater STOMP Avenue.

7   STOMP has now toured all over the United States and most of the world. One reason STOMP is so popular is that anyone can enjoy it. There are no words or story. People from all cultures can understand it, regardless of the language they speak.

Vocabulary Skills

Write the words from the passage that have the meanings below.

1. hitting things together to create a sound

   _____
   Par. 2

2. passing down ideas or ways of doing something

   _____
   Par. 3

3. tempting

   _____
   Par. 3

4. the first time something is seen; an introduction

   _____
   Par. 5

5. a period of ten years

   _____
   Par. 6

Check the meaning of the underlined word in each sentence.

6. STOMP is a hit all over the world.

   _____ to strike or beat

   _____ something very popular

7. The group called *Pookiesnackenburger* had their own television show.

   _____ a performance

   _____ to display or allow to be seen

8. STOMP continues to draw large crowds.

   _____ to make a picture of

   _____ to attract

Find the compound words from the selection that contain the words below.

9. balls _____
   Par. 1

10. day _____
    Par. 2

11. lamp _____
    Par. 4

Reading Skills

Write **T** before the sentences that are true. Write **F** before the sentences that are false.

1. _____ The performers in STOMP use common objects and turn them into instruments.

2. _____ Luke Cresswell, one of the founders of STOMP, played the trumpet.

3. _____ There is a street called STOMP Avenue in New York City.

4. _____ STOMP's first performance was at London's Bloomsbury Theatre.

5. _____ STOMP was formed by two Latin American musicians.

6. In Britain, what does the word *busker* mean?

   _____

7. Why couldn't Luke Cresswell use a traditional drum set when he was performing?

   _____

   _____

Study Skills

1. Use the numbers 1–5 to put the words below in alphabetical order.

   _____ rhythm

   _____ rib

   _____ rhinoceros

   _____ ribbon

   _____ riddle

The Best Hoofer of All

How did Savion Glover bring tap dancing into the 21st century?

1   What comes to mind when you think of tap dancing? You might picture a black-and-white movie with a performer dressed in a tuxedo. Tap dancing might not seem like something popular and modern. If that is how you picture tap, then you have never seen Savion Glover dance! This choreographer, dancer, director, and producer has changed the way people think about tap dancing today.

2   Savion Glover was born in New Jersey in 1973. He showed a talent for drumming when he was only four years old, so he began going to school at the Newark Community School of the Arts. By the time he was seven, he had begun taking rhythm tap classes at the Broadway Dance Center in New York. Rhythm tap is a special kind of dance that uses all the parts of the foot to create sounds.

3   When Savion began taking tap lessons, his family could not afford the special shoes he needed. Savion had to wear a pair of cowboy boots to his first lesson! Just a few years later, Savion landed his first role in a Broadway performance, *The Tap Dance Kid*.

4   Savion continued working in a variety of areas. He learned much of what he knew about tap dancing from masters like Sammy Davis, Junior and Gregory Hines. He participated in other Broadway productions, and he even made a movie. Savion also became well-known for his recurring role on the children's television show *Sesame Street*.

5   In 1995, Savion choreographed and starred in a production called *Bring in 'Da Noise, Bring in 'Da Funk*. The show, which followed African American history from the times of slavery through the 20th century, was extremely popular. People loved its energy. They were amazed at how the story could be expressed through dance. *Bring in 'Da Noise, Bring in 'Da Funk* won four Tony Awards, the highest honor a musical can receive. One of those awards was for best choreographer, Savion Glover.

6   The style of tap that Savion is best known for is often called *hoofing*, or street tap. It is a hard-hitting form of tap, and the movements are more acrobatic than those of traditional tap. Savion's work combines elements of jazz, funk, hip-hop, rock 'n' roll, and the blues to create something unique and exciting. People love to watch Savion's feet move. It is hard to keep up with them, but that is part of the fun in watching Savion Glover perform!

Vocabulary Skills

Write the words from the passage that have the meanings below.

1. someone who directs the movements of a dance performance

   _____
   Par. 1

2. experts

   _____
   Par. 4

3. was a part of

   _____
   Par. 4

Write the words from the selection that match the abbreviations below.

4. Jr. _____

5. NY _____

6. NJ _____

A word that sounds the same as another word but has a different spelling and meaning is a **homophone**. Circle the homophone that correctly completes each sentence below.

7. Savion's family could not afford a _____ of special tap dancing shoes. (pear, pair)

8. Savion wore cowboy boots to his first tap dancing _____. (lesson, lessen)

9. One movie Savion _____ was with director Spike Lee. (made, maid)

Reading Skills

1. Check the words that describe Savion Glover.

   _____ energetic   _____ motivated

   _____ nosy   _____ quiet

   _____ enthusiastic

2. In what show was Savion's first professional performance?

   _____

   _____

3. What story did *Bring in 'Da Noise, Bring in 'Da Funk* tell?

   _____

   _____

4. Who did Savion study to become better at tap dancing?

   _____

   _____

Study Skills

Use the poster below to answer the questions that follow.

The Alden Theater presents . . .

Savion Glover's Improvography

Wednesday, August 16th
at 8:00 P.M.

Tickets go on sale August 2—
Call 614-555-SHOW

Tickets $22-35

1. What is the price range for tickets to see *Improvography*?

   _____

2. What is the name of the theater that is hosting the performance?

   _____

3. What date do tickets go on sale?

   _____

Looking for Something Green

Will Fiona and Nora ever get used to living in the city?

1 Fiona and Nora stared out the window of the apartment. If they looked up State Street to the right, they could see several skyscrapers with shiny windows that glittered like jewels in the midmorning sun. If they looked down the street to their left, they could see a parking garage and an impressive looking building their mother had told them was the downtown library. Straight below them was a tangle of traffic that seemed to stretch as far as they could see. They could hear the honking of horns and the shouting of street vendors.

2 "It's so different here," sighed Fiona. "I miss our old farmhouse. When we looked out the window at home, all we could see were acres of green grass and trees. I don't think I can see a single green thing from this window in any direction."

3 "Well," said Nora, "that man is wearing a green jacket. And I see a green truck. Look! That woman is carrying a potted plant that has a lot of green leaves!"

4 Fiona gave her little sister a look. "You know that's not what I'm talking about," she said. "I just feel like everything here is made of stone and steel and glass. We don't even have a lawn or a tree that we can sit under and read. What if we wanted to have a cook-out like we used to do in our backyard? Where will Mom plant her flowers? What if we wanted to play ball?"

5 Mom walked into the room just in time to hear what Fiona was saying. "Okay, girls," said Mom. "I think it's time we went on a walk. We're going to go exploring. Our mission is to find ourselves a little piece of green space right here in the city."

6 "Mom," said Fiona, "I don't think there is any green space here. We live in the city now, not the country."

7 "Come on," said Mom, grabbing her daughters by the hand. "Let's see what we can find."

8 Fiona, Nora, and their mother walked past the vendors selling hot dogs and pretzels. They walked past the skyscrapers with shiny windows, the tangle of traffic, and the bustle of people in business suits. Suddenly, Fiona and Nora saw a bit of grass and a park bench. They turned the corner and began to grin. They saw an enormous grassy park filled with trees. There was even a pond with a fountain. A girl on a bicycle stopped to let two ducks waddle past her.

9 As Fiona, Nora, and Mom made their way toward the pond, Mom smiled and said, "What do you think, girls?"

10 Fiona and Nora smiled back. "We found our little piece of green in the city," said Nora.

Vocabulary Skills

Write the words from the story that have the meanings below.

1. makes a lasting feeling or image

   _____
   Par. 1

2. areas of land that are each equal to 4,840 square yards

   _____
   Par. 2

3. goal; purpose

   _____
   Par. 5

4. people who sell things

   _____
   Par. 8

5. to move around in a busy manner

   _____
   Par. 8

A **simile** compares two things using the words *like* or *as*. Find the simile in paragraph 1, and write it on the line below.

6. _____

Compound words are divided into syllables between the two words that make the compound. For example, *play/ground*. Divide the words below into syllables using a slash *(/)*.

7. f a r m h o u s e

8. b a c k y a r d

9. h o m e s i c k

Reading Skills

Read the descriptions below. Write **F** next to the phrase if it describes Fiona. Write **N** if it describes Nora.

1. _____ says she can't see anything green from the window

2. _____ feels like everything is made of steel, stone, and glass

3. _____ points out several green things on the street below

4. _____ says she misses their old farmhouse

5. _____ says they found their piece of green in the city

6. What do you think "green space" is?

   _____

7. What problem do Fiona and Nora have in this story?

   _____

8. Where do you think Fiona and Nora used to live before they moved to the city?

   _____

9. Nora points out three green things she can see from the window. What does Fiona mean when she says, "You know that's not what I'm talking about," to her sister?

   _____

   _____

Study Skills

The word you look up in a dictionary is called an **entry word**. An entry word is usually a base word. For example, if you want to find the meaning of *happier*, you would look up the base word *happy*. Write the entry word you would look for in a dictionary next to each word below.

1. glittered _____

2. honking _____

3. libraries _____

4. exploring _____

A Garden in the Clouds

Will Fiona and Nora find a place where they can have a garden in the city?

1   Fiona and Nora were becoming accustomed to life in the city. They were learning their way around, and they were discovering all kinds of exciting things. The best library they had ever been to was right across the street from their apartment. It had an enormous selection of books, and they had already made friends with Ms. Applebaum, one of the librarians. Sometimes, she put books aside that she thought Fiona and Nora might enjoy.

2   The sisters still missed some things about living in the country, but they had learned that they just needed to look a bit harder to find similar things in the city. After they had discovered the nearby park with their mother one day, they spent a lot of time there. They roller-bladed on the trail that ran around the perimeter of the park. Their dad made friends with the man who sold food for the ducks, and he always gave them an extra handful.

3   The one thing that Fiona and Nora still missed about their old farmhouse was having a place for a garden. Both girls had inherited their mother's green thumb. Last summer, they had grown so many tomatoes they were able to make enough spaghetti sauce to last most of the winter.

4   One afternoon, Fiona, Nora, and Mom decided to take a different route to the park. They liked to explore the side streets on their way there. Nora looked up when a large cloud passed overhead. She noticed something that looked like a tree on top of the building beside her.

5   "That looks like a tree on the roof!" she exclaimed. Fiona and Mom looked up. They couldn't see very well because they stood directly below the building. They walked a bit further down the street, and then they crossed over to the other side to get a better view.

6   "You're right, Nora," said Fiona. "I think there's actually a whole garden up there! I can see a trellis with some flowers creeping up it. And there are some more pots along the far side of the roof."

7   "It looks like they have a rooftop garden," said Mom. "I've heard of them, but I've never actually seen one before. People who live in cities sometimes use the space on the top of their buildings for gardening."

8   "Do you think we could start one on the roof of our building, Mom?" asked Fiona.

9   Mom smiled. "We'll have to check with the superintendent of our building first," she replied. "But I doubt it will be a problem. I've seen a sign for stairs leading to the roof. I've even seen a family taking a picnic dinner and a telescope up there."

10   Nora grinned. "Sometimes, you just have to look a little harder to find what you're looking for in the city."

Vocabulary Skills

Write the words from the story that have the meanings below.

1. used to or familiar with

   _____
   Par. 1

2. choice

   _____
   Par. 1

3. the area around something

   _____
   Par. 2

4. received from a relative

   _____
   Par. 3

5. a structure that supports climbing plants

   _____
   Par. 6

6. the landlord or manager of a building

   _____
   Par. 9

An **idiom** is a group of words that has a special meaning. For example, the idiom *hit the hay* means *go to bed*. Write the idiom from paragraph 3 on the line under its meaning.

7. a talent for growing plants

   _____

Read each word below. Then, write the letter of its antonym on the line beside the word.

8. _____ enormous   **a.** different

9. _____ exciting   **b.** tiny

10. _____ same   **c.** summer

11. _____ winter   **d.** boring

Fill in the blanks below with the possessive form of the word in parentheses.

12. The _____ friendship made the girls feel at home. (librarian)

13. _____ talent for gardening had been passed on to Nora and Fiona. (Mom)

Reading Skills

1. Check the phrase that best describes the author's purpose.

   _____ to tell a story about two sisters discovering rooftop gardens

   _____ to persuade the reader to start a rooftop garden

   _____ to share information about the best type of plants to use in a rooftop garden

Dialogue is what a character says. The words in dialogue are always in quotation marks.

2. On the line below, write the words that are dialogue in paragraph 5.

   _____

3. Check the word or words that best describe what type of selection this is.

   _____ historical nonfiction

   _____ folktale

   _____ fiction

4. Do you think Mom will help the girls start a rooftop garden of their own? Why or why not?

   _____

   _____

Study Skills

Use a dictionary to help you divide these words into syllables.

1. apartment _____

2. enormous _____

3. spaghetti _____

Green Roofs

Have you ever seen a rooftop garden?

1   Why would anyone want to plant a garden on a roof? People are finding out that it is good for the environment and good for them. The roof of a building can get extremely hot, especially if it is covered in tar. Dark colors absorb the light of the sun, which causes them to become hotter than things that are light in color.

2   Cities can be as much as four to ten degrees warmer than rural areas. Green rooftops can actually help cool the air in cities. A single green roof will not do much to change the temperature of a city. However, when more buildings begin to convert their rooftops to green spaces, a real difference can occur. Buildings that are cooler also use air conditioning less often. This reduces the amount of energy a building uses, which is good for the environment.

3   Cities are usually more polluted than other areas. The addition of plants to rooftops can even help clean the air. Plants use carbon dioxide and produce oxygen. Because people breathe oxygen, a large number of plants in an area creates more breathable air. Gardens in the city can also provide a place for birds and bugs to live.

4   One unusual rooftop garden is located above Children's Hospital in St. Louis, Missouri. The garden covers an area of 7,500 square feet. It is a place for the children and their parents to relax and be close to nature without leaving the hospital. The garden has flowers, fountains, and even a goldfish pond. There are also paths that children can walk on in slippers or with bare feet.

5   Another interesting garden is on the rooftop of the Royal York Hotel in Toronto, Canada. A large herb garden has been planted on the roof. The hotel's chefs can pick all of the herbs they use fresh from the roof. Other hotels and restaurants maintain gardens where they grow fruits and vegetables to use in cooking. They just need to make sure that there are gardeners to care for the plants. Rooftop gardens can dry out quickly in the summer sun, and vegetables need frequent watering.

6   Why don't all buildings have green rooftops? One reason is that they can be more expensive than traditional rooftops. However, they may save a company on heating and cooling bills in the future. Also, a roof needs to be flat and strong enough to support the weight of the garden.

7   Many people do not know about rooftop gardens and how good they can be for the environment. But word is starting to get out. You may want to keep your eyes on the skies when you walk the streets in your town or city. You never know when you might catch a glimpse of a secret garden many feet above the ground.

Vocabulary Skills

Write the words from the passage that have the meanings below.

1. take in or soak up

   _____
   Par. 1

2. related to life in the country

   _____
   Par. 2

3. change from one thing to another

   _____
   Par. 2

4. makes less

   _____
   Par. 2

5. a quick look

   _____
   Par. 7

Write a compound word using two words in each sentence.

6. The pond contains fish that have a gold color.

   _____

7. The garden is located on the top of the roof.

   _____

8. A house for a bird can be placed in the garden.

   _____

Reading Skills

1. Why do the rooftops of buildings get so hot?

   _____

2. How big is the rooftop garden at the Children's Hospital in St. Louis, Missouri?

   _____

3. Do you think that more buildings will begin to convert their roofs to green spaces? Explain your answer.

   _____

   _____

4. What is planted in the rooftop garden of the Royal York Hotel?

   _____

5. A **summary** is a short sentence that tells the most important facts about a topic. Check the sentence below that is the best summary for paragraph 2.

   _____ Cities are warmer than rural areas.

   _____ Rooftop gardens can cool the air in cities and reduce the amount of energy used.

   _____ Buildings with rooftop gardens use less air conditioning.

Study Skills

An **outline** is used to put ideas in order. It shows the important facts in a story. Use the facts from paragraph 2 to complete Part I. Use the facts from paragraph 4 to complete Part II.

I. Often warmer in the city than in the country

   A. green roofs help cool air

   B. _____

   C. reduces energy buildings use

II. Rooftop garden at Children's Hospital in St. Louis

   A. 7,500 square feet

   B. _____

   C. has flowers, fountains, and pond

   D. _____

Wasteful or Resourceful?

How green is your school? What about your home or the places your parents work?

1   What can people do to help the places they go every day become friendlier to the environment? Large buildings are often hard on the environment. The good news is that there are many ways even the biggest offenders can make improvements.

2   One problem is the amount of energy that is used every day in large buildings. Rooftop gardens are one way to reduce the amount of energy needed to air condition a building in the summer and heat it in the winter. But rooftop gardens are not the only solution. Some companies have installed solar panels. This allows them to gather energy from the sun and then turn it into electricity. Solar panels can be expensive, but companies that want to make protecting the environment a priority think it is worth the money.

3   Other companies have all kinds of special gadgets that help save energy. For example, in some offices, lights automatically go out when a person leaves a room. The plumbing is set up in a way that allows water to be reused. In new buildings, recycled materials might even be a part of the walls or the floor. Tile can be made using recycled glass. Floors can be made from old tires. Walls can even be insulated with newspaper or bales of straw.

4   You do not need to live in a green building or go to a green school in order to help the environment. There are lots of things you can do on your own. For example, turn off the water when you brush your teeth. Turn off the lights when you leave a room. If you can walk or ride your bike somewhere, do that instead of riding in a car.

5   Does your school recycle paper? If it does not, see if you can work with a teacher to start a recycling program. Do you know what happens to the food that is not used in your school's cafeteria? Maybe it can be donated to a local food bank.

6   You can also tell people you know about ways they can help the environment. The more people you tell, the more people will become aware of things they can reuse and recycle. The sooner that happens, the sooner we'll be able to see a healthy change in the world around us.

Vocabulary Skills

Write the words from the passage that have the meanings below.

1. people who are guilty of something

   _____
   Par. 1

2. working on its own; without being controlled

   _____
   Par. 3

3. covered with a material that keeps warmth or sound from passing through it

   _____
   Par. 3

Check the meaning of the underlined word in each sentence.

4. One way to help the environment is to <u>save</u> energy.

   _____ rescue

   _____ conserve

5. Turn off the <u>light</u> when you leave a room.

   _____ something bright that allows you to see

   _____ not heavy

6. Even an old <u>tire</u> can be recycled and put to good use.

   _____ a rubber circle that surrounds a wheel

   _____ to become sleepy or weary

The prefix **mid-** means *the middle part*. For example, *midday* means *middle of the day*. Add the prefix **mid-** to each word below. Then, use each new word in a sentence.

7. night _____

   _____

8. summer _____

   _____

Reading Skills

1. How do solar panels work?

   _____

2. What types of recycled materials can tile and floors be made of?

   _____

3. Name two things you can do at home or at school to help the environment.

   _____

   _____

Study Skills

Use the brochure below to answer the questions that follow.

Celebrate Earth Day!

Who: You, your friends, and your family

How: By cleaning up the litter at McDougal Park (and staying for a free cook-out party)

When: Saturday, April 24 from 10:00 A.M. until 1:00 P.M.

Where: Meet at the baseball diamond at McDougal Park

Why: To keep our neighborhood clean and green!

1. Who can attend the Earth Day celebration?

   _____

2. What time are people meeting on Saturday?

   _____

3. What service will the volunteers be performing?

   _____

Poetry Slam

Have you ever written a poem?

1   "For the next two weeks, we're going to be talking about and writing poetry," Ms. Jorge told her class. "What comes to mind when you think about poetry?" she asked.

2   "Feelings and personal thoughts," Maya said.

3   "Rhyming words," said Maurice.

4   "Descriptive words," said Taylor.

5   "Images that tell a story," said Ana.

6   "Those are all excellent answers," said Ms. Jorge. "One reason I love poetry is because of its diversity. You can find a poem to fit any mood or feeling. Some poems make you laugh, and others make you think. Poems can remind you of things you have forgotten, and they can take you places you have never been."

7   "I didn't hear any of you use the words *exciting* or *competitive* to talk about poetry," said Ms. Jorge. "What do those words make you think of?"

8   Maya raised her hand. "They make me think of sports," she answered. "Poetry seems quieter and more serious."

9   Ms. Jorge smiled. "We're going to learn about a form of poetry today that might change your mind. A poetry slam is a competition for poets. Each poet has three minutes to deliver his or her poem. The judges are all chosen from the audience. The poets are judged on the content of the poems and on the way they present the poems. After a poet finishes, the judges hold up signs to show the scores they've given the poet. The scores range from one to ten, with ten being a perfect score."

10   "That almost sounds like an Olympic event," joked Taylor.

11   Ms. Jorge nodded. "It's a different way of becoming involved with poetry," she said. "Anyone can try it. Throughout history, poetry has been a part of the oral tradition. It is meant to be spoken or read aloud. Many types of poetry would never have survived if they had not been passed down through the generations by word of mouth."

12   "Are there poetry slams for kids?" asked Maurice.

13   "Yes, they have been popping up all around the country in the last few years," answered Ms. Jorge. "There is even a Youth Poetry Slam League and a national competition."

14   "Don't kids get nervous reciting their poetry in front of a big audience?" wondered Ana.

15   "I'm sure they do get nervous," said Ms. Jorge. "But they also enjoy having a chance to share their feelings and get new perspectives on things. Some of the poets like the excitement and the competitive atmosphere. Others like the support of being with and performing for other poets."

16   Ms. Jorge walked to her desk and picked up a stack of paper. "Does anyone know where we'll be going on our next field trip?" she asked. When no one had an idea, she continued. "The city of Riverview will be holding its first youth poetry slam at the Book Nook. I'm passing around applications right now. I encourage all of you to think about performing!"

Vocabulary Skills

Write the words from the story that have the meanings below.

1. variety; different types

   _____
   Par. 6

2. to speak or present

   _____
   Par. 9

3. the amount something can vary or be different

   _____
   Par. 9

4. spoken aloud

   _____
   Par. 11

5. particular ways of viewing something

   _____
   Par. 15

Read each word below. Then, write the letter of its synonym on the line beside the word.

6. _____ responded   **a.** select

7. _____ often   **b.** varied

8. _____ choose   **c.** replied

9. _____ different   **d.** frequent

A **word family** is a group of words that have the same letter combinations. For example, the words *could*, *would*, and *should* are in the same word family, because they all contain the **-ould** combination. Circle the words in each row that are part of the word family in parentheses.

10. (*-ight*) bring   bright   tonight   tomorrow

11. (*-ought*) fought   thin   thought   then

12. (*-ight*) midday   light   linger   midnight

Reading Skills

Write **F** before the sentences that are facts. Write **O** before the sentences that are opinions.

1. _____ Poetry can be exciting.

2. _____ Ms. Jorge's class will be going on a field trip to a poetry slam.

3. _____ Poetry slams can be interesting to attend.

4. _____ Poetry has been a part of the oral tradition throughout history.

5. _____ Ms. Jorge enjoys poetry.

6. Do you think any of Ms. Jorge's students will participate in the poetry slam? Explain your answer.

   _____

   _____

   _____

   _____

7. What is a poetry slam?

   _____

   _____

   _____

8. Why do you think Taylor says that a poetry slam sounds like an Olympic event?

   _____

   _____

9. Name two things that Ms. Jorge says kids enjoy about poetry slams.

   _____

   _____

   _____

   _____

Where the Poetry Begins

What is your favorite poem? Who is your favorite poet?

1   Who is your favorite poet? For many young people, the answer is Shel Silverstein. Shel's first book was published in the 1960s, and since then his children's books have sold more than 20 million copies! Young people recognize that Shel really understood his audience.

2   Shel Silverstein was born in Chicago, Illinois, in 1932. He began writing poetry when he was young. He was not familiar with the work of any famous poets, so he invented his own style. This turned out to be a good thing, because style is one of the most distinctive things about Shel's poetry.

3   Although he was best known for writing children's literature, Shel was creative in many ways. He began his career in the arts as a cartoonist. He also was a talented singer, songwriter, composer, and illustrator. In fact, Shel illustrated all of his children's books himself. This is one reason the pictures seem to accompany the poetry so perfectly.

4   *Where the Sidewalk Ends*, first published in 1984, is one of the most beloved children's books of all time. But what makes Shel's poetry so timeless and popular? His poems are often hilarious, and young people love Shel's type of humor.

5   In one poem, he told the story of a girl who refused to take out the garbage. It piled up higher and higher until it finally threatened to take over the town. Many kids have experienced the feeling of not wanting to do a chore. They love how out of control the author let the situation get because they know that it would never happen that way in real life.

6   In another popular poem, a girl pretends to be sick so that she will not have to attend school. Shel made fun of the situation by having the character exaggerate her symptoms to the point where they became ridiculous. The punch line of the poem occurs at the end. The girl discovers that it is Saturday, and she would not have had to go to school anyway.

7   Shel also liked to play with language in his poetry. He often used elements like alliteration in his work. *Alliteration* is the use of words that begin with the same sounds. In the poem about the girl who refused to take out the garbage, the character's name is Sarah Cynthia Sylvia Stout. This type of alliteration can make poetry fun to read aloud. Shel's poems also often rhymed and had a good rhythm, two more elements that make his work easy and interesting to read.

8   In 1999, Shel Silverstein died in his home in Key West, Florida. Children and adults will miss his quirky humor and incredible imagination. But a bit of Shel Silverstein is captured in his work, which will live on and bring joy to children for many generations to come.

Vocabulary Skills

Rewrite the following address without using the abbreviations.

1. Dr. Hannah Tyrrell
   19052 Inglewood Dr.
   Lincoln, NE 68512

   _____

   _____

   _____

Fill in the blanks below with the possessive form of the word in parentheses.

2. Shel Silverstein is best known for his _____ literature. (children)

3. One of Shel _____ books is called *Falling Up*. (Silverstein)

4. The _____ name in one poem is Sarah Cynthia Sylvia Stout. (character)

Reading Skills

1. Number the events below to show the order in which they happened.

   _____ Shel's first book was published.

   _____ Shel died in 1999.

   _____ Shel began his career as a cartoonist.

   _____ Shel Silverstein was born in Chicago.

   _____ *Where the Sidewalk Ends* was published.

2. What does it mean when the author says that Shel Silverstein illustrated all his children's books himself?

   _____

   _____

3. About how many copies of Shel's books have been sold?

   _____

4. Write your own example of alliteration.

   _____

   _____

5. Check the words that describe Shel Silverstein.

   _____ funny

   _____ lazy

   _____ talkative

   _____ artistic

   _____ clever

Study Skills

A **time line** shows the order in which things happened. Use the time line below to answer the questions that follow.

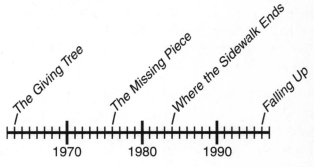

1. What was the most recent book published?

   _____

2. Which book was published in 1984?

   _____

3. In what year was *The Giving Tree* published?

   _____

A Poetic Visitor

What would you ask a poet who came to visit your classroom?

1   "Class, I'd like to introduce Kerry Donnelly," said Ms. Jorge. "Ms. Donnelly has written four books of children's poetry. Two of her books are award winners. We're lucky she was able to take the time to speak with us today."

2   Ms. Donnelly smiled at the class. "Thanks for having me," she said. She leaned against the edge of Ms. Jorge's desk. "Did you all know I went to elementary school here? I actually wrote my first poem in Mr. Wen's class, right across the hall.

3   "My best friend was moving to Washington, and I couldn't imagine life without her," continued Ms. Donnelly. "Mr. Wen asked us to write a poem about something we felt passionate about. I passionately didn't want Madelyn to move to Washington, so I wrote about her and our friendship and all the things I'd miss. For some reason, that poem actually made me feel better.

4   "The day before Madelyn moved, I gave her the poem I'd written. She said it made her feel better, too, because she knew at least one other person in the world understood how she was feeling. I think that's one of the most valuable things about poetry."

5   Ms. Donnelly stood up and put out her hands. "I'd like to hear your questions," she said. "You can ask me anything you like about poetry and writing, and I'll do my best to answer your questions."

6   Maurice raised his hand. "Do you know what you are going to say when you sit down to write?" he asked.

7   Ms. Donnelly shook her head. "Usually, I don't know what I want to say until I actually see the words appearing on the page. I just have to make sure that I sit down and write something every single day. That way, I'm sure to capture the good stuff when it's ready to be written."

8   "Where do you get your ideas?" asked Maya.

9   "That's a good question," said Ms. Donnelly. "I have twin sons who are in the sixth grade. They and their friends and classmates have been the source of many ideas. I also grew up in a family of five kids, so my reminiscences of my siblings and my own childhood appear pretty regularly in my work."

10   "What would you be if you couldn't be a poet?" asked Ana.

11   Ms. Donnelly smiled but didn't say anything for a minute. "That's a very hard question. There are many other things I'd like to be, but they are all in addition to being a poet. I can't think of a single job I'd rather have instead."

12   "And that," said Ms. Jorge to the class, "is the very best kind of job."

Vocabulary Skills

Write the words from the story that have the meanings below.

1. having very strong feelings

   _____
   Par. 3

2. very important; worth a great deal

   _____
   Par. 4

3. memories

   _____
   Par. 9

4. brothers and sisters

   _____
   Par. 9

In each row, circle the word that does not belong.

5. book   desk   newspaper   magazine

6. vacation   poem   story   essay

7. friend   companion   vehicle   pal

Read each pair of words listed below. If the words are synonyms, write **S** on the line. If the words are antonyms, write **A** on the line.

8. _____ remember   forget

9. _____ smiled   grinned

10. _____ often   infrequently

11. _____ brief   long

12. _____ leave   depart

Reading Skills

1. Find one sentence that shows Ms. Donnelly is happy to be a poet. Write it on the lines below.

   _____

   _____

2. Check the phrase that best describes the author's purpose.

   _____ to tell a story about a poet who visits a classroom

   _____ to tell the reader about the lives of famous poets

   _____ to explain how to write a poem

Circle the word that best completes each sentence.

3. Ms. Donnelly felt _____ about her best friend moving away.

   strongly   excited   joyful

4. Ms. Donnelly is eager to share her _____ with the class.

   worries   experiences   confusion

Study Skills

A library's reference system can help you find a book. Use the information below to answer the questions that follow.

Call No:	455.62 SU
Author:	Sullivan-Todd, Kathy
Title:	My Life in Poetry
Publisher:	Darby House Publishing, 2004

1. What is the title of the book?

   _____

2. What year was the book published?

   _____

3. Which book would be located closer to the book with the call number above—the book with call number 455.62 VO or the book with call number 455.62 DA?

   _____

An Everyday Poet

What parts of your life would be good material for a poem?

1   Naomi Shihab Nye has lots of things to write about. She never seems to run out of ideas. Naomi writes poetry for young people and adults, but she is also the author of essays, children's picture books, songs, and a novel for teenagers. In addition, she has edited several poetry anthologies.

2   Where does Naomi get her ideas? She is a great observer of the world around her. She sees poetry in the details of everyday life, like the way things smell or taste, the sounds of nature, the voices of her family, and the colors of a flower or a bird's wing or a strawberry.

3   Naomi's poetry is also often influenced by places she has lived and visited. Naomi was raised by her Palestinian father and American mother. She grew up in St. Louis, Missouri; Jerusalem, Israel; and San Antonio, Texas. Each of these places has unique flavors that Naomi has captured with her rich, descriptive language.

4   Naomi also writes about her dual cultures and the conflict between the Israelis and Palestinians in the Middle East. Today, Naomi lives with her family in San Antonio. She knows many people who have a Mexican-American heritage, and she works their experiences into her poetry. Naomi focuses on the ways that people of different cultures and backgrounds are similar rather than different. She has even traveled to the Middle East and Asia to promote international goodwill through the arts. Naomi firmly believes in the power of writing to change the world and help people find common ground.

5   Naomi Shihab Nye began writing poetry as soon as she learned how to write. She published her first poem when she was only seven years old! Since that time, Naomi has written and edited more than 20 books. She advises young writers to write about their daily lives—the things they observe and the feelings they have. That's a good reminder for any writer!

Vocabulary Skills

Write the words from the passage that have the meanings below.

1. collections of writing by different authors

   _____
   Par. 1

2. someone who watches and pays attention

   _____
   Par. 2

3. to bring to people's attention

   _____
   Par. 4

An **idiom** is a group of words that has a special meaning. Write the idiom from paragraph 4 on the line below its meaning.

4. things people can agree on

   _____

A word that sounds the same as another word but has a different spelling and meaning is a **homophone**. Circle the homophone that correctly completes each sentence below.

5. Naomi was _____ by parents of different nationalities. (raised, razed)

6. Naomi _____ for children and for adults. (rights, writes)

Reading Skills

1. Check the line beside the word or words that best describe what type of nonfiction selection this is.

   _____ historical nonfiction

   _____ biography

   _____ how-to

2. A **summary** is a short sentence that tells the most important facts about a topic. Check the sentence below that is the best summary for paragraph 3.

   _____ Naomi uses descriptive language in her work.

   _____ Naomi grew up in St. Louis, Jerusalem, and San Antonio.

   _____ Naomi's poetry is influenced by the places she has lived.

3. The author says that each of the places Naomi has visited or lived has its own "unique flavors." What does this mean?

   _____

   _____

Study Skills

Use the table below to answer the questions that follow.

Title	Type of Book	Date Published
Sitti's Secrets	picture book	1994
Habibi	novel	1996
Come With Me: Poems for a Journey	poetry	2000
19 Varieties of Gazelle:Poems of the Middle East	poetry	2002

1. What type of book is *Habibi*?

   _____

2. Which book was published in 2000?

   _____

3. In what year was *Sitti's Secrets* published?

   _____

Can You Spell N-E-R-V-O-U-S?

Will Daniel be able to help Noah calm his nerves and compete in a school spelling bee?

1 Noah sat on the front steps of his family's apartment building. He absently bounced a tennis ball on the sidewalk as he stared off into space. Noah didn't even notice his brother coming down the sidewalk until Daniel stood right in front of him.

2 "Where were you, Noah?" Daniel asked his brother, settling beside him on the step. "It seemed like you were a million miles away. You didn't even hear me calling you, did you?"

3 Noah shook his head. He caught the tennis ball in one hand and looked at his older brother. "Daniel, have you ever had stage fright?" he finally asked.

4 "Sure," said Daniel. "Plenty of times. Do you remember that play I was in a few years ago? I must have been in fourth grade. I knew my lines, but I was terrified to have to recite them in front of an audience. I also have a little bit of stage fright right before my basketball games start. I feel okay during practice, but as soon as I see the crowd of people in the stands, my heart beats so fast that it feels like popcorn popping in my chest."

5 "I know just what you mean," said Noah. "That's how I feel just *thinking* about the spelling bee next week."

6 "I didn't know you made it to the finals," said Daniel. "Good job!"

7 "It's not good at all," said Noah, starting to bounce the ball again. "I'm worried I'll get nervous and freeze on stage. I might forget how to spell everything—even my own name! I don't know what to do." Noah looked miserably at his brother.

8 "Noah, I know that you're not going to forget how to spell your name," Daniel reassured his brother. "I'll help you get through this. Here's what you need to do. You have to practice as much as you can before the day of the competition. I'll go to the auditorium with you to practice, if you want. That way you'll feel comfortable there."

9 Noah began to look a little less miserable. "Then, I'll teach you this exercise my hockey coach taught me," continued Daniel. "You close your eyes and picture yourself doing the thing that you're worried about. You go through the entire situation in your mind so you can see what it feels like to do it and do it well. It might sound strange, but believe me, it works."

10 "I'm still nervous," said Noah, "but I feel a little better. You'll really help me prepare for this?"

11 Daniel grinned and put his arm around his brother's shoulder. "Of course I'm going to help you. I'm a lousy speller. I can't help being impressed by your aptitude for spelling. Quick, spell *aptitude*!" he joked.

12 Noah just rolled his eyes. "T-H-A-N-K-S, Daniel. You're a pretty good brother."

Vocabulary Skills

Write the words from the story that have the meanings below.

1. not paying attention to what one is doing

   _____
   Par. 1

2. repeat something from memory

   _____
   Par. 4

3. a talent or natural ability

   _____
   Par. 11

4. A **simile** compares two things using the words *like* or *as*. Find the simile in paragraph 4, and write it on the line below.

   _____

   _____

5. What were the two things compared to each other in question 4?

   _____

6. Choose one item from question 5, and use it to create your own simile on the lines below.

   _____

   _____

Reading Skills

Read the descriptions below. Write **N** next to the phrase if it describes Noah. Write **D** if it describes Daniel. Write **B** if it describes both Noah and Daniel.

1. _____ is the older brother

2. _____ is on a basketball team

3. _____ is nervous about a spelling bee

4. _____ gets stage fright sometimes

5. _____ gives his brother good advice

6. What problem does Noah have in this story?

   _____

   _____

7. Name two times Daniel has experienced stage fright.

   _____

   _____

8. What was Noah thinking about when Daniel was calling him at the beginning of the story?

   _____

   _____

9. Why does Noah feel less nervous by the end of the story?

   _____

   _____

Study Skills

An **outline** is used to put ideas in order. It shows the important facts in a story. Use the facts from paragraph 4 to complete Part I. Use the facts from paragraph 9 to complete Part II.

I. Daniel describes his experiences with stage fright

    A. stage fright for 4th grade play

    B. _____

    C. not nervous at practice

II. Daniel explains relaxation exercise

    A. close your eyes

    B. _____

    C. sounds strange but works

Spelling Their Way to Success

What would it be like to be a contestant in one of the most famous spelling bees in the world?

1   Have you ever participated in a school or community spelling bee? If you have, you know how exciting it is and how intense the competition can be. No one knows this better than the contestants in the Annual Scripps Howard National Spelling Bee in Washington, D.C. Every year, the best spellers come together to compete for the $12,000 grand prize and the honor of winning such a prestigious competition.

2   The first event was held in 1925 and was sponsored by a Kentucky newspaper, the *Louisville Courier-Journal*. A national bee has been held every year since then, except for 1943, 1944, and 1945 because of World War II. There were only nine contestants that first year. Today, there are more than 250 competitors. The sponsors, mostly newspapers, hold competitions in their communities. The winners of these spelling bees meet in Washington, D.C. for the national competition.

3   There are many rules and restrictions for the national bee. The contestants must be under 16 years of age and must not be in a grade higher than the eighth grade. There may be as many as five rounds. All of the spelling is done orally, except in the first round when the contestants must take a written test. After a spelling word is given to a contestant, he or she is allowed to ask for the word's pronunciation, definition, and language of origin. The contestant can even request that the word be used in a sentence.

4   You might wonder how all of these pieces of information could help someone spell an unfamiliar word. The competitors spend many hours studying the spellings of specific words. But even more importantly, they learn patterns that they can use when they do not know a word.

5   Being able to break a word down into its parts can also help. Imagine having to spell the word *arachnophobia*. This sounds like a difficult word, but the definition, *a fear of spiders*, contains a couple of clues. If you know the

Greek word *phobos* means *fear* and the Greek word for spider is *arachne*, *arachnophobia* becomes much simpler to spell.

6   No matter how much studying the contestants do, there is no way for them to predict what the word will be when it is their turn to take the microphone. Here is a list of some of the winning words from the last seven decades of national bees: *chlorophyll*, *crustaceology*, *insouciant*, *chihuahua*, *sarcophagus*, *logorrhea*, *esquamulose*, and *milieu*. If you can spell any of these words, you just might have a future as a Scripps Howard National Spelling Bee champ.

Vocabulary Skills

Write the words from the passage that have the meanings below.

1. important and highly respected

   _____
   Par. 1

2. people or companies who provide financial support

   _____
   Par. 2

3. original source; beginning

   _____
   Par. 3

4. know about in advance

   _____
   Par. 6

Check the sentence in which the underlined word has the same meaning as it does in the story.

5. _____ Dominic was careful not to be stung by a <u>bee</u> when he walked across the lawn.

   _____ My aunt is going to a quilting <u>bee</u> next Saturday.

6. _____ Do you have time to play a <u>round</u> of golf with me today?

   _____ The baby played with the <u>round</u> rubber ball.

Fill in the blanks below with the possessive form of the word in parentheses.

7. The _____ words are often hard for even adults to spell. (winners)

8. Each _____ goal is to become the new spelling champ. (contestant)

9. A contestant may ask for a _____ definition. (word)

Reading Skills

1. Why wasn't a national bee held in 1943, 1944, or 1945?

   _____

2. Name two words that winners of the national bee have spelled.

   _____

3. What is one technique contestants use to spell unfamiliar words?

   _____

4. Check the sentence that best states the main idea of the selection.

   _____ Spellers cannot predict what words they will be asked to spell.

   _____ A contestant in the Scripps Howard National Spelling Bee can ask for a word's pronunciation, definition, and language of origin.

   _____ The Scripps Howard National Spelling Bee in Washington, D.C. is a time for the best spellers to compete for a grand prize.

Write **T** before the sentences that are true. Write **F** before the sentences that are false.

5. _____ During the first round, contestants take a written test.

6. _____ The Scripps Howard National Spelling Bee is held in the state of Washington.

7. _____ Contestants must be older than 16.

8. _____ The first national bee was held in 1925.

Cooking Up a Tasty *Cinco de Mayo*

Have you ever prepared a meal from another culture?

1   Alicia and Marco wandered down the sidewalk taking in the sounds, sights, and smells all around them. Alicia loved the swirling colors of the dancers' skirts. Marco tapped his feet in time to the familiar beat of the *mariachi* band. The air was filled with the wonderful aroma of meat and vegetables cooking over a hot grill.

2   Finally, Alicia and Marco reached a large tent. "This is it, Marco," said Alicia, pointing to a banner that read: *12th Annual Cinco de Mayo Cooking Classes.* Alicia and Marco ducked inside the tent and let their eyes adjust to the light that seemed dim in comparison to the bright afternoon sun.

3   "Let me guess," called a woman wearing a colorful embroidered blouse. "You two must be Alicia and Marco Ruiz."

4   The brother and sister nodded. "Our dad signed us up for the cooking class," said Marco.

5   "He thinks everyone should know how to cook," added Alicia.

6   The woman smiled. "He's right! My name is Mrs. Juarez. No one else is registered for this session, so it looks like it will just be the three of us."

7   "You can start by washing your hands over there," she said, pointing to a sink. "Then, we'll talk about some of the ingredients that are traditionally used in Mexican cooking. We'll also learn how to make a few healthful and tasty dishes. Do either of you have a favorite Mexican dish?"

8   Marco was drying his hands on a red dishtowel. "I was hoping we might learn to make *gazpacho*. It's one of my mom's favorites in the summer."

9   "*Gazpacho* is an excellent cold soup to make on a hot day. What kind of ingredients do you think we'll need?" asked Mrs. Juarez.

10   "Hmmm," said Marco. "I know there are tomatoes, cucumbers, and celery in it. My family likes spicy foods, so there is probably some kind of pepper in it, too."

11   "That's right," said Mrs. Juarez. "I use green and red peppers for flavor and a jalapeño pepper for zing."

12   "How about you, Alicia?" asked Mrs. Juarez. "Do you have any favorites?"

13   "I love *empanadas*," replied Alicia. "But I've never made them myself before."

14   "What kind of ingredients do you think we'll need to make *empanadas*?"

15   "I'm not sure what ingredients are used in the dough, but our dad always makes them with pumpkin filling," said Alicia. "I think they have some cinnamon and nutmeg in them, too."

16   "Very good! I see that both of you pay attention to the flavors in the foods you eat. That is very important. I like the two dishes you have chosen. Both of them use several traditional Mexican ingredients. I thought we could also make one of my favorite dishes, *arroz con pollo.* Do you have any ideas about what that is?"

17   "*Arroz* means *rice*, and *pollo* is *chicken*," said Alicia.

18   "So, *arroz con pollo* is *chicken with rice*," finished Marco.

19   "Excellent!" said Mrs. Juarez, walking toward a refrigerator at the far end of the tent. "Are you ready to begin?" she asked.

20   "I can't wait," said Marco. "All this talk about food is making me hungry!"

Vocabulary Skills

Write the words from the story that have the meanings below.

1. a pleasant scent or smell

   _____
   Par. 1

2. get used to

   _____
   Par. 2

3. not very bright

   _____
   Par. 2

4. decorated with designs made by needle and thread

   _____
   Par. 3

Circle the homophone that correctly completes each sentence below.

5. Marco and Alicia _____ inside the tent. (ducked, duct)

6. *Empanadas* are made with pastry _____ that is stuffed with filling and then baked or fried. (doe, dough)

7. Alicia and Marco took in all the _____ and sounds at the *Cinco de Mayo fiesta*. (sights, sites)

Write a compound word using two words in each sentence.

8. An area on which you can walk by the side of the road is a _____.

9. Marco wiped his hands on a towel used to dry a dish, or a _____.

10. To cook their meal, Alicia and Marco used a book with recipes, or a _____.

Reading Skills

1. What do you think Mrs. Juarez means when she says she uses a jalapeño pepper for zing?

   _____

2. Why wasn't anyone else in Alicia and Marco's cooking class?

   _____

3. Do you think that Alicia and Marco will cook anything for their parents? Why or why not?

   _____

Read the descriptions below. Write **A** next to the phrase if it describes Alicia. Write **M** if it describes Marco.

4. _____ wants to learn how to make *gazpacho*

5. _____ loves *empanadas*

6. _____ enjoys watching the dancers at the *fiesta*

Study Skills

Write the name of the reference source you could use to find out the information in each question below.

encyclopedia	dictionary
atlas	

1. Where could you find out how to pronounce the word *mariachi*?

   _____

2. Where could you find out more information about *Cinco de Mayo*?

   _____

3. Where could you look to find out how far Mexico City is from Houston, Texas?

   _____

Now You're Cooking!

Do you ever help your parents prepare meals at home?

Before you begin:

- Never use the stove or a knife without an adult's supervision.

- Always remember to keep the handle of the skillet turned in so you cannot accidentally bump into it.

Tortilla Casserole

1 tablespoon vegetable oil

$\frac{1}{2}$ cup chopped frozen onion

$\frac{1}{2}$ green bell pepper, diced

1 14-ounce can diced tomatoes

$\frac{1}{2}$ cup bottled tomato salsa

$\frac{1}{2}$ teaspoon dried oregano

$\frac{3}{4}$ teaspoon salt

2 15-ounce cans black beans, drained and rinsed

8 small corn tortillas

1 cup shredded Monterey Jack cheese

1 cup shredded cheddar cheese

1. Here are some other things you will need: a measuring cup, a teaspoon, a tablespoon, a cutting knife, a colander, a wooden spoon, a bowl, cooking spray, aluminum foil, a skillet, a spatula, and a large, oval baking dish.

2. First, preheat the oven to 350°F. Then, chop the green bell pepper. Place the oil, pepper, and onion in the skillet, and cook over medium heat. Sauté the vegetables for about five minutes.

3. Remove the skillet from the burner. Open both cans of beans, and place them in the colander. Rinse the beans in cool water, and drain well.

4. Add tomatoes, salsa, oregano, and salt to the skillet, and stir well. Next, add the beans to the mixture.

5. Coat the baking dish with cooking spray. Combine the two cheeses in a bowl. Then, spread one-third of the bean mixture on the bottom of the dish. Top with four tortillas, and sprinkle with one-third of the cheese. Now, add another layer of the bean mixture, four more tortillas, and another third of the cheese. Add the last layer of beans, and cover the dish with aluminum foil. Reserve the remaining cheese.

6. Bake the casserole for about 40 minutes. Then, remove the foil and add the remaining cheese. Put the casserole back in the oven, and bake it until the cheese topping is hot and bubbly. Allow the casserole to cool slightly before serving. This recipe makes six servings.

Vocabulary Skills

Write the words from the recipe that have the meanings below.

1. a kitchen tool used for draining liquid

   _____
   Step 3

2. to allow the liquid to flow away

   _____
   Step 3

Check the meaning of the underlined word in each sentence.

3. Spread part of the bean mixture in the dish.

   _____ a blanket or covering for a bed

   _____ to place a layer over a surface

4. The foil keeps the casserole from becoming too dry while it is baking.

   _____ a thin sheet of aluminum

   _____ to keep from being successful

Reading Skills

1. Number the steps below to show the order in which they happen.

   _____ Add the beans to the tomato mixture.

   _____ Sauté the vegetables in the skillet.

   _____ Coat the baking dish with cooking spray.

   _____ Preheat the oven.

   _____ Bake the casserole until the cheese on top is bubbly.

2. Check the line beside the word or words that best describe what type of nonfiction selection this is.

   _____ how-to

   _____ biography

   _____ persuasive text

3. Check the phrase that best describes the author's purpose.

   _____ to tell a story about a family who makes a tortilla casserole

   _____ to explain how to make tortilla casserole

   _____ to show the history of casseroles in American cooking

4. What are the two types of cheeses that are used in this recipe?

   _____

   _____

Study Skills

An **index** is located at the end of many nonfiction books. It is an alphabetical listing of all the topics in a book. You can look in the index to find out where to look for information about a particular topic. Use the index below to answer the questions.

Index

1. On which page can you find a recipe for flan?

   _____

2. Which entry in the index has two recipes listed below it?

   _____

3. What recipe would you find on page 32?

   _____

A Big Victory for a Small Army

What do people celebrate on Cinco de Mayo?

1   Have you ever attended a *Cinco de Mayo* festival? If you have not, you do not know what you are missing. In Spanish, the words *cinco de mayo* mean *fifth of May*. It is a day for celebration and pride in Mexican heritage. It is celebrated both in Mexico and in parts of the United States, especially the Southwest, where there is a larger Hispanic population.

2   In 1862, the French attacked the Mexican army. They were fighting for control of Mexico. They planned to quickly defeat the Mexican army and allow Emperor Maximilian of Austria to become Mexico's ruling monarch. The French did not anticipate many problems in the battle for power in Mexico. Their army was larger, stronger, and better trained than the Mexican

army. This is why it came as a great surprise to the French when they were defeated in just a few hours at the Battle of Puebla, under the direction of General Ignacio Zaragoza, on May 5, 1862.

3   This victory was an enormous triumph for Mexico. Unfortunately, it did not last long. The French returned in 1863 with even greater force and conquered the country. The French occupation lasted only until 1867, when Mexico was able to take back power with some support from the United States. *Cinco de Mayo* is a celebration of the spirit of the Mexican people.

4   *Cinco de Mayo fiestas* (*fee ESS tahs*), or celebrations, vary from place to place. One of the biggest of all takes place in the Mexican town of Puebla, where the French army was defeated in 1862. The festivals often last for more than one day. There is plenty of traditional Mexican food, as well as music, dancing, games, parades, decorations, and fireworks. There may also be a reenactment of the Battle of Puebla. People dress up as the French and Mexican soldiers. After a pretend battle, the Mexican general wins a swordfight with the French general, and the celebrating continues.

5   One Mexican tradition that is popular with children at *Cinco de Mayo fiestas* is the *piñata* (*pin YAH tah*). A *piñata* is a colorful object often made of papier-mâché and cardboard. It is stuffed with all kinds of treats, such as candy and small gifts. Children take turns being blindfolded and trying to break open the *piñata* with a large stick so the goodies can spill out on the ground.

6   The next time the fifth of May is coming near, see if you can find a *Cinco de Mayo fiesta* near you. If you can't, invite your friends over and hold one of your own. Ask an adult to help you make some simple, traditional Mexican dishes. Make a *piñata*, play some *mariachi* music, and remember the small Mexican army that bravely protected their country.

Vocabulary Skills

A **word family** is a group of words that have the same letter combinations. Circle the words in each row that are part of the word family in parentheses.

1. (*-ight*)   blight   delight   blink   tonight

2. (*-ould*)   should   shelter   counter   could

The prefix **re-** means *again*. The prefix **pre-** means *before*. Add **re** or **pre** to each underlined word below to form a word that matches the definition.

3. to <u>enact</u> again _____

4. to <u>arrange</u> before _____

5. to <u>fill</u> again _____

Circle the homophone that correctly completes each sentence below.

6. The types of celebration _____ from place to place. (vary, very)

7. Children _____ open the *piñata* with a stick to get to the treats inside. (brake, break)

Reading Skills

1. What happens during a reenactment of a battle?

_____

2. What is a *piñata*?

_____

3. Why is *Cinco de Mayo* such an important celebration even though the French returned a year later and took power?

_____

_____

4. Check the sentence below that is the best summary for paragraph 2.

_____ The French were surprised to be defeated by the Mexican army in 1862.

_____ The French wanted Emperor Maximilian to become the new ruler of Mexico.

_____ The Mexican army was smaller than the invading French army.

Study Skills

Fiesta! Celebrate Cinco de Mayo on Saturday morning, May 5!

Sample the best Mexican food north of the border all day long!

Don't forget to bring your blanket and stay for the fireworks at dusk.

11:00 Parade begins

12:00 Speech by Mayor Gutierrez

1:00 Mariachi band contest

2:00 Make-your-own piñata party

3:00 Reenactment of the Battle of Puebla begins

1. Who is giving a speech at noon?

_____

2. What happens at 1:00?

_____

3. When will the fireworks begin?

_____

A Fitness Challenge

Will Eva and Kwame be able to convince the students in their class to get in shape?

1   Eva and Kwame stood in front of their fifth-grade classroom beneath a banner that read *Celebrate Fitness Awareness Week*! Eva held a colorful poster that showed the muscles of the human body. Kwame smiled at Eva, took a deep breath, and began the presentation.

2   "Think about sinking a basketball into a hoop," Kwame said to his class. "Imagine playing the piano, licking an ice-cream cone, doing a handstand, winking at a friend, and brushing your hair. What do all of these things have in common?" He waited a moment and then continued. "None of them would be possible without the hundreds of amazing muscles in your body. Did you know that there are more than six hundred muscles in the human body?"

3   "The ones we can control are called *voluntary muscles*. These are the muscles you use to do things like kick a ball or shake hands. The ones we can't control are called *involuntary muscles*. The heart is one example of an involuntary muscle. Now, Eva will tell you a little bit more about the kinds of muscles in the human body."

4   Eva stepped forward. "There are three main categories of muscles," she began. "Smooth, skeletal, and cardiac muscles. Smooth muscles are involuntary. Your brain and body give directions to these muscles without you thinking about it. Smooth muscles help your eyes focus. They are also found in your stomach. How many people have ever thrown-up?" she asked.

5   Almost every member of the class raised a hand. "Those are your smooth muscles at work," said Eva. "When you are sick, they contract, or become tighter. This pushes the food in your stomach back up, and you throw up.

6   "Cardiac muscles are the muscles of your heart," continued Eva. "They perform one of the most important functions in your body. They contract and relax to pump blood through your entire body.

7   "The last type of muscle is the skeletal muscle," Eva told her class. "These are muscles that you can control. They are attached to portions of your skeleton by tissues called *tendons*. When you want to pick up something, for example, your brain sends a message to your muscles. Tendons help the muscles move your arm and pick up the object."

8   "What is the best kind of exercise for your muscles?" Kwame asked. "It is aerobic exercise. It makes your heart stronger and your skeletal muscles more powerful. There are many ways to get aerobic exercise. Bike riding, hiking, playing softball, jumping rope, swimming, and roller-blading are just a few examples."

9   "In honor of Fitness Awareness Week," said Eva, "we'd like to ask everyone to spend at least 30 minutes exercising your muscles each day this week."

10   "Record your activities, and every person who has completed 30 minutes of exercise each day will be awarded a prize at the end of the week," said Kwame. "You'll get your picture in the Santa Rosita newspaper for Fitness Awareness Week and a free water bottle!"

Vocabulary Skills

Write the words from the story that have the meanings below.

1. different subject areas

   _____
   Par. 4

2. to produce a clear picture or image

   _____
   Par. 4

3. jobs; uses

   _____
   Par. 6

4. something that allows the body to use more oxygen and helps the heart get stronger

   _____
   Par. 8

Find an antonym in the story for each of the words below.

5. above _____
   Par. 1

6. shallow _____
   Par. 1

7. backward _____
   Par. 4

8. relax _____
   Par. 5

Words that have a single middle consonant are usually divided into syllables before the consonant. For example, *e/vil* or *o/pen*. Divide the words below into syllables using a slash *(/)*.

9. f o c u s

10. e v e r

11. r e l a x

12. a b o u t

Reading Skills

1. In paragraph 2, Kwame lists several different activities. How are these activities similar?

   _____

2. How are voluntary and involuntary muscles different?

   _____

3. What idea are Eva and Kwame trying to persuade their classmates into doing?

   _____

4. Name two types of aerobic exercise that are not mentioned in the story.

   _____

5. Do you think that Kwame and Eva will get their pictures in the Santa Rosita newspaper? Explain your answer.

   _____

   _____

Study Skills

A library's reference system can help you find a book. Use the information below to answer the questions that follow.

Call No:	331.68 RE
Author(s):	Redwing, Jake and Alice
Title:	The Kids' Guide to Fitness and the Body
Publisher:	Body and Mind Publishing, Inc.

1. Who are the authors of the book?

   _____

2. What is the name of the publisher?

   _____

3. Which book would be located closer to the book with the call number above—the book with call number 331.52 RA or the book with call number 331.68 RA

   _____

Muscles in the Wild

How are the muscles of different animals suited to their needs?

1   You probably know many of the things that you can do with the hundreds of different muscles in your body. But have you ever thought about how the muscles in an animal's body are different from yours? An animal's muscles are made to do the things that are most important for its survival.

2   Lions are hunters. They depend on their ability to hunt other animals to survive. Lions must be fast in order to catch their prey. The powerful muscles in their rear legs allow them to run at speeds of more than 30 miles per hour. They can also leap a distance of more than 35 feet. The strong muscles in their chests and front legs help them capture their prey.

3   Snakes also use their muscles for hunting prey and for movement, but their muscles function in very different ways than lions' do. Because snakes do not have any limbs, they need a form of locomotion other than walking, crawling, or flying. Pound for pound, snakes have more muscles than most animals. They contract, or tighten, and then release their powerful muscles. This creates a wavelike motion down the length of the snake's body. These waves push against the ground or other objects to move the snake forward. This is just one of several ways snakes get from one place to another.

4   Snakes' muscles are also equipped to allow them to swallow things that seem much too large. For example, a snake may eat an egg that is larger than the width of its body. How does the snake accomplish this amazing feat? Can you imagine eating an entire watermelon in a single gulp? The snake's strong neck muscles tighten and release to push the egg along as the snake swallows. The pressure of the muscles is so strong that it cracks the shell and allows the snake to digest the egg's contents.

5   The elephant's trunk contains an enormous amount of muscle. Scientists believe that the trunk alone has more than 100,000 muscles! This is because the elephant uses its trunk much in the same way that people use their hands and fingers. Even though the trunk is large, it can perform surprisingly delicate tasks. For example, an elephant can pick up a small twig or leaf from the ground. The trunk can also be a powerful tool. An elephant can use its trunk to pick up a tree by its roots or even to lift a baby elephant.

6   The specialized muscles of these animals seem pretty incredible. But the muscles in your body work exactly the way you need them to. After all, it might be fun to be able to leap a distance of 30 feet, but as a human being, there is just not much need for it.

Vocabulary Skills

Write the words from the passage that have the meanings below.

1. arms, legs, wings, or flippers

   _____
   Par. 3

2. the ability to move from one place to another

   _____
   Par. 3

3. let go; loosen or relax

   _____
   Par. 4

4. used for a specific purpose

   _____
   Par. 6

5. Check the sentence in which *roots* has the same meaning as it does in paragraph 5.

   _____ The roots of the large tree extend deep underground.

   _____ June's father helped her research their family's roots.

6. Check the sentence in which *pound* has the same meaning as it does in paragraph 3.

   _____ Please do not pound so loudly at my door.

   _____ The chef will need a pound of flour to make enough bread for dinner.

Reading Skills

1. Why do a snake's neck muscles need to be strong?

   _____

2. About how far can a lion leap?

   _____

3. According to the selection, what is one way snakes and lions are similar?

   _____

Circle the word that best completes each sentence.

4. A lion's strength is important for its

   _____.

   interest   survival   body

5. An elephant can _____ many types of tasks with its trunk.

   accomplish   forget   create

Study Skills

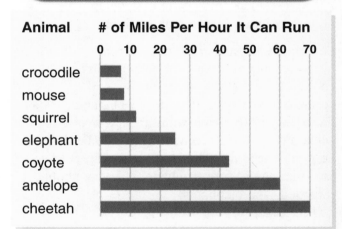

| Animal | # of Miles Per Hour It Can Run |

1. Which is the fastest animal listed above?

   _____

2. Which two animals run at about the same speed?

   _____

3. About how fast can a coyote run?

   _____

4. Which animal runs about 12 miles per hour?

   _____

The Art of the Elephants

What makes a drawing or a painting a piece of art?

1   If your cat walked across something you were painting and left footprints behind, would you consider your cat an artist? What if your bird could hold a colored pencil in its beak and make marks on a piece of paper? These ideas might sound like a joke to you, but some people have been taking animal art very seriously.

2   In 1995, two Russian-American artists, Vitaly Komar and Alex Melamid, first heard about the troubled elephants of Thailand. Elephants were used for hundreds of years in Thailand's logging industry to haul timber from forests in areas where there were no roads. When the forests of Thailand began to slowly disappear, the government put a stop to logging. All of a sudden, there were many elephants who no longer had a way to make a living.

3   Some elephants were abused. Others had to try to survive on their own and couldn't find enough to eat. There were once tens of thousands of elephants living in Thailand. Today, there are less than five thousand. Komar and Melamid knew that something had to be done to help the elephants. Then, they came up with an idea that would forever change the way people regarded Thai elephants.

4   Komar and Melamid visited elephant camps in Thailand. There they began to show the *mahouts*, or elephant trainers, how to teach the elephants to paint. At first, the mahout has to guide the elephant's trunk. The elephants became more comfortable doing this with practice—and lots of sweet snacks—and finally started to paint on their own.

5   The strange idea that Komar and Melamid had to save the elephants actually began to work. They helped found several elephant art schools in Thailand and in other Asian countries. The elephants and their mahouts go there to learn about painting and to get the supplies they need. Today, people buy elephant artwork from galleries all around the world. Some are even willing to pay more than $2,000 for the work of the elephant artists!

6   Some people have compared the cheerful, brightly-colored artwork to the work of abstract painters like Jackson Pollock and Vasily Kandinsky. Other people are just happy to buy art that is so unique and original and that supports such a good cause. The next time you see a piece of colorful abstract art, find out who the artist is. You just may be surprised at what you learn!

Vocabulary Skills

Write the words from the passage that have the meanings below.

1. carry; transport

   _____
   Par. 2

2. looked at; considered

   _____
   Par. 3

3. create; establish

   _____
   Par. 5

4. places where art is displayed

   _____
   Par. 5

5. not resembling anything real

   _____
   Par. 6

Find an antonym in the story for each of the words below.

6. rapidly _____
   Par. 2

7. temporarily _____
   Par. 3

8. depressing _____
   Par. 6

Reading Skills

1. Check the phrase that best describes the author's purpose.

   _____ to share information about the elephant artists of Thailand

   _____ to persuade the reader to buy a piece of elephant artwork

   _____ to inform the reader about the different types of animals living in Thailand

2. What problem were the elephants of Thailand having before Komar and Melamid stepped in?

   _____

3. About how many elephants are there in Thailand today?

   _____

4. Name one artist whose work some people believe resembles the elephant artwork.

   _____

5. What is the name for the elephants' style of painting?

   _____

Study Skills

1. What body of water lies south of the majority of Thailand?

   _____

2. Which country can be found along the western edge of Thailand?

   _____

3. What direction would you go from Bangkok to get to China?

   _____

4. Which country lies along most of the northern and eastern borders of Thailand?

   _____

Jack the Dripper

Why is the work of Jackson Pollack so important in the art world?

1   If someone scribbled on a piece of paper, would you consider it to be a work of art? What if the piece of paper were as big as a wall and there were layers and layers of scribbles? The paintings of artist Jackson Pollack are sometimes seen as "just scribbles." However, Pollack forced people to think about what they accepted as art. In the process, he changed painting forever.

2   Pollack was the type of artist who was determined to find his own style. But during the 1930s, most critics agreed that his paintings looked a lot like work done by the artists he

most admired: Pablo Picasso, Joan Miro, Diego Rivera, and his teacher, Thomas Hart Benton. However, the New York art dealer Peggy Guggenheim saw potential in his work and asked Pollack to create a large mural for the entrance hall to her home.

3   This painting would be Jackson Pollack's breakthrough. The mural was 18 feet long, but it had no recognizable elements in it, just drips and splatters of paint. People were very intrigued and excited by what Pollack had done.

4   Critics described Pollack's new paintings as more similar to a piece of music than to a realistic painting or a photograph. For instance, when you listen to a song or melody that has no words, it does not represent anything in nature. The music is simply sound for its own purpose. Pollack's abstract paintings were like music for the eyes. The colorful drips and splatters danced their way across the canvas. Even though they did not create an image, they were energetic and exciting to look at.

5   In 1949, *LIFE* magazine published a series of photographs showing Pollack working in his studio. The way he painted was almost as shocking as the finished paintings. Instead of using an easel, he laid his huge canvases on the floor to make the dripping and splattering easier.

6   It was definitely not a clean way to paint. In fact, many of Pollack's paintings contain bits from his studio floor, like nails and coins, as well as footprints where he stepped on the canvas! His technique has been called *action painting*. This is because, unlike a traditional painter who sits at an easel, Pollack walked around and swung his arms, dripping and splattering the paint. He even earned the nickname "Jack the Dripper." Many artists saw what Pollack did and felt free to be able to create art in any way they felt inspired to.

Vocabulary Skills

Write the words from the passage that have the meanings below.

1. a possibility that hasn't yet become real

   _____
   Par. 2

2. a large painting that is done directly on a wall

   _____
   Par. 2

3. a sudden advance that allows one to continue

   _____
   Par. 3

4. able to be known or remembered

   _____
   Par. 3

5. interested; curious about

   _____
   Par. 3

6. causing great surprise

   _____
   Par. 5

Find the simile in paragraph 4, and write it on the line below.

7. _____

Find a synonym in the story for each of the words below.

8. altered _____
   Par. 1

9. respected _____
   Par. 2

10. completed _____
    Par. 5

Underline the compound word in each sentence. Then, write the two words that make up each compound.

11. Creating a mural for Peggy Guggenheim was a breakthrough for Pollack.

    _____   _____

12. Pollack's footprints can be seen in some of his pieces.

    _____   _____

13. In the past, nobody had attempted to make art like Jackson Pollack's.

    _____   _____

Reading Skills

1. What has Pollack's technique been called?

   _____

2. Name two artists whom Pollack admired.

   _____

3. Is this passage a fantasy, or does it take place in reality?

   _____

4. How did Pollack change painting forever?

   _____

5. Why did critics think that Pollack's style of painting was more similar to music than to realistic painting?

   _____

   _____

Study Skills

Use a dictionary to help you divide these words into syllables.

1. d e s p e r a t e l y

2. p o t e n t i a l

3. r e a l i s t i c

4. p h o t o g r a p h s

5. t r a d i t i o n a l

6. l i b e r a t e d

Art School

What kind of art will Samir and Matthew make on their first day of class?

1 Samir and Matthew sat at a long table that was covered with flecks of paint. The walls were almost completely hidden behind row after row of paintings, drawings, collages, and photographs.

2 "Do you think all these pieces were done by kids our age?" Samir asked Matthew in a loud whisper.

3 "I don't know," replied Matthew. "I hope not. I don't think I could make anything that looks this professional. I wonder if we're in the wrong class."

4 Samir nodded in agreement. "You and I are pretty talented cartoonists, but I don't think either one of us is as experienced as the people in this class."

5 The boys' conversation was interrupted by a tall woman with gray hair that was pinned up on top of her head in a clump of curls. She wore jeans, a bright red shirt, and dangly earrings that spelled out the word *art* in thin pieces of twisted metal. "I'd like to welcome you all to the summer art program. My name is Tess Kaye, and I'll be your instructor for the next six weeks."

6 She leaned against her desk and continued. "Before we started class, I couldn't help hearing some of your comments. I don't want anyone to feel intimidated. We have some wonderful artwork displayed here from the spring session. Those students were all beginners, too. I know we have just as many talented artists in this class, so I want everyone to do their best to relax and have fun."

7 Samir and Matthew exchanged looks. They still weren't convinced, but they were willing to try. The first project they were going to do was a still life. Ms. Kaye arranged some twigs, leaves, and rocks on a small platform. The students could draw, paint, or create a collage. They could make a picture that looked realistic, or they could use their imaginations to create something that was their own interpretation of what they saw.

8 Samir and Matthew worked hard on their projects for the entire two-hour class. Neither one realized how quickly the time was passing until they heard Ms. Kaye call their names. She stood behind them and looked closely at the pieces they had been working on.

9 Samir was finishing his painting. The twigs, leaves, and rocks looked realistic, except that Samir had chosen to use unusual colors. Instead of painting in shades of gray, brown, and green, Samir chose bright turquoise blue, lime green, and a sunny, cheerful yellow.

10 Matthew had chosen to draw the still life in pencil. He drew from the perspective of a small cricket at the edge of the drawing. Each item in the drawing looked enormous through the eyes of the cricket.

11 "I'm so impressed!" exclaimed Ms. Kaye. "Today is only the first day of class. This was just going to be a warm-up exercise, but you both have done such a nice job. Do you mind if I hang your pieces on the board until next week?" she asked.

12 Samir and Matthew smiled and shook their heads. As they walked out into the bright afternoon sunlight, they slapped hands. Their first art class had gone much better than expected!

Vocabulary Skills

Write the words from the story that have the meanings below.

1. artwork made by gluing different materials onto a surface

   _____
   Par. 1

2. made to feel timid or frightened

   _____
   Par. 6

3. persuaded to do or believe something

   _____
   Par. 7

4. understanding or seeing something in a certain way

   _____
   Par. 7

Circle the homophone that correctly completes each sentence below.

5. There were small _____ of paint on the table. (flecks, flex)

6. Ms. Kaye arranged a _____ on the platform. (seen, scene)

7. Each _____ of art is unique. (piece, peace)

Write **S** if the possessive word is singular. Write **P** if it is plural.

8. _____ boys' artwork

9. _____ Ms. Kaye's comments

10. _____ Samir's painting

11. _____ students' conversations

Reading Skills

1. What kind of earrings was Ms. Kaye wearing?

   _____

2. Why was Samir's painting unusual?

   _____

3. What do you think a still life is?

   _____

4. What problem did Matthew and Samir have at the beginning of the story?

   _____

   _____

5. What is one way in which Mathew and Samir are different?

   _____

   _____

6. Write a summary of paragraph 6 on the lines below.

   _____

   _____

Study Skills

Maple Springs Community Summer Art Program

Classes begin on June 24.
Sign up online or in person.

Beginning Art	Tues. 1–3
Sculpture	Mon. and Wed. 10–12
Printmaking	Thurs. 6–9
Photography	Tues. and Thurs. 1–3

1. How can you sign up for classes?

   _____

2. When does the sculpture class meet?

   _____

3. Which classes meet only one day a week?

   _____

4. Which class meets in the evening?

   _____

The Petite Picasso

Read the story below to learn about the artwork of young Alexandra Nechita, an artist with amazing talent and a big heart.

1   Do you know what you'd like to be when you grow up? It takes most people many years and lots of experimentation to figure this out. For the young artist Alexandra Nechita, it never really seemed to be a question. From the day she began drawing at the age of two, she was an artist.

2   Alexandra Nechita was born in Romania in 1985 and moved to California when she was still a baby. As a toddler, she loved coloring in her coloring books. Her parents were worried that she should be spending less time coloring and more time being active and playing with other children. When her parents took away her coloring books, Alexandra began drawing her own pictures and coloring them in.

3   By the time Alexandra was seven years old, she had begun painting with acrylic and oil paints. She asked her parents for larger and larger canvases. When Alexandra took a local art class, her teacher was amazed at the young artist's unique style of painting. Alexandra's work was similar in some ways to cubist paintings by artists like Picasso.

4   These artists did not use a realistic style of painting. They allowed their imaginations to play an important part in their work. The figures of people in cubist paintings often had sharp corners and angles. Sometimes, they had multiple faces or sets of eyes. The interesting thing was that little Alexandra had never seen the work of these artists. People who wrote about her called her "Petite Picasso," which means *little Picasso*. This was a great compliment, but Alexandra's style of painting was all her own.

5   Alexandra's first public show was in 1994 at the Los Angeles Public Library when she was only eight years old. People were amazed at how young Alexandra was, but mostly they loved her imaginative artwork. It seemed like the work of a much more mature and accomplished artist.

6   It did not take long for Alexandra and her work to become famous. She appeared on television programs and in newspapers and magazines all over the world. Even though she is still a teen, Alexandra's career has continued to progress at an amazing pace. Her artwork has been shown internationally in galleries and museums. The sale of a single piece can earn the young artist more than $100,000. But that is not why Alexandra paints. She just cannot imagine doing anything else that would bring her such joy and satisfaction.

7   One reason Alexandra does appreciate the price her art demands is because it allows her to donate money to her favorite charities, such as the Special Olympics, an organization for athletes with special needs. Alexandra Nechita is a talented young woman who has already accomplished so much in her lifetime. What will the future hold for her?

Vocabulary Skills

Write the words from the passage that have the meanings below.

1. trying out different things

   _____
   Par. 1

2. more than one; several

   _____
   Par. 4

3. like an adult

   _____
   Par. 5

4. a feeling of being content and fulfilled

   _____
   Par. 6

Read each pair of words listed below. If the words are synonyms, write **S** on the line. If the words are antonyms, write **A** on the line.

5. _____ unique   common

6. _____ amazed   astonished

7. _____ joy   happiness

8. _____ public   private

The prefix **ir-** means *not*. Add **ir** to each word below. Then, use each new word in a sentence.

9. responsible _____

   _____

10. replaceable _____

   _____

Reading Skills

1. Why was it so unusual that Alexandra painted in the style of Cubists when she was small?

   _____

2. Find one sentence in the passage that shows Alexandra loves what she does. Write it below.

   _____

   _____

3. Check the line beside the word or words that best describe what type of selection this is.

   _____ biography

   _____ fiction

   _____ how-to

4. Check the words that describe Alexandra.

   _____ creative   _____ ambitious

   _____ generous   _____ scientific

   _____ impatient

5. Number the events below to show the order in which they happened.

   _____ Alexandra had her first public show.

   _____ Alexandra's works were shown in galleries and museums around the world.

   _____ Alexandra's parents thought she should spend less time coloring.

   _____ Alexandra began painting with acrylic and oil paints.

   _____ Alexandra was born in Romania.

Study Skills

Write the entry word you would look for in a dictionary next to each word below.

1. coloring _____

2. worried _____

3. continued _____

4. internationally _____

Planet of Dreams

Have you ever looked through a telescope? If you have, what did you see?

1 "Lena," whispered Dad. "Are you awake? You said to wake you up if I could get a clear image of Saturn through the telescope. Do you want to get up for a few minutes and come see it with me?"

2 Lena opened her eyes and yawned. She glanced at the clock and saw that it was a little before midnight. "Thanks for coming to get me, Dad. I'm glad it ended up being a clear night. Is it pretty amazing?" she asked, turning on the small lamp on her nightstand.

3 Lena's dad just grinned. "I'm not even going to say a word. You just have to see it yourself."

4 Lena put on one of her brother's cozy, worn-in sweatshirts over her pajamas. She and her dad sat on the wicker chairs on the back porch with the big telescope between them. Lena's dad made a few adjustments, and then Lena looked through the small opening.

5 "Wow!" Lena exclaimed. "Dad, this is incredible! I see a gold-colored sphere, and I can even see two of Saturn's rings. What is the smaller sphere I'm seeing beside it?"

6 "That's Titan," replied her dad, "one of Saturn's moons. So far scientists have discovered that Saturn has 31 moons, but it's possible that there are more still waiting to be discovered."

7 "Do you think that people will ever get to visit Saturn, Dad?" asked Lena dreamily.

8 "I doubt it," he answered. "Saturn is mostly composed of hydrogen and helium, which are both gases. The core is made of harder materials, but people wouldn't be able to walk on the surface. It can also be extremely windy on Saturn. In fact, I've read that winds can exceed one thousand miles an hour!"

9 "I guess I'll just have to be happy seeing it through a telescope," sighed Lena.

10 Once Lena was settled snugly back in her bed, she closed her eyes and quickly fell into a deep sleep.

11 *A tall, distinguished-looking gentleman stepped onto a large stage with red velvet curtains. He approached the microphone. "This year's award for Greatest Contribution to the World of Interplanetary Study goes to Ms. Lena Rinaldo for her discovery of a new moon around Saturn. In addition, Ms. Rinaldo has designed a spacesuit that can tolerate winds of nearly two thousand miles an hour. Her design brings us one step closer to sending humans to the ringed planet one day."*

12 *Lena took the microphone and addressed the large audience that had gathered in her honor. "Thank you for this generous award," she began. "Today is a dream come true for me. I have strived for this my entire career. I'd like to announce that Saturn's newest moon will be named* Alejandro, *in honor of my father." She winked at her dad, who was sitting proudly in the front row of the auditorium next to Lena's mother and brother.*

13 A car door slammed, and Lena opened her eyes. She took in the sunlight streaming in the window of her familiar bedroom and smelled the scent of coffee and eggs coming from the kitchen. She sighed, put on her slippers, and headed to the bathroom to brush her teeth.

Vocabulary Skills

Write the words from the story that have the meanings below.

1. made of

   _____
   Par. 8

2. be greater than

   _____
   Par. 8

3. respected and wise

   _____
   Par. 11

4. worked toward

   _____
   Par. 12

Compound words are divided into syllables between the two words that make the compound. For example, *play/ground*. Divide the words below into syllables using a slash *(/)*.

5. n i g h t s t a n d

6. s w e a t s h i r t

7. s u n l i g h t

8. s p a c e s u i t

Fill in the blanks below with the possessive form of the word in parentheses.

9. Lena can see _____ rings through the telescope. (Saturn)

10. _____ dad knows a lot about the planets. (Lena)

11. The _____ discovery of 31 moons surprised Lena. (scientists)

Reading Skills

1. Do you think Lena will be a scientist one day? Explain your answer.

   _____

   _____

2. What is one reason why Lena's dad thinks people will never be able to visit Saturn?

   _____

3. What part of the story is a fantasy for Lena? What part takes place in reality?

   _____

   _____

4. The **protagonist** is the main character in a story. Who is the protagonist in this story?

   _____

Study Skills

Write the name of the reference source you could use to find out the information in each question below.

encyclopedia	dictionary
thesaurus	

1. Where could you find the definition of the word *interplanetary*?

   _____

2. Where could you learn more about the conditions on Saturn?

   _____

3. Where could you find a synonym for the word *incredible*?

   _____

The Ringed Planet

How much do you know about one of our solar system's most fascinating planets?

1   The famous astronomer Galileo was the first to see that Saturn was shaped differently than the other planets. He thought the bulges on each side were caused by two other planets sitting right next to Saturn. The Cassini-Huygens spacecraft is named after the 17th century astronomers who concluded that Saturn was actually ringed: Giovanni Cassini and Christiaan Huygens.

2   The Cassini-Huygens spacecraft was launched in October of 1997, but it took seven years to reach its destination—the planet Saturn. On July 1, 2004, the Cassini orbiter began circling the sixth planet from the sun. It will continue sending information back to Earth for the next four years.

3   On January 14, 2005, the Huygens probe was dropped onto Titan, one of Saturn's many moons. For about 90 minutes, it sent back data and images of the moon. People around the world were amazed to see pictures of Titan's rocky surface. Scientists were able to identify what looked like a shoreline, drainage channels, and large boulders. Every piece of information they receive is one more clue in solving the mysteries of our solar system.

4   Although four other spacecrafts have flown by Saturn, Cassini will be the first one to stay for a while. During its four years of orbiting, Cassini will take photographs and scientific measurements that will be transmitted back to scientists on Earth. Even before it arrived at its final stop, Cassini was amazing astronomers with the best photographs ever taken of Jupiter, as well as rare views of Saturn's moon Phoebe.

5   One of the trickiest parts of the mission was maneuvering the spacecraft through Saturn's famous rings. The rings are thought to be the remnants of a moon that was somehow destroyed in the past. Its many pieces still orbit the planet and create a solid-looking ring.

6   The rocks and ice that form the rings vary greatly in size, from as small as dust particles to as big as a car. Trying to get Cassini-Huygens through there was a risky and complex challenge. However, the international team of scientists did it successfully.

Vocabulary Skills

Write the words from the passage that have the meanings below.

1. came to a decision

_____
Par. 1

2. the place something or someone is going

_____
Par. 2

3. sent by one person or thing to another

_____
Par. 4

4. carefully moving or guiding

_____
Par. 5

5. remains; leftovers

_____
Par. 5

Compound words are divided into syllables between the two words that make the compound. For example, *play/ground*. Divide the words below into syllables using a slash (/).

6. s p a c e c r a f t

7. s o m e h o w

8. t a k e o f f

In each row, circle the word that does not belong.

9. Galileo   Cassini   Huygens   Jupiter

10. Jupiter   meteor   Saturn   Earth

11. sun   moon   Titan   Phoebe

12. amaze   astonish   disappoint   surprise

Reading Skills

1. Check the line beside the word that best describes what type of passage this is.

_____ informational

_____ fiction

_____ myth

2. What did Galileo think the bulges on either side of Saturn were caused by?

_____

3. How long did it take the Cassini-Huygens spacecraft to travel from Earth to Saturn?

_____

4. How do scientists think the rings of Saturn were created?

_____

Study Skills

1. Which planet is closest to the sun?

_____

2. Between which two planets is Earth located?

_____

3. What is the name of the fifth planet from the sun?

_____

Kitt Peak National Observatory

Is there an observatory located near you?

1 The Kitt Peak National Observatory in Arizona is one of the most important astronomical research sites in the world. With 21 different telescopes aimed at the stars, Kitt Peak astronomers have made many discoveries that help us better understand the universe. For instance, research conducted at Kitt Peak has produced new information about how stars are formed. Research there has also helped find better ways to measure the incredible distances across the galaxies.

2 Kitt Peak is located 55 miles southwest of Tucson in the Quinlan Mountains that rise from the Sonoran Desert. This land is part of the Tohono O'odham Nation, the Native American people who have lived there for many centuries. Kitt Peak was originally called *Ioligam*, the Tohono O'odham word for the manzanita bush that grows there.

3 In the mid-1950s, scientists started a search for the best place to put a national observatory. From more than 150 potential mountain sites, Kitt Peak was chosen as the best location. Today, Kitt Peak is just one part of the National Optical Astronomy Observatory. The NOAS also has telescopes in New Mexico, Hawaii, and Chile. These telescopes work together so that there is always the best possible view of outer space.

4 Kitt Peak National Observatory offers daily tours of its facilities, but it also has a special night program that allows anyone to come and enjoy a close-up view of the universe. The Nightly Observing Program lets visitors look through either of two powerful telescopes to see astronomical features not visible to the naked eye.

5 At Kitt Peak, you might see any of the planets. You might also see meteors and comets that pass by. If you see a thick band of light flowing across your view, that is probably the Milky Way galaxy. Galaxies are groups of millions, and even billions, of stars that are grouped together and move as one through the universe. The Milky Way is the galaxy that contains our solar system.

6 Some other interesting things you might see are nebulae and clusters. Nebulae (the plural form of *nebula*) are enormous clouds of gas and dust where stars are formed. Astronomers give them descriptive names such as the *Swan Nebula* and the *Cat's Eye Nebula*. Clusters are groups of stars that are always seen together. A couple of clusters you might see are the Butterfly Cluster and the Wild Duck Cluster. While some astronomical objects are named, many astronomical objects are only referred to by numbers.

Vocabulary Skills

Write the words from the passage that have the meanings below.

1. places; locations

   _____
   Par. 1

2. guided or directed

   _____
   Par. 1

3. possible

   _____
   Par. 3

4. buildings that are used for a specific purpose

   _____
   Par. 4

5. words that describe something

   _____
   Par. 6

Write the words from the passage that match the abbreviations below.

6. HI _____

7. AZ _____

8. NM _____

Read each sentence below. Then, write the word from the **-ight** word family that best completes the sentence.

9. Kitt Peak offers a special _____ program where you can use powerful telescopes to view the universe.

10. You _____ be able to see a meteor or a comet.

11. The words *site* and _____ are homophones, or words that sound the same but are spelled differently and have different meanings.

Reading Skills

1. Check the line beside the word that best describes what type of nonfiction selection this is.

   _____ biography

   _____ informational

   _____ persuasive

2. On the lines below, write a sentence that summarizes paragraph 1.

   _____

   _____

3. In which mountain range is Kitt Peak located?

   _____

Study Skills

Rates for Guided Tours at Kitt Peak	
Adults:	$2.00 per person
Children (ages 6–12):	$1.00 per person
Children under 6:	free
Tohono O'odham Members:	free

1. Who can get a free guided tour at Kitt Peak?

   _____

2. How much would it cost for two adults to take the tour?

   _____

3. How much would it cost for two 10-year-olds and one 5-year-old to take the tour?

   _____

Anchors Aweigh!

What will Sarah and Pilar learn about boating safety?

1   At eight o'clock on Saturday morning, Sarah and Pilar stood on the dock and helped load supplies onto the small white sailboat. Pilar's grandpa was a tall man with deeply suntanned skin and crinkles around his eyes. Her grandma had tightly curled gray hair that she wore in a red kerchief. She held a steaming cup of coffee and smiled brightly at the girls.

2   "Sarah," said Mrs. Roma, "Pilar tells us this is the first time you've been sailing. Are you excited? We have such beautiful weather today." She looked up at the sky that was as blue as the bottom of a swimming pool.

3   "I'm really excited," said Sarah. "I've always wanted to go sailing. We only moved to Ohio from Iowa a couple of years ago. I'm still getting used to living next to such a big body of water. My cousin from Iowa came to visit us once, and she thought that Lake Erie was part of an ocean!"

4   Mrs. Roma nodded. "I can see why she might think that. Even though it doesn't have salty water like the ocean, it is certainly much bigger than what most people think of as a lake."

5   "We're almost ready to go," said Pilar's grandpa. "Why don't we all climb aboard, and then we can go over some basic safety tips with the girls," he suggested.

6   As soon as everyone was seated on the deck, Mr. Roma handed out life jackets. "These are called *PFDs*," he told Sarah and Pilar. "That stands for *personal flotation device*, which is just another word for *life jacket*. These need to be worn anytime you're out on the water, no exceptions." The girls nodded.

7   "Let's see if we have all the rest of our basic equipment." Mrs. Roma handed Sarah and Pilar a list. "If you read the items on the list, Grandpa and I will check to make sure that we have them onboard."

8   "Whistle, flashlight, and mirrors?"

9   "Check."

10   "Oars?"

11   "Check."

12   "Bucket and ropes?"

13   "Check."

14   "First aid kit?

15   "Check."

16   "Blanket?"

17   "Check."

18   "Good job, ladies," said Mr. Roma. "It looks like we're ready to set sail for Kelleys Island. Any questions?"

19   "What are the whistle, flashlight, and mirror for?" Pilar asked her grandpa.

20   "That's a good question. We always bring them along for safety in case we run into trouble or hit some bad weather. We can use those supplies to let people know where we are if they can't see us. For example, you can use a flashlight to signal SOS, which means *help*. Just make three quick flashes, three longer flashes, and then three more quick flashes. Anything else?"

21   The girls shook their heads. "Then, it's anchors aweigh, mates!" shouted Mr. Roma. "We're off on our sailing adventure!"

Vocabulary Skills

Write the words from the story that have the meanings below.

1. a landing area for ships and boats

_____
Par. 1

2. into or onto a vehicle

_____
Par. 5

3. one of the floors on a ship or boat

_____
Par. 6

4. things that don't follow the standard rules

_____
Par. 6

Check the sentence in which *moved* has the same meaning as it does in paragraph 3.

5. _____ My aunt was moved to tears by the letter you wrote her.

_____ Ivan moved to Tallahassee, Florida, last year.

Find the simile in paragraph 2, and write it on the line below.

6. _____

Check the correct meaning of the underlined word.

7. Mr. Roma <u>rearranged</u> the supplies on the boat.

_____ arranged again
_____ able to arrange
_____ someone who arranges

8. None of the dishes on the boat were <u>breakable</u>.

_____ before breaking
_____ breaking again
_____ able to break

9. The <u>midday</u> sun was hot on Sarah's dark hair.

_____ before day
_____ middle part of the day
_____ not day

Reading Skills

1. Check the sentence that best states the main idea of the selection.

_____ Pilar asks her grandpa what the flashlight, mirror, and whistle are for.

_____ Sarah moved to Ohio from Iowa a couple of years before.

_____ Sarah and Pilar go on a sailing trip with Pilar's grandparents and learn some safety tips about boating.

Write **F** before the sentences that are facts.
Write **O** before the sentences that are opinions.

2. _____ Sarah and Pilar helped load supplies on the boat.

3. _____ Sailing is a good way to relax.

4. _____ *PFD* stands for *personal flotation device.*

5. _____ Mrs. Roma is a better sailor than Mr. Roma.

6. _____ The characters in this story all live in Ohio.

7. How do you signal SOS?

_____

8. Do you think that Sarah and Pilar will go sailing with Pilar's grandparents again? Why or why not?

_____

Traveling with Only the Wind and a Sail

Do you know how a sailboat uses the wind to take the sailor where he or she wants to travel?

1   Many people today are asking which energy sources are the safest and most efficient. In fact, there is one resource that creates no pollution and can be found almost anywhere, even right outside your front door—wind! Human beings have been using wind as an energy source for thousands of years. One of the main ways people have used wind is to propel boats across water, a form of transportation called *sailing*.

2   Sails are large pieces of cloth suspended above the boat. They are used to catch the wind and move the boat forward. When the wind comes from behind the boat, the process is pretty simple. The boat is pushed in the same direction the wind is blowing. This is called *sailing before the wind*. But what if you don't want to go in that direction? Sailing would not be a very good way to travel if you could only move where the wind took you.

3   The sail is designed to rotate so that it can be used in different ways depending on the direction the wind is blowing. When the wind comes from the side, the sail is turned so that the air moving across it creates a vacuum. Now, instead of pushing, the wind is actually pulling

4   One problem still remains. How do you sail straight into the wind? The answer is that you cannot. When the wind is blowing from the front of the boat, the sailor must zigzag back and forth to go in that direction. First, the boat sails off to the right of the wind. Then, the sail is quickly rotated to the opposite side, and the boat sails to the left of the wind. This is called *tacking*.

5   Although the sail is the most visible part of the boat, an equally important element is located beneath the water. The keel is like a fin that comes out of the bottom of the boat and keeps it moving forward. When the wind is blowing from the side, the boat naturally wants to turn and travel in the opposite direction. Extending down into the water, the knifelike shape of the keel slices through the water and holds the boat in a forward position. Both the sail and the keel are needed to get the boat to its destination.

6   The next time you feel a cool breeze or a gust of wind sweeps a piece of paper from your hand, think about the power of the wind. It's strong enough to take you anywhere you'd like to travel, just as long as you have a strong sail and the knowledge to harness the power of the wind.

Vocabulary Skills

Write the words from the passage that have the meanings below.

1. bringing about a result without wasting time or energy

   _____
   Par. 1

2. to cause something to move

   _____
   Par. 1

3. hung; attached from above

   _____
   Par. 2

4. turn

   _____
   Par. 3

5. able to be seen; obvious

   _____
   Par. 5

Read each word below. Then, write the letter of its antonym on the line beside the word.

6. _____ forward   **a.** pulling

7. _____ pushing   **b.** different

8. _____ creates   **c.** insignificant

9. _____ similar   **d.** destroys

10. _____ important   **e.** backward

Write **S** if the possessive word is singular. Write **P** if it is plural.

11. _____ the boat's sails

12. _____ the sailors' skills

13. _____ the sailboats' course

14. _____ the wind's power

Reading Skills

1. What does it mean to *sail before the wind*?

   _____

2. Why does a sail need to be able to rotate?

   _____

3. When does a sailor need to travel in a zigzag pattern?

   _____

4. What purpose does a sailboat's keel serve?

   _____

5. Check the phrase that best describes the author's purpose.

   _____ to share information about how a sailboat works

   _____ to entertain the reader with a story about funny experiences with sailing

   _____ to inform the reader about great sailors of the past century

6. Check the line beside the word that best describes what type of selection this is.

   _____ informational

   _____ fiction

   _____ autobiography

Study Skills

Use a dictionary to help you divide these words into syllables.

1. e f f i c i e n t

2. v a c u u m

3. o p p o s i t e

4. n a t u r a l l y

5. d e s t i n a t i o n

Sailing Toward Victory

What is the America's Cup, and how did it get its start?

1   The America's Cup is one of the oldest competitions that is still in existence today. The first race was held in 1851. A 100-foot-long American schooner, representing the New York Yacht Club, and 16 British ships competed in a race around the Isle of Wight in the English Channel. The American boat won the race. The America's Cup, named after the boat *America*, not the country, was born.

2   For the next 132 years, the United States continued its winning streak during 25 challenges. This is the longest winning record in sports history. It seemed that the United States was unbeatable until Australia finally managed to win the cup in 1983. Since that time, only two other foreign countries have won the America's Cup.

3   The way the competition works is that the winning country from the previous America's Cup is the defender. Yachts from around the world compete for a chance to challenge the defender. In 1970, so many countries wanted to compete against the United States that the Challenger Selection Series was begun. The winner of this series of races earns the honor of competing against the previous America's Cup winner. In 1983, this competition became known as the Louis Vuitton Cup.

4   One way that the America's Cup is different from other competitions is that the winners do not keep the cup forever. Instead, the original cup that was made in London in 1848 is passed along from one winning team to the next. This tradition was almost permanently stopped in 1997. A vandal broke into the place where the cup was being held and nearly destroyed it with a sledgehammer. It took a silversmith three months of painstaking work to repair it.

5   From the beginning, the winner of the America's Cup was determined by which team was the first to win four races in a series of seven. This changed in 1995, when the winner was required to be the best in five out of nine races.

6   Many other elements of the competition have changed during its long history. The location of the competition depends on the hosts, or the winners of the previous competition. The length of the legs, or sections, of the race, and the way boats are classified have also changed over time. The one element that has remained constant throughout the many America's Cup challenges is that the races are fiercely competitive. The sailors on the winning team have no doubt that they have earned the title of the most skilled and fastest sailors in the world. That is, until the next America's Cup race.

Vocabulary Skills

Write the words from the passage that have the meanings below.

1. the condition of being or existing

   _____
   Par. 1

2. coming before in time

   _____
   Par. 3

3. difficult; needing a lot of care and effort

   _____
   Par. 4

4. unchanging

   _____
   Par. 6

5. Check the sentence in which *race* has the same meaning as it does in paragraph 1.

   _____ People of many races attended the international festival in my town.

   _____ Habib and I will run the race downtown on Saturday.

6. Check the sentence in which *streak* has the same meaning as it does in paragraph 2.

   _____ My school soccer team has been on a winning streak this entire season.

   _____ There was a large streak on the mirror where Jess had wiped it with a towel.

Reading Skills

Circle the word that best completes each sentence below.

1. The challenger _____ against the defender.

   competes   rebels   supports

2. In the Louis Vuitton Cup, boats compete to see who will challenge the _____ champion.

   original   future   current

3. The _____ is passed from one winning team to the next.

   tradition   trophy   competition

4. Name one thing that was similar about all America's Cup races before 1983.

   _____

5. Name two countries that you think have the best chance of winning the America's Cup in 2007.

   _____

6. Where did the first America's Cup take place?

   _____

Study Skills

Year	Name of Winning Boat	Country
1983	*Australia II*	Australia
1987	*Stars & Stripes*	United States
1988	*Stars & Stripes*	United States
1992	*America³*	United States
1995	*Black Magic*	New Zealand
2000	*New Zealand*	New Zealand
2003	*Alinghi*	Switzerland

1. Which country listed in the table above has the most wins?

   _____

2. What is the name of the winning boat from 1992?

   _____

3. Which country owns the *Alinghi*?

   _____

Bee Safe

Have you ever been stung by a bee? If you haven't, can you imagine what it feels like?

1   Sarah had decided that she loved everything about sailing. She loved the gentle rocking of the boat and the breeze against her face. She loved seeing water in every direction, and she loved feeling like she was on an adventure.

2   As the boat approached Kelleys Island, Mr. Roma had the girls help him prepare to dock. "Is anyone getting hungry yet?" asked Mrs. Roma. She held a large wicker picnic basket. "I packed quite a lunch, so I hope you brought along your appetites."

3   Once the boat was docked, the girls removed their life jackets and left them on the deck of the boat. Mr. Roma gave them each a hand as they stepped onto the dock. It took them a moment to become accustomed to standing on solid land again after the constant rocking motion of the boat. Sarah and Pilar walked ahead and found a pretty, grassy area with a good view of the lake. They waved to Pilar's grandparents who joined them a moment later with the picnic basket and a worn plaid quilt.

4   Pilar and Sarah each grabbed a side of the quilt and spread it out over the grass. They took off their sandals and helped Mrs. Roma unpack the lunch. They ate sandwiches, pretzels, and fresh peaches that dribbled juice down their chins. Pilar's mom had contributed oatmeal chocolate-chip cookies, and they were so good that everyone ate two. Pilar's grandpa even ate a third when he thought no one was looking.

5   After lunch, the girls began a game of catch, while Mr. and Mrs. Roma read the newspaper and did a crossword puzzle together. All of a sudden, Sarah gave a small yelp and swatted at her arm.

6   "What's wrong, Sarah?" asked Pilar.

7   "I think I just got stung by a bee," said Sarah. She examined her arm closely. "I can see it starting to swell already," she added.

8   "We should show my grandma," said Pilar. "She used to be a nurse. She'll know what to do."

9   Mrs. Roma looked at the small red welt on Sarah's arm. "Have you been stung before, Sarah?" she asked. "Do you know if you're allergic?"

10   "I've been stung a few times," replied Sarah. "My dad and I garden together a lot, and that's usually when it happens. I've never had a bad reaction before."

11   "I'm relieved to hear that," said Mrs. Roma. "Pilar, can you run and get me the first-aid kit from the boat?"

12   When Pilar brought back the kit, Mrs. Roma used a pair of tweezers to remove the small, black stinger from Sarah's arm. Then, she washed the area with soap and some of the bottled water they'd brought along on their trip. Finally, she handed Sarah one of the ice packs that had kept the sandwiches cool in the picnic basket.

13   "This will soothe it and help bring the swelling down a bit," said Mrs. Roma, patting Sarah on her back. "I must say, you're an excellent patient. Pilar's grandpa is not nearly as calm when he gets stung or gets a splinter that I have to remove."

14   Mr. Roma chuckled. "Well, Captain Sarah, it looks like your courage has been well appreciated. You just may earn a medal of bravery before this journey is done."

Vocabulary Skills

Write the words from the story that have the meanings below.

1. got closer to

_____
Par. 2

2. old; well-used

_____
Par. 3

3. gave to a cause

_____
Par. 4

4. response; way of acting or behaving

_____
Par. 10

5. glad; not worried

_____
Par. 11

Words that have a single middle consonant are usually divided into syllables before the consonant. For example, *a/bove* or *o/pen*. Divide the words below into syllables using a slash (/).

6. w a t e r

7. a l o n g

8. m o m e n t

Write a compound word using two words in each sentence.

9. Pilar watched a beautiful boat with a large white sail glide past.

_____

10. Sarah had a sting from a bee on her arm.

_____

11. Pilar's grandparents read a paper that contained the news.

_____

Reading Skills

1. What is the name of the island where they had their picnic?

_____

2. Why was Pilar's grandma a good person to have nearby when Sarah was stung by a bee?

_____

Read the sentences below. Write **B** next to the sentence if it tells about something that happened before Sarah was stung. Write **A** if it tells about something that happened after.

3. _____ Pilar and Sarah began playing Frisbee.

4. _____ The girls helped Mrs. Roma unpack the lunch.

5. _____ Sarah looked at the red welt on her arm.

Study Skills

Use the table below to answer the questions that follow.

Sailboats Docked at the Lake Erie Sailing Club		
Name	Length	Dock Number
Annabelle Lee	26 feet	6
Windswept	44 feet	18
The Castaway	28 feet	55
Clementine	34 feet	119

1. Which boat listed above is the smallest?

_____

2. How long is *The Castaway*?

_____

3. Which boat is docked at Dock 18?

_____

Busy, Busy Bees

Did you know that bees have a complicated way of communicating with each other?

1   Think of the last time you saw a bee. Perhaps it was busily gathering nectar from a flower in your garden. Maybe it was flying around a sweet drink you had at a picnic. Did you ever think about where that bee might live and what it does once it flies away? Chances are it lives a more interesting and complex life than you ever suspected.

2   Today, the honey bee can be found on every continent except Antarctica. It can survive only as a member of a colony, where each bee plays a very specific role. In each honey bee colony, there are three types of bees: the queen bee, the worker bees, and the drones.

3   The queen is different from the rest of the bees in a colony in several ways. She is the only bee in the colony to reproduce, so she is the mother of all the other bees in the colony. She can lay an enormous number of eggs —as many as 1,500 every day! The weight of all those eggs is about the same as the queen's entire body.

4   She has a smooth, curved stinger instead of a straight, barbed, or spiky, stinger like the worker bees. Worker bees die after stinging, because they cannot remove their barbed stingers. The queen bee can sting repeatedly without injuring herself.

5   Another difference between queen and worker bees is that a queen bee can live for one to three years, while a worker bee lives only an average of six weeks.

6   A colony of honey bees is mostly made up of worker bees. A single colony may contain as many as 80,000 worker bees. They are called worker bees for a very good reason. Their job is to build and maintain the nest, gather nectar and pollen to make honey, and care for the young bees. If the hive becomes too warm for the eggs and young bees, the worker bees fan their wings to make it cooler. When the hive becomes too cool, they huddle around the eggs and young bees to warm them.

7   The third type of honey bee is called a *drone*. The drones are the male bees. They do not have stingers or tools for working. They cannot even feed themselves. Their only purpose is to mate with the queen bee to produce new worker bees.

8   One of the most fascinating things about honey bees is their way of communicating. Bees are able to tell each other where to find food by doing complicated "dances." These dances can tell bees how far away food can be found and in which direction it is located. The moves they make are so clear that scientists who have studied bee communication can actually watch a dance and follow a bee's directions.

Vocabulary Skills

Write the words from the passage that have the meanings below.

1. hard to understand

   _____
   Par. 1

2. over and over again

   _____
   Par. 4

3. a group of animals that live together

   _____
   Par. 6

4. to crowd closely together

   _____
   Par. 6

5. very interesting and appealing

   _____
   Par. 8

Circle the homophone that correctly completes each sentence below.

6. Each type of honey bee has a different _____ in the colony. (roll, role)

7. The queen's body _____ is about the same as that of the eggs she carries. (weight, wait)

8. A queen bee can _____ an enormous number of eggs. (lei, lay)

Write **S** if the possessive word is singular. Write **P** if it is plural.

9. _____ the queen's eggs

10. _____ bees' colony

11. _____ the hive's temperature

12. _____ the workers' jobs

13. _____ the flower's nectar

Reading Skills

Read the descriptions below. Write **Q** next to the phrase if it describes queen bees. Write **W** if it describes worker bees.

1. _____ dies after stinging

2. _____ builds the nest

3. _____ has a smooth, curved stinger

4. _____ lays more than a thousand eggs a day

5. _____ cools eggs by fanning their wings

6. What is one place in the world where honey bees cannot be found?

   _____

7. How long can a queen bee live?

   _____

Study Skills

Use the facts from paragraph 6 to complete Part I of the outline. Use the facts from paragraph 8 to complete Part II.

I. Worker bees

   A. make up most of the colony

   B. build and maintain the nest

   C. _____

   D. _____

   E. monitor the temperature for the young bees

II. Bee communication

   A. give directions to food through dancing

   B. _____

   C. scientists can follow the clear directions

Planet Rock

Have you ever tried indoor rock climbing?

1   Dante and Ethan said goodbye to Dante's dad, who had dropped them off at the door of Planet Rock. They each carried a birthday present for Katsu, who was turning eleven. No one in their class other than Katsu had been rock climbing before, and Dante and Ethan had asked him a million questions about it. They could hardly wait to have an opportunity to try it themselves.

2   Katsu and his parents were standing near the front desk when Dante and Ethan arrived. "Happy birthday!" they said.

3   "Thanks!" said Katsu. "Are you guys ready to put on some harnesses and hit the rocks?" he asked. Dante and Ethan nodded.

4   A woman named Nicole was going to be their instructor. Nicole had been Katsu's teacher when he first started climbing three years before. "Katsu, will you be my assistant today?"

5   "Sure," agreed Katsu. "I'm really excited to have Dante and Ethan try climbing. I think they'll love it as much as I do."

6   "Okay," said Nicole. "Communication is really important in climbing, so we want to make sure that we are all using the same vocabulary.

7   "Whenever you're climbing, you'll need to wear a harness for safety," Nicole continued. "My assistant here will demonstrate how to put on and fasten a harness properly." Katsu put on his harness slowly, making sure that his friends could see.

8   "*Belay* is another term that you'll need to know. It means to *secure a climber with a rope*. Katsu's dad is also a climber, so he knows how to belay Katsu. If your parents come climbing with you sometime, they can take a short class that teaches them how to belay."

9   Nicole held up a metal ring. "This is called a *carabiner*," she said. "It is a sort of hook. You'll use it to attach your belay device to your harness." Katsu demonstrated how the carabiner worked. After a few more minutes of instruction, the boys were ready to attempt their first climb. They put on the helmets that Nicole had handed them.

10   "Katsu, do you want to go first?" asked Nicole. "As you're climbing, I can give Dante and Ethan a few more tips."

11   Dante and Ethan watched as their friend made his way up the wall. They were impressed by how confident and in control he was. "Are we going to climb the same wall?" asked Dante excitedly.

12   "Yes," said Nicole. "It's a bit more work than it seems to be after you've watched someone experienced do it. Just remember to take your time and have fun. Rock climbing gets under your skin pretty quickly. After my first time, I couldn't wait to try it again."

13   Katsu's dad spotted Katsu as he descended. "That was great!" said Katsu, grinning widely. "Who's next?"

14   Ethan raised his hand. "I think I'm about to get bitten by the climbing bug!" he said, as he secured his rope.

Vocabulary Skills

Write the words from the story that have the meanings below.

1. a set of straps used to attach a person or an animal to something

   _____
   Par. 7

2. feeling sure

   _____
   Par. 11

3. came down

   _____
   Par. 13

Read each pair of words listed below. If the words are synonyms, write **S** on the line. If the words are antonyms, write **A** on the line.

4. _____ properly   incorrectly

5. _____ try   attempt

6. _____ ascended   descended

Write the idiom from paragraph 12 on the line next to its meaning.

7. to enjoy and get used to something unexpected _____

   _____

Check the correct meaning of the underlined word.

8. Ask a <u>dependable</u> person to belay you.

   _____ depend again

   _____ able to depend on

   _____ someone who depends

9. The climber will <u>reattempt</u> to climb the tallest wall.

   _____ attempt before

   _____ able to attempt

   _____ attempt again

Reading Skills

1. Do you think this story takes place in reality, or is it a fantasy? Why?

   _____

   _____

2. Do you think that Dante and Ethan will want to go rock climbing again? Why or why not?

   _____

   _____

3. What is the purpose of a carabiner?

   _____

4. **Hyperbole** is an exaggerated statement. For example: *I am so hungry, I could eat a horse.* Find the hyperbole in paragraph 1, and write it on the line.

   _____

   _____

Study Skills

Guide words are printed at the top of each page in a dictionary. The guide word at the left is the first word on the page. The guide word at the right is the last word on the page. Check each word that could be found on a page having the guide words shown in dark print.

1. **bawl–beeswax**

   _____ beginner   _____ beautiful
   _____ bayou

2. **immigrant–impressive**

   _____ incapable   _____ illustrate
   _____ imposter

3. **reflection–relish**

   _____ reflex   _____ relative   _____ recline

Rock On!

How are the various types of rock climbing different from one another?

1 People have always climbed mountains, either to hunt wild animals that lived there or to find good grazing for their domestic animals. Today, people mostly climb for excitement, adventure, and even competition.

2 There are three basic types of climbing: alpine climbing, ice climbing, and rock climbing. The first two are done on mountains and use teams of people to get to the top. Sometimes, alpine and ice climbing can take days to complete. Rock climbers, however, are more concerned with the physical part of climbing and will find a rock face or cliff anywhere they can, even if it is indoors!

3 There are two kinds of rock climbing. Free climbing is when a person uses only his or her hands and feet to ascend the cliff or rock wall. Ropes are still used as a safety precaution in case the climber slips, but the ropes cannot be used in any other way. The climber wedges his or her fingers into cracks and holes, or grabs onto rocks that stick out. Free climbers use all of their muscles to ascend the wall. To keep their hands dry, climbers apply gymnasts' chalk and wear athletic tape to ensure a firm grip. They also wear special shoes that have sticky rubber soles.

4 The other type of climbing is aid climbing. In this type of climb, the person can use a variety of different tools. Ropes are still used for safety, but now they can also be used to help pull the climber up. For long climbs, there is even a sling that can be brought along so that the climber can sit and rest.

5 Before a new climber tries scaling the side of a steep, rocky cliff or wall, he or she needs to practice somewhere safe. One method is called *bouldering*. Climbers find a site where large rocks are available close to the ground. They can practice their maneuvers without worrying about falling a great distance. Another great place for practicing is at an indoor rock-climbing facility.

6 Rock climbing competitions are usually held at these indoor spaces as well. One kind of race is all about speed. Two identical walls are set up next to each other, and the climbers simply race to the top.

7 The other type of competition is more about decision making. Each competitor is given the same amount of time to climb the same wall, and whoever gets to the highest point wins. The climber must decide which path is best to get to the top. Sometimes, the climber starts off in one direction only to find out that it leads to a dead end. The climber must then climb back down and try a different path. The competitors do not get to watch each other climb. Otherwise, they would see each other's mistakes and have an unfair advantage.

Vocabulary Skills

Write the words from the passage that have the meanings below.

1. to go up

   _____
   Par. 3

2. an action that is taken to protect against danger or mistakes

   _____
   Par. 3

3. climbing up to the top

   _____
   Par. 5

4. planned movements

   _____
   Par. 5

5. exactly the same

   _____
   Par. 6

Words that have two middle consonants are divided into syllables between the consonants. For example, *pic/ture* or *bas/ket*. Divide the words below into syllables using a slash (/).

6. p r a c t i c e

7. c l i m b e r

8. m i s t a k e

9. a l p i n e

Reading Skills

1. Check the sentence that best states the main idea of paragraph 2.

   _____ Alpine climbing, ice climbing, and rock climbing are the three main types of climbing.

   _____ Alpine and ice climbing are usually done in teams.

   _____ Rock climbers look for walls or cliffs to climb almost anywhere.

Write **F** before the sentences that are facts.
Write **O** before the sentences that are opinions.

2. _____ Free climbers use chalk and tape to keep their hands dry.

3. _____ People who enjoy rock climbing are adventurous and brave.

4. _____ Bouldering is one way new climbers can practice somewhere safe.

5. _____ In aid climbing, a person can use different types of tools.

6. _____ Rock climbing competitions are very interesting to watch.

7. Why do you think rock climbing competitions are usually held indoors?

   _____

   _____

Study Skills

Use the index below to answer the questions.

Index

Best outdoor climbs (also listed by
   state) 14–15, 16, 17, 18–20, 21, 22–25
Climbing safety 2–9
Climbing with kids 51–63
Equipment 26–33
Indoor facilities 64–68, 75
Tips for beginners 10

1. What is another way the best outdoor climbs are listed?

   _____

2. Which pages have information about climbing with kids?

   _____

3. What type of information would you find on page 10?

   _____

Forehead in the Sky

Why would a person risk his or her life to climb to the top of the highest mountain on Earth?

1   Today, mountain climbing and rock climbing are popular "extreme sports." Mount Everest in the Himalayan Mountains is the ultimate test of a climber's skill and courage. But Mount Everest is not just any mountain. Believed to be the highest mountain in the world, Mount Everest rises 29,035 feet into the sky. In fact, it is getting taller all the time! Scientists have discovered that due to geological forces, Mount Everest is gaining a few millimeters in height every year.

2   The conditions on Mount Everest are some of the most extreme in the world. January is the coldest month on the mountain. Temperatures average about -33°F but can drop to -76°F. During the warmest month, July, temperatures still only average -2°F. In addition to frigid temperatures, the weather on Mount Everest is also often unpredictable. Massive blizzards can suddenly blow in and completely obstruct vision. In the middle of winter, gusts of wind can reach more than 170 miles per hour. These winds are considered hurricane force!

3   Many people cannot understand why anyone would choose to climb a mountain in such dangerous conditions. But humans have always loved a chance to test themselves against the elements of nature. The people who choose to climb mountains love the challenge and the thrill of accomplishing such an amazing feat.

4   On a historic day in 1953, Edmund Hillary and Tenzing Norgay became the first people to reach the summit of Mount Everest. Hillary was an explorer from New Zealand, and Norgay was his Sherpa porter. The Sherpas are the mountain people of Nepal. They are often hired as guides and porters by foreign explorers. At the time of their expedition, Norgay was an experienced climber of Mount Everest, though he had never reached the summit.

5   Hillary and Norgay were not the first people to attempt to climb Mount Everest. Many others before them had tried and failed to conquer the enormous mountain. Some even lost their lives in snowstorms or avalanches. It was a combination of skill, luck, determination, and courage that allowed Hillary and Norgay to succeed where others before them had not. Both men received honors for their accomplishment. Hillary was knighted, and Norgay received the highest award a civilian, or someone not in the military, could receive.

6   Since Hillary and Norgay's famous journey, many other adventurous people have made the dangerous climb up Mount Everest. More than 4,000 people have attempted to climb Mount Everest, and more than 170 have died. Something is so intriguing about Mount Everest that people are still willing to risk their lives to climb it. Maybe that's because it's the highest mountain in the world—a mountain the Nepali people call *Sagarmatha*, or *Forehead in the Sky*.

Vocabulary Skills

Write the words from the passage that have the meanings below.

1. to get in the way of

   _____
   Par. 2

2. the top or highest point

   _____
   Par. 4

3. to overcome or get control of

   _____
   Par. 5

Read each word or phrase below. Then, write the letter of the abbreviation that matches in the space beside it.

4. _____ feet   **a.** Mt.

5. _____ miles per hour **b.** ft.

6. _____ Mount   **c.** mm.

7. _____ millimeters   **d.** m.p.h.

Find a synonym in the selection for each of the words below.

8. freezing _____
   Par. 2

9. hazardous _____
   Par. 3

10. trip; journey _____
    Par. 4

11. daring _____
    Par. 6

Reading Skills

1. On the lines below, write one sentence from the selection that shows the author was trying to persuade you that climbing Mount Everest is a dangerous goal.

   _____

   _____

   _____

Circle the word that best completes each sentence below.

2. The height of Mount Everest is _____ slightly every year.

   decreasing   increasing   moving

3. Every year, many people _____ to reach the summit of the mountain.

   regret   pretend   attempt

4. The _____ of an avalanche is always on the minds of the climbers.

   threat   awareness   belief

Study Skills

Use the graph below to answer the questions that follow.

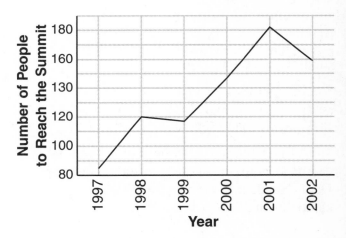

1. In which year did the greatest number of people reach the summit?

   _____

2. How many people reached the summit in 1998?

   _____

3. In which year did only 85 people reach the summit?

   _____

On the Road to the Presidency

Does your school elect class officers? Have you ever run for a class office?

1 Ahmad sat at a table in the school cafeteria. The election for fifth-grade class president was only about two weeks away, and Ahmad knew it was time to begin seriously campaigning.

2 "I think you need a catchy slogan," said Will, twirling a pencil as he thought. "You need something that people will remember when it's time to vote. *Make Your Vote Count! Vote for Ahmad for President!* or *Ahmad—Your Voice in School Politics.*"

3 "Those aren't too bad," said Ahmad. "Let's start keeping a list, and we'll pick the best slogans for our signs and fliers."

4 "How about *Articulate, Authentic, and Approachable: Always Ahmad*?" asked Maura. She was the class spelling bee champ, and she couldn't help using her extensive knowledge of words whenever possible.

5 Will grinned. "It's got a nice ring to it, but it might be a little too wordy."

6 "People won't forget that Olivia was the fourth-grade president last year. They'll like the fact that she has experience," Carlos said.

7 Ahmad nodded. "I know, but I think that I can bring some fresh ideas to school politics. Does anyone know what Olivia's plans for the campaign are?"

8 Olivia, Bennett, and Jenna sat at the kitchen table at Olivia's house. They were eating crackers and peanut butter as they discussed what to put on the signs they planned to make that afternoon. They had bought posterboard in bright colors they thought would attract attention. At the center of the table was a plastic bin that held a jumble of writing utensils—markers, pens, colored pencils, and crayons.

9 "Where should we start?" asked Bennett, brushing the cracker crumbs from his hands. "What do you want people to know about you?" he asked.

10 Olivia thought for a moment. "I want them to know I'm a hard worker," she said. "I have experience as class president. I also have a lot of ideas for how to make this a great school year."

11 "I think that experience is really important," commented Jenna. "That is one of the things my parents looked for in the last presidential election. They said they wanted to vote for someone who had proven he would be the kind of leader they were looking for."

12 *"Olivia for President—All Original, All Experience,"* suggested Bennett.

13 "How about *Olivia for President, Opportunity for All*?" said Jenna.

14 "I like both of those," said Olivia. "The first one reminds the voters of my experience. The second one lets people know I will listen to their ideas and work for and with them." Olivia took out a fat red marker and began the first poster. "I don't know what I'd do without my fabulous campaign crew!" she exclaimed.

Vocabulary Skills

Write the words from the story that have the meanings below.

1. a short phrase that describes a person's or group's ideas or beliefs

   _____
   Par. 2

2. covering a wide range

   _____
   Par. 4

3. objects or tools used for a specific purpose

   _____
   Par. 8

Write the idiom from paragraph 5 on the line next to its meaning.

4. sounds good _____

Circle the homophone that correctly completes each sentence below.

5. Olivia thinks that her ideas will make the school year _____. (grate, great)

6. The students are _____ to post their signs on the bulletin boards in the hallways. (aloud, allowed)

Underline the compound word in each sentence. Then, write the two words that make up each compound.

7. Ahmad's classmates are eager to help him run his campaign.

   _____   _____

8. Olivia has a background in school politics.

   _____   _____

Reading Skills

1. Check the words that describe Olivia.

   _____ confident   _____ thoughtful

   _____ lazy   _____ ambitious

2. What does Ahmad think his strength as president would be?

   _____

3. What does Jenna think Olivia should emphasize in her campaign?

   _____

4. **Alliteration** is the use of words that begin with the same sound. Find the alliteration in paragraph 4, and write it on the line.

   _____

   _____

Study Skills

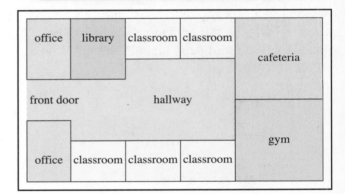

Use the map of Ahmad's and Olivia's school to answer the questions that follow.

1. What two rooms is the library located between?

   _____

2. How many classrooms are there?

   _____

3. Is the cafeteria closer to an office or to a classroom?

   _____

All Tied Up

How will Ahmad and Olivia's classmates decide who will become the next class president?

1   "I have the results for this year's fifth-grade elections," said Ms. Pond, waving an envelope at the class. She opened the envelope and read the names of the winners for class secretary, treasurer, and vice-president. Then, she paused for a moment.

2   "For the first time, we have a tie for president. Ahmad and Olivia each received the same number of votes. You can have a few minutes to talk about this with one another," said Ms. Pond. "I'd like you to try to come up with a solution that is fair to both candidates."

3   Ahmad and Olivia waited in the hall. After a few minutes, Ms. Pond motioned for them to come back into the classroom. "The class has decided that they'd like to hear both of you take a few minutes to tell us why you'd like to be president," she told Ahmad and Olivia. "Who would like to go first?"

4   "I will," said Olivia, walking to the front of the room. "There are a lot of changes and improvements that I'd like to make as class president," she began. "For example, I'd like to start a ski club this winter. A few parents that I've spoken to are willing to drive and chaperone the students who are interested.

5   "A number of students that I've spoken to don't think it's fair that we have to wait until seventh grade to have a class dance. I'd like to have a bake sale to raise enough money for our first ever fifth-grade dance."

6   Olivia paused and took a deep breath. "I hope that you'll look at my record from last year and see that I take my promises seriously. I would love to be your president. Thank you."

7   Ahmad took Olivia's place at the front of the room. "It's important to me to listen to your ideas and concerns," said Ahmad. "I would have a suggestion box so that I could keep in touch with your needs. I also would like to start a club for students who are interested in volunteering in the community. I volunteer at an animal shelter, but we could also tutor younger kids, help out at a food bank, or visit nursing homes.

8   "I would like to have a fifth-grade page in the school's monthly newsletter. We could update the rest of the students and the parents about the things that are going on in our class. I would do my best to be a good president. Thank you," said Ahmad, returning to his seat.

9   The class was quiet for a moment. Then Li Chen, who had just been elected vice-president, raised her hand. "Ms. Pond, I think that Ahmad and Olivia both have some excellent ideas." Her classmates nodded. "Could Ahmad and Olivia be co-presidents? That way we could benefit from both their ideas."

10   Ms. Pond smiled. "Ahmad and Olivia, what do you think? Does that sound like a fair solution to you?"

11   They both nodded and grinned. "Hi, Prez," said Olivia, holding out her hand for Ahmad to shake.

Vocabulary Skills

Write the words from the story that have the meanings below.

1. changes that make things better

_____
Par. 4

2. to supervise a group of young people

_____
Par. 4

3. to provide a service without getting paid for it

_____
Par. 7

4. to affect in a positive way

_____
Par. 9

Find an antonym in the story for each of the words below.

5. problem _____
Par. 2

6. unwilling _____
Par. 4

7. noisy _____
Par. 9

8. unjust _____
Par. 10

Write **S** if the possessive word is singular. Write **P** if it is plural.

9. _____ Olivia's plans

10. _____ this year's election

11. _____ students' votes

12. _____ Ahmad's ideas

13. _____ parents' opinions

Reading Skills

1. Number the events below to show the order in which they happened.

_____ Ms. Pond read the names of the different class officers.

_____ Ms. Pond told the class she had the election results.

_____ Ahmad said he would like to create a volunteering club.

_____ Li Chen suggested that Ahmad and Olivia be co-presidents.

_____ Ahmad and Olivia waited in the hallway.

In **first-person point of view**, the reader knows the thoughts and feelings of the person telling the story. In **third-person point of view**, the reader only knows what an outsider knows about a character. Mark each sentence below **F** for first-person and **T** for third-person.

2. _____ I wonder if Ahmad and Olivia would mind being co-presidents?

3. _____ Olivia walked to the front of the room.

4. _____ Ahmad said he would do his best to be a good president.

5. _____ I can't believe that I am going to be class secretary!

Study Skills

Check each word that could be found on a dictionary page having the guide words shown in dark print.

1. **acquaint—adhesive**

_____ achieve _____ acute _____ admiral

2. **meander—mellow**

_____ merry _____ measure _____ meditate

3. **urgent—utter**

_____ us _____ uproar _____ utilize

The Race for President

How does the Electoral College work?

1   You might be just old enough to remember some of the controversy that surrounded the presidential election of 2000. In one of the closest political races in United States history, more people voted for Vice-President Al Gore than Texas governor George W. Bush. How did Bush become President then? It is because he received a larger number of electoral votes.

2   The person with the most votes in the race for President of the United States is not necessarily the winner. Instead, the United States has a system called the *Electoral College* in which candidates are awarded a set number of votes for each state they win. For example, the candidate who receives the most votes in Florida earns 25 electoral votes and in Nebraska earns 5. This is partly because more people live in Florida than in Nebraska.

3   There are a total of 538 electoral votes available from all of the states, including three votes from the District of Columbia. To become President, the candidate must receive at least half of the electoral votes, or a minimum of 270 votes.

4   In the 2000 election, Al Gore actually received 500,000 more votes than George W. Bush. However, Bush received 271 electoral votes compared to Gore's 266. It was a very close race, but the election results in Florida were even closer. With nearly 6,000,000 votes cast, the final official count put Bush ahead by only 537 votes. Because Florida's 25 electoral votes could swing the presidency either way, many people wanted to recount the votes to be confident about which man had won.

5   For more than a month, people recounted votes, and the candidates and their supporters waited anxiously for the results. Finally, on December 12, 2000, the Supreme Court of the United States decided that enough recounting had been done. The accepted totals meant that George W. Bush would be President. Even though Al Gore was not happy about this decision, he conceded the election. He said that his supporters should put all of their energy into respecting the new President.

6   Some people believe that the Electoral College system is not a fair way to elect our Presidents. They feel that when a candidate wins the election in a state, the votes for the other candidate do not count. The winner receives all of the electoral votes, no matter how close the race might have been.

7   Supporters of the Electoral College system believe that it helps smaller, less populated states have a voice in the election. They feel that if the winner was simply the person with the most votes, candidates would campaign only in big cities and in states like California, Texas, and Florida. The Electoral College ensures that every part of the United States has a voice in an election. As the 2000 presidential election proved, even the three electoral votes available in Wyoming would have changed the final result.

Vocabulary Skills

Write the words from the passage that have the meanings below.

1. a public event or issue about which two sides have different views

   _____
   Par. 1

2. the least

   _____
   Par. 3

3. feeling nervous and uncertain

   _____
   Par. 5

4. gave up or gave in

   _____
   Par. 5

5. lived in; occupied by

   _____
   Par. 7

6. makes sure

   _____
   Par. 7

Read each word below. Then, write the letter of its abbreviation in the space beside it.

7. _____ Wyoming   **a.** CA

8. _____ Florida   **b.** D.C.

9. _____ California   **c.** TX

10. _____ Texas   **d.** WY

11. _____ District of Columbia **e.** FL

12. Check the sentence in which *swing* has the same meaning as it does in paragraph 4.

   _____ Dad installed a new swing in the backyard.

   _____ The candidate hoped to swing the crowd's opinion.

Reading Skills

1. Check the line beside the word that best describes what type of selection this is.

   _____ informational

   _____ persuasive

   _____ fiction

2. What is the smallest number of electoral votes a candidate must receive to win the presidency?

   _____

3. Why do some states have more electoral votes than others?

   _____

   _____

4. Why do some people feel that the Electoral College is not a fair way to elect the president?

   _____

   _____

   _____

5. Why do some people believe that the Electoral College is a good system to elect the president?

   _____

   _____

   _____

6. Why did people want the votes in Florida to be recounted?

   _____

   _____

   _____

Treasure Hunt

Have you ever participated in a scavenger hunt?

1   It was the last day of school before summer vacation. The students in Mr. Chandler's class were full of energy and excitement as their end-of-the-school-year party began.

2   "Are you all ready for a scavenger hunt?" asked Mr. Chandler. "I'd like everyone to get into teams of four. I'm going to distribute lists of things that you'll be able to find inside the school and on the playground. The first team to find every item on the list wins the grand prize."

3   Mr. Chandler continued to talk as he handed out the list. "Remember, you don't want to go too quickly. If you don't take the time to read the list carefully, you may collect the wrong things. For example, number six is a blue pen. If you accidentally grab a black pen, you'll have to waste time by going back to look for a blue one. Use your best powers of observation, and may the best team win!"

4   Each team worked a little differently. Some teams huddled in groups, deciding how to divide the list. Others scattered in several directions at once, quickly adding things to their basket as they went.

5   "We need a yellow highlighter," announced Alex to the other teams. "Does anyone have an extra they would be willing to exchange? I have a large paper clip and an extra cap eraser that I can trade."

6   "I'm headed to the cafeteria," whispered Sheryl to Huang. "We need a fork and a small packet of salt."

7   Maya and Devon had a quick whispered conference by the door. Then, Maya slipped outside to the playground where she gathered an oak leaf, two pine needles, and four pebbles.

8   Bryan and Rosa ran into another team in the hallway on their way back from the library. Both teams laughed as they tried to hide what they were carrying.

9   After about half an hour of teamwork, Sheryl, Huang, Maya, and Devon realized that they had checked off every item on their list. They ran back to their classroom and handed Mr. Chandler the basket. Moments later, a second team raced up to Mr. Chandler's desk. The members of the first team held their breath as their teacher carefully examined each item in their basket. They knew that if they made any mistakes, it was possible that the team standing behind them could win.

10   There was a tense moment when Mr. Chandler had to measure a piece of paper to make sure it was the correct size. Mr. Chandler finally cleared his throat. "It looks like we have a winner," he announced. "The members of the winning team, Sheryl, Huang, Maya, and Devon, will each receive a school sweatshirt and two free tickets to a movie of their choice at the Palace Theater.

11   "For those of you who haven't won anything yet today, don't be too concerned. There will be plenty of other fun games this afternoon!" exclaimed Mr. Chandler.

Vocabulary Skills

Write the words from the story that have the meanings below.

1. hand out

   _____
   Par. 2

2. the act of paying careful attention

   _____
   Par. 3

3. separated or in many directions

   _____
   Par. 4

4. a meeting to discuss a specific topic

   _____
   Par. 7

5. nervous

   _____
   Par. 10

The suffix **-ation** means *state, condition, act, or process of*. For example, the word *expectation* means *the act of expecting*. Add **ation** to each word, and write the new word on the line. Then, use the new word in a sentence. Remember that you may have to drop the final **e** before adding the suffix.

6. prepare _____

   _____

7. inspire _____

   _____

8. imagine _____

   _____

9. Write the idiom in paragraph 9 on the line below its meaning.

   waited anxiously

   _____

Reading Skills

1. Check the sentence below that is the best summary for paragraph 3.

   _____ Mr. Chandler handed out the list to the students.

   _____ Mr. Chandler gave the students tips about being careful during the scavenger hunt.

   _____ Mr. Chandler said, "May the best team win!"

2. What does each team have to do during the scavenger hunt?

   _____

3. Name three items that are on the list Mr. Chandler distributes.

   _____

4. What does Alex offer to exchange for a yellow highlighter?

   _____

Study Skills

Write the entry word you would look for in a dictionary next to each word below.

1. continued _____

2. announced _____

3. carrying _____

4. standing _____

5. heavier _____

The Search for Undersea Treasure

What happens to the treasures found in shipwrecks that are decades, or even centuries, old?

1   Whenever a shipwreck is discovered, there are two different ways to think about the remains. Some people value the shipwreck for its financial worth. They are explorers who have spent a lot of their own time and money searching for the wreck. When they finally locate it, they believe that the ship and its contents should be theirs. These people are usually referred to as *treasure hunters*.

2   Other people, however, see shipwrecks as a valuable opportunity to study history. For them, a ship lying at the bottom of the sea is a valuable snapshot of how citizens from past cultures lived and traveled. Maritime, or marine, archaeologists are the scientists who study underwater historical sites.

3   Both the treasure hunters and the archaeologists have a good point. Many shipwrecks are discovered because of the treasure hunters. They are motivated to spend personal resources on research and equipment because they might find gold, jewelry, and expensive antiques scattered across the ocean floor. After investing so much of their own money, it seems as though they have earned the right to collect the treasure.

4   On the other hand, scientists argue that shipwreck sites are more valuable as historical artifacts that can benefit everyone. By studying these sites, they hope to have a better understanding of human history. They want to prevent treasure hunters from disturbing the sites and taking away the historical artifacts. This idea seems like a valid argument as well.

5   The solution to this dilemma has been for scientists and treasure hunters to compromise and even work together. Treasure hunters usually let scientists spend as much time as they need to study the wreck and its cargo. In return, scientists have provided better equipment and resources for exploration.

6   One of the most important technologies for searching underwater is *sonar*. Sonar uses sound waves to "see" in the darkest depths of the ocean. Sound waves are projected through the water. When they run into something, they bounce back to receptors on the ship. The shape and size of objects underwater are determined by how long the waves take to return to the sonar equipment.

7   Robots are the latest tool to be used for finding shipwrecks. Because of the intense pressure found deep underwater, it is very difficult for humans to travel far below the surface. However, robots with cameras and sonar can be sent to incredible depths. JASON Jr. was the robot used by Dr. Robert Ballard to discover the *Titanic* at a depth of about 13,000 feet!

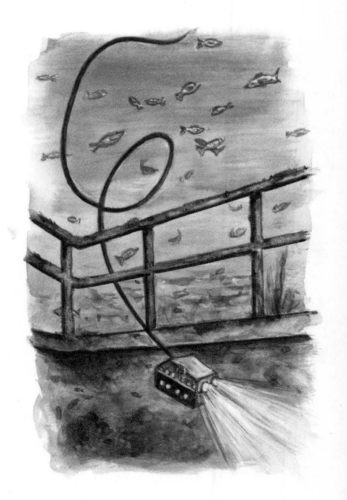

Vocabulary Skills

Write the words from the passage that have the meanings below.

1. having a reason to do something

   _____
   Par. 3

2. reasonable or acceptable

   _____
   Par. 4

3. an agreement reached by two opposing sides, each of which had to give up part of what they wanted

   _____
   Par. 5

4. receivers

   _____
   Par. 6

5. very strong

   _____
   Par. 7

Words that end in **le** are usually divided into syllables before the consonant that precedes the **le**. For example, *ta/ble* or *han/dle*. Divide the words below into syllables using a slash (/).

6. p e o p l e   8. d a n g l e

7. n o b l e   9. r a m b l e

Reading Skills

1. Check the phrase that best describes the author's purpose.

   _____ to inform

   _____ to persuade

   _____ to entertain

2. How are archaeologists and treasure hunters similar?

   _____

   _____

3. How are they different?

   _____

   _____

4. In the opinion of archaeologists, what is valuable about shipwrecks?

   _____

   _____

5. How have archaeologists and treasure hunters compromised?

   _____

6. In paragraph 6, the word *see* is set in quotation marks. What was the author's purpose for doing that?

   _____

   _____

Write **F** before the sentences that are facts. Write **O** before the sentences that are opinions.

7. _____ Treasure hunters have the right to use the contents of a shipwreck in any way they like.

8. _____ Dr. Robert Ballard discovered the *Titanic*.

9. _____ Both the treasure hunters and the archaeologists have a good point.

Study Skills

A **pronunciation key** is a list of sound symbols and key words. They show how to pronounce words. Use the pronunciation key on the inside back cover of this book to write the words that match these pronunciations.

1. /tre′ zher/ _____

2. /sī′ en tist/ _____

3. /rē sȯr′ sez/ _____

4. /əth′ er/ _____

The Wreckage of the *Belle*

What would you expect to find in the wreckage of a 300-year-old ship?

1   In 1686, a French ship called the *Belle* sank in Texas's Matagorda Bay. It would be more than 300 years before archaeologists were able to excavate the site. It turned out to be well worth the wait. The *Belle* held clues to historical events and information about the last journey of the famous French explorer, René-Robert Cavelier, Sieur de La Salle.

2   The *Belle* was part of an expedition of four French ships that were headed for the mouth of the Mississippi River. The ships sailed far off course and landed on the coast of Texas, about 400 miles from where they had meant to go.

3   The crew and settlers faced many hardships, such as conflicts with the Native American people in the area, disease, and malnutrition. In spite of their troubles, the group settled in a place they named *Fort St. Louis*. During a winter storm, the *Belle* sank in Matagorda Bay.

4   In 1995, after years and years of searching, a marine archaeologist named J. Barto Arnold finally came across the wreckage of the *Belle*. It took nearly a year for the Texas Historical Commission to excavate the site. They installed a structure called a *cofferdam* that made the work of the archaeologists much easier. The cofferdam was a large, circular piece of steel that was placed around the wreckage of the ship. Water was pumped out of the area inside the cofferdam. This allowed the archaeologists to work in a dry area instead of deep underwater.

5   One of the most interesting things about the artifacts that were found on the *Belle* is that they show what kinds of materials people coming to settle a new land needed. After so many years, you might think that almost everything would have decayed, or rotted away. Luckily, the thick mud that covered the bottom of the ship helped preserve things that might have been lost forever.

6   About a million artifacts were found in the wreckage. Among the items were cloth, bone, wood, the hull (or body) of the ship, three bronze cannons, thousands of glass beads, bells, and pottery.

7   It was a lot of work to carefully remove all those artifacts from the ocean floor, and it will take just as much attention to preserve them. Every single item will be cleaned, identified, and preserved. Many pieces are on display in Texas museums today, but it will be a long time before archaeologists have learned everything they can from this amazing discovery!

Vocabulary Skills

Write the words from the passage that have the meanings below.

1. to uncover something by digging

_____
Par. 1

2. a journey for a specific purpose

_____
Par. 2

3. placed something in position

_____
Par. 4

4. things created by humans during a certain period of history

_____
Par. 5

5. to protect something for the future

_____
Par. 7

In each row, circle the word that does not belong.

6. explore   preserve   protect   save

7. expedition   hull   trip   journey

8. history   artifact   sailed   archaeologist

Find the compound words from the selection that contain the words below.

9. water _____
Par. 4

10. thing _____
Par. 5

11. for _____
Par. 5

Reading Skills

1. How did the cofferdam make the work of the archaeologists easier?

_____

_____

2. Why were the archaeologists pleased that a layer of mud covered the bottom of the boat?

_____

3. Name three things that were found in the wreckage of the *Belle*.

_____

4. Where were the four boats in the French expedition supposed to be headed?

_____

Write **T** before the sentences that are true. Write **F** before the sentences that are false.

5. _____ The *Belle* sank in 1656.

6. _____ The explorer La Salle led the French expedition.

7. _____ The *Belle* was an Italian ship.

8. _____ Almost everything in the wreckage of the boat had decayed and was no longer recognizable.

9. _____ A marine archaeologist discovered the wreckage of the *Belle*.

Study Skills

Write the number of the encyclopedia volume that would have the most information for each of these topics.

1. _____ La Salle

2. _____ shipwrecks

3. _____ archaeology

4. _____ Mississippi River

La Salle

Read to learn about La Salle's exploration of North America.

1   When Europeans first arrived in North America, they had no idea what the land looked like or how big it was. For this reason, explorers traveled across the continent in all directions trying to map the territory and discover what resources were available. One of the most famous of these European explorers was René-Robert Cavelier, Sieur de La Salle, more simply known as "La Salle."

2   La Salle was born in France in 1643, but his desire for adventure took him west across the Atlantic Ocean. In 1666, La Salle settled in the eastern part of Canada, controlled by France at that time, and established himself as a fur trader. During his first years in North America, La Salle explored areas closer to his home, but by 1678 he was ready for a substantial journey.

3   La Salle prepared his ship, called *Le Griffon*, to sail around the Great Lakes. It was very common at that time to find ships sailing the oceans, but *Le Griffon* would be the first ship to sail the Great Lakes. By the time La Salle returned, he had explored Lake Erie, Lake Huron, and Lake Michigan. He also established forts for France along the way.

4   La Salle's next adventure, and the one he might be best known for, was a trip down the Mississippi River. Although the river had been used for centuries by the indigenous people of the area, La Salle became the first European to travel its entire length. Aided by Native American guides, La Salle canoed south until reaching the Mississippi Delta, the area where the river empties into the Gulf of Mexico. To honor his home country, La Salle named the region *Louisiana* after King Louis XIV of France.

5   In 1683, La Salle returned to France and was named viceroy of North America in recognition of his accomplishments. The next year he left France again, this time to establish a French colony at the mouth of the Mississippi River. Unfortunately, La Salle's adventure did not go as planned. Instead of arriving at the Mississippi Delta, La Salle and his crew landed at Matagorda Bay in Texas, thinking it was the western area of the delta. It was almost four years before La Salle realized his mistake.

6   Hoping that his northern friends would be able to help him relocate the colony, La Salle recruited a group of men to join him on a journey to Canada. This was the one adventure La Salle never completed. Because of poor conditions during the journey north, La Salle's men mutinied and took his life. In 1687, La Salle's explorations came to an end.

Vocabulary Skills

Write the words from the passage that have the meanings below.

1. having great weight or meaning

   _____
   Par. 2

2. native; having always lived in a certain area

   _____
   Par. 4

3. acknowledgment

   _____
   Par. 5

4. enlisted or enrolled new members

   _____
   Par. 6

5. took part in a rebellion against a leader

   _____
   Par. 6

Circle the homophone that correctly completes each sentence below.

6. For some time, La Salle worked as a _____ trader. (fir, fur)

7. La Salle was the first to _____ the Great Lakes. (sail, sale)

8. It took about _____ years for La Salle to realize that he had not landed at the mouth of the Mississippi. (four, for)

Underline the word with a prefix in each sentence. Then, write the meaning of the word on the line.

9. La Salle hoped that some friends could help him relocate the colony.

   _____

10. Midway through his last journey, La Salle was killed.

    _____

Reading Skills

1. Check the words that best describe La Salle.

   _____ adventurous

   _____ unfriendly

   _____ courageous

   _____ funny

   _____ determined

Read the sentences below. If the event described happened before La Salle returned to France in 1683, write **B** on the line. If it happened after, write **A**.

2. _____ La Salle and his crew landed at Matagorda Bay.

3. _____ La Salle established himself as a fur trader.

4. _____ La Salle was killed when his men mutinied.

5. _____ La Salle named Louisiana after King Louis XIV.

6. Where was La Salle when he thought he had reached the mouth of the Mississippi?

   _____

7. What was the name of the first ship to sail the Great Lakes?

   _____

8. How did the state of Louisiana get its name?

   _____

9. What group of people used the Mississippi for many years before the European explorers arrived?

   _____

Behind the Scenes at the Zoo

What would it be like to work at a zoo?

1 Miki and Takashi stood with their parents behind the fence at Monkey Island on a sunny Saturday afternoon. They watched the monkeys frolic on the rocks and soak up the sun.

2 "Look, Miki!" exclaimed Takashi. "That one has a baby on her back!"

3 "I wish I could come here every day," said Miki to her family. "I don't think I'd ever get tired of seeing the animals."

4 "It sounds like you might like to be a zookeeper," Mr. Yamamoto said thoughtfully. "Do you see that woman wearing the tan pants and top? I'm pretty sure she is a zookeeper. If you're interested, we could ask her whether she has a few minutes to tell us about her job."

5 Miki introduced herself and explained that she wanted to learn about a career in zookeeping. The woman, whose name was Annette, joined Miki, Takashi, and Mr. and Mrs. Yamamoto at a picnic table in a grassy area near Monkey Island.

6 "How long have you been a zookeeper?" asked Takashi.

7 Annette smiled. "I've been working here for almost 15 years," she said. "I have a degree in zoology, like most of the other zookeepers here."

8 "Is a degree in zoology a requirement for your job?" asked Miki.

9 Annette shook her head. "No, but a degree related to the study and behavior of animals definitely helps. A few of the zookeepers have degrees in biology, and some others have worked in veterinary medicine."

10 "What are the best and worst parts about being a zookeeper?" asked Miki.

11 "Well, seeing the animals every day is the best part," said Annette. "Zookeepers often form a strong bond with the animals under their care. Sometimes, we have to remind ourselves that the zoo animals are wild creatures, not pets," she added.

12 "I think the worst part is that the work can be difficult and unpleasant," continued Annette. "The cages are often smelly, and we have to work in all kinds of weather. The zookeepers have to make sure the animals are clean and well fed and that they are kept in appropriate conditions."

13 "Do you ever teach the animals to do tricks?" wondered Takashi.

14 "That's a good question, Takashi," said Annette. "Some visitors to the zoo do expect that the animals here will know how to perform. We are careful not to teach the animals to do things just to entertain people. Some animals, like the monkeys, enjoy playing, so we play games with them. Animals who are very intelligent need to have some intellectual stimulation, so we try to provide that as well."

15 "So, what do you think, Miki? Does it sound like zookeeping is something you might be interested in pursuing?" asked Annette.

16 "I'm even more excited by the idea now than I was before!" said Miki.

17 "I think that cleaning the litter box at home should be your chore now," joked Takashi. "I don't want to be a zookeeper, but it would be good practice for you!"

Vocabulary Skills

Circle the homophone that correctly completes each sentence below.

1. Zookeepers have to work in all kinds of _____. (whether, weather)

2. Annette finished cleaning the _____ cage at two o'clock. (bear's, bare's)

3. The zookeeper _____ some meat to the lions. (through, threw)

Write **S** if the possessive word is singular. Write **P** if it is plural.

4. _____ zookeepers' duties

5. _____ Miki's questions

6. _____ Annette's opinion

7. _____ animals' behavior

Reading Skills

Mark each sentence below **F** if it is in first-person point of view and **T** if it is in third-person point of view.

1. _____ Annette enjoys her job.

2. _____ I have to remind myself that the zoo animals are still wild creatures.

3. _____ Takashi thinks Miki should start changing the litter box at home.

4. _____ I would love having a job where I could work with animals every day.

5. Do you think Miki will continue to look for more information about becoming a zookeeper? Why or why not?

_____

6. On the lines below, write one sentence from the story that shows that Miki might enjoy a job as a zookeeper.

_____

_____

7. Why does Mr. Yamamoto tell Miki she should talk to the zookeeper?

_____

8. Why don't zookeepers usually teach the zoo animals to do tricks?

_____

_____

Study Skills

Use the information below to answer the questions that follow.

Green Valley Zoo

Hours of Operation

Monday	Closed
Tuesday–Friday	10–6
Saturday	9–6
Sunday	12–5

Admission:

Adults	$8
Children 3–12	$4
Children under 3	Free

1. Which day of the week is the zoo closed?

_____

2. What are the zoo's hours on Sunday?

_____

3. How much is admission for one adult and one 10-year-old child?

_____

An Unlikely Friendship

Have you ever observed two animals of different species form a friendship?

1   Have you ever heard of a friendship between a cat and mouse? An unlikely friendship developed between a domestic black cat named *Muschi*, which means *pussycat* in German, and an Asiatic shaggy black bear named *Maeuschen*, or *little mouse*. A relationship between these two creatures may seem even less likely than one between a cat and a real mouse. Yet Muschi and Maeuschen seem to live quite happily in Maeuschen's cage at the Berlin Zoo in Germany.

2   No one is quite sure how the friendship first began. One day, zookeepers noticed the tiny black cat in the bear's outdoor pen. They were surprised to see how well the small cat seemed to get along with the half-ton bear. Because the two animals were living together peacefully, the zookeeper allowed the cat to stay in the bear's cage. The pair and their unusual friendship became a special attraction at the zoo.

3   After several years, the time came to build Maeuschen a new, larger cage. The bear was moved into temporary housing while the new cage was constructed. Muschi was not moved with her friend, and she made her displeasure quickly known. She paced back and forth outside Maeuschen's temporary cage, crying to be let in. The zoo workers finally took pity on Muschi and allowed her to move back in with Maeuschen. The cat and bear happily cuddled together, and then went back to their normal routine of lying in the sun and sharing meals.

4   Muschi isn't the only cat to have made friends with an animal more than a hundred times her size. In 1972, psychologist Francine Patterson was teaching a gorilla named Koko how to communicate using American Sign Language. Koko loved listening to books about cats and seeing pictures or photographs of cats. For the gorilla's birthday, Patterson allowed Koko to choose a kitten as a pet.

5   You might think that a kitten would be terrified of such a large animal, but All Ball (as Koko named her kitten) seemed perfectly comfortable cradled in the gorilla's enormous hands. Koko was ecstatic to have a pet of her own and treated All Ball with gentleness and tenderness.

6   It seems that animals sometimes have their own ideas about who would make a good companion or friend. These ideas may come as a surprise to humans, who generally expect animals to form bonds with others of the same species. This doesn't appear to concern the animals, though, who just go about their business until the opportunity for a new, maybe very different, friend comes along.

Vocabulary Skills

Write the words from the selection that are homophones for the words below.

1. pear _____
   Par. 2
2. billed _____
   Par. 3
3. paste _____
   Par. 3
4. fourth _____
   Par. 3

The suffix **-ness** means *the condition or quality of being*. For example, *lateness* means *the condition or quality of being late*. Write a word to match each definition below. Then, write a sentence using each word.

5. the condition or quality of being gentle

   _____

   _____

6. the condition or quality of being tender

   _____

   _____

7. the condition or quality of being kind

   _____

   _____

Reading Skills

1. What do *Muschi* and *Maeuschen* mean?

   _____

   _____

2. What is humorous about the names *Muschi* and *Maeuschen*?

   _____

   _____

3. Why were Muschi and Maeuschen separated?

   _____

   _____

4. How did Francine Patterson and Koko communicate with one another?

   _____

   _____

5. How did Koko treat All Ball?

   _____

   _____

6. Check the sentence that best states the main idea of the selection.

   _____ Koko showed a great deal of interest in stories about cats.

   _____ Some animals can occasionally form strong friendships with animals from other species.

   _____ Muschi and Maeuschen live at the Berlin Zoo in Berlin, Germany.

Study Skills

Write the name of the reference source you could use to answer each question below.

encyclopedia	dictionary
atlas	

1. What are the eating habits of the Asiatic black bear?

   _____

2. Where is Berlin, Germany?

   _____

3. How would you divide the word *temporary* into syllables?

   _____

Cats, Cats, Cats

How many different breeds of cats can you identify?

1   Have you ever had a cat for a pet? If you have, you know how rewarding their friendship can be. Cats are known for being independent creatures, but they come to rely on the affection and attention they receive from their human friends.

2   Domestic cats are similar to their wild cousins in many ways. Both types of cats have claws they can retract, or pull in, sharp senses of hearing and smell, excellent night vision, and muscular and flexible bodies.

3   There is an old saying that cats have nine lives. Of course cats do not possess any more lives than any other creature, but they are very agile. Although the domestic cat is much smaller than a human being, its body contains more bones than a human being's. In addition, cats are able to use their tails for balance and to keep themselves from falling.

4   You are probably familiar with the names and appearances of several different dog breeds, but did you know that there are also about 40 different breeds of cats? There are fewer purebred cats than there are dogs, and this may be one reason that the varieties of cats are not as well recognized. Some of the differences between breeds are quite subtle, and only breeders or experts would be able to identify them.

5   Other differences are more obvious. For example, the Maine coon cat is very large and may weigh more than 25 pounds. That is about twice as much as an average cat weighs! The Maine coon cat also has a striped, bushy tail and very long fur. The cat received its name from the legend that it is part raccoon, which is said to explain its size and striped tail.

6   Another interesting breed of cat is the Manx. The Manx has a very small stub of a tail or no tail at all. Also, its front legs are shorter than its back legs. Some people think that with its stubby tail and odd style of running it looks more like a rabbit than a cat.

7   Other types of cats are prized for their beautiful coloring. The Russian blue is one breed of cat with striking coloring. The Russian blue's fur is short but very thick. It has a double coat, which means that it has a layer of soft, downy fur below the fur that is visible on the surface. The top coat has an unusual bluish-gray color that appears to be silver on the tips.

8   Although it's interesting to learn about all the different varieties of cats that exist around the world, it is also important to remember how many homeless cats there are. In animal shelters all across the country, thousands and thousands of cats wait for a good home with a loving family. Even though there is something special about each variety or breed of cat, there are just as many special things about cats that are a combination of breeds. It can be even more exciting for a new owner to experience the surprise of learning the hidden characteristics of his or her feline friend.

Vocabulary Skills

Find an antonym in the passage for each of the words below.

1. dull _____
   _{Par. 2}

2. clumsy _____
   _{Par. 3}

3. thin _____
   _{Par. 7}

4. hard _____
   _{Par. 7}

Write **S** if the possessive word is singular. Write **P** if it is plural.

5. _____ the breed's characteristics

6. _____ cats' muscles

7. _____ Russian blue's fur

8. _____ humans' bones

Reading Skills

Circle the word that best completes each sentence below.

1. Cats use their tails for _____.

   running   balance   protection

2. There are many _____ in the colors and patterns of cats' fur.

   characteristics   coats   variations

3. Some people think that cats are _____ creatures.

   independent   wild   lonely

4. Name two ways in which domestic cats and wild cats are similar.

   _____

   _____

5. How is the Manx cat different from other cats?

   _____

   _____

6. What is the legend surrounding the name of the Maine coon cat?

   _____

   _____

7. In paragraph 8, what is the author trying to persuade the reader of?

   _____

   _____

8. On the lines below, write a summary sentence for paragraph 8.

   _____

   _____

Study Skills

Write the part of a book you would use to find the information to answer each question below.

| table of contents | glossary |
| index | |

1. On what page does chapter 7 begin?

   _____

2. How is the word *Persian* pronounced?

   _____

3. On what page could you find information about litter box training?

   _____

4. Does the book include a chapter about choosing the right cat for your lifestyle?

   _____

The Power of Cats

Keep reading to learn more about the relationship of ancient Egyptians with their cats.

1   Why do people keep cats as pets? Cat owners know that cats make excellent companions. They are playful, intelligent, loving animals. Cats let their owners know they are happy by rewarding them with a loud, rumbling purr or a lick on the arm. They also have the ability to be alone for several days at a time. All these aspects of cat ownership make it easy to see why millions of people today choose to share their homes with cats.

2   The ancient Egyptians, who began keeping cats as pets more than 4,000 years ago, probably appreciated the same things about cats that we do today. But the reason they first formed relationships with cats was because the wild cats were keeping animals like mice and rats away from their supplies of grain. They probably began leaving food for the wild cats to encourage them to stay nearby and control the number of rodents. Once this happened, the cats became accustomed to living among people. It's likely that they were brought into homes, tamed, and bred by the Egyptians.

3   There is also evidence that the ancient Egyptians brought cats with them on hunting trips. They would have trained the cats the way that other civilizations have used dogs— to retrieve animals, like fish or birds, for their owners.

4   Archaeologists have been able to learn much about cats in ancient Egypt because of clues that have been found in the tombs of Egyptians and in Egyptian artwork. Pictures that were painted on the insides of tombs often show cats as part of everyday life in Egypt. Archaeologists have even found thousands of mummified cats. In Egyptian culture, this means that cats were highly respected. Some mummified cats have even been found with mice, rats, and saucers of milk buried in their tombs!

5   There have also been many statues and other sculptures found depicting cats. In fact, one of the Egyptian goddesses, known as *Bast* or *Bastet*, is often shown to have the body of a woman and the head of a cat. She was one of the best-loved goddesses in ancient Egypt, and she was thought to be the protector of women, children, and cats.

6   The next time you pet a cat on the head or scratch it under the chin, remember the history of cats in ancient Egypt. And if a cat expects you to treat it a bit like royalty, maybe now you'll understand why!

Vocabulary Skills

Write the words from the passage that have the meanings below.

1. ways that something can be viewed

   _____
   Par. 1

2. enjoyed; was thankful for

   _____
   Par. 2

3. facts that help one come to a conclusion

   _____
   Par. 3

4. bring back

   _____
   Par. 3

5. representing or standing for

   _____
   Par. 5

Circle the pair of synonyms in each set of words below.

6. encourage   control   grateful   appreciative

7. ancient   importance   statue   significance

8. rewarding   smart   intelligent   sculpture

The nouns below have base words that are verbs. Fill in the blanks to show the verb and suffix that combine to form each noun.

Noun	Verb	Suffix
9. replacement	_____	_____
10. breakable	_____	_____
11. enjoyment	_____	_____
12. washable	_____	_____
13. arrangement	_____	_____

Reading Skills

Write **F** before the sentences that are facts. Write **O** before the sentences that are opinions.

1. _____ Cats are excellent companions.

2. _____ Ancient Egyptians appreciated that cats kept the number of rodents under control.

3. _____ The artwork on the inside of Egyptian tombs is beautiful.

4. _____ Archaeologists have found mummified cats in Egyptian tombs.

5. _____ The Egyptian goddess Bast is often shown to have the body of a woman and the head of a cat.

6. Why did the ancient Egyptians first form relationships with cats?

   _____

7. How have archaeologists learned so much about cats and the ancient Egyptians?

   _____

Study Skills

Read the dictionary entry below and answer the questions that follow.

companion /kəm pan′ yən/ *n.* a friend; one that keeps another company

1. What part of speech is *companion*?

   _____

2. On the line below, write the word *companion* with slash marks to show where the syllable breaks are.

   _____

3. Which syllable is stressed in *companion*?

   _____

Sam Carmichael, Egyptologist

Will Sam solve the mystery of the pyramids one day?

1   Sam Carmichael and his dad sat on the couch with their legs propped up on the coffee table and a large metal bowl of popcorn in between them. They were watching a special program about Egyptian pyramids. Someday, Sam and his dad planned to take a trip to Egypt. Sam hoped that all the mysteries surrounding the construction and contents of the pyramids wouldn't be solved by then.

2   During a commercial, Sam turned to his dad. "What do you think is located in the pyramid chamber that the robot found?" he asked.

3   "I don't know, Sam," replied Mr. Carmichael. "I'm curious why the exploration into that chamber hasn't continued. It has been several years since the robot drilled through the door and extended the camera into the next chamber. I would have thought that trying to open the other sealed door would have been the next logical step."

4   Sam nodded and grabbed a handful of popcorn. "I know," he said. "I'm also curious to hear more about the room that the amateur Egyptologists believe they've found. If they're correct in thinking that it has never been opened in the last four thousand years, it could have some incredible stories to tell."

5   The commercial ended, and the program resumed. Sam and his dad both turned their attention back to the television where the amateur Egyptologists, Gilles Dormion and Jean-Yves Verd'hurt, were being interviewed about their theories of a hidden room.

6   *"And now, we'd like to talk with our expert, Sam Carmichael," said the program's host. "Dr. Carmichael, can you tell us a little about your discovery?"*

7   *Sam adjusted his tie and cleared his throat. "Of course," he began. "I assumed that there was a significant amount of information that was contained in the room Dormion and Verd'hurt discovered. I knew we couldn't wait much longer, so I visited the Egyptian Supreme Council of Antiquities and made my case. They granted me a limited amount of time in which I could bring in my crew of archaeologists and attempt to access the room."*

8   *"Did you ever expect that your work would have such an impact on the study of ancient Egyptian history?" asked the host.*

9   *Sam smiled. "I'd always hoped to be part of a team that had the privilege of making this kind of discovery. My father has always encouraged my interest in archaeology and the Egyptian pyramids, so some of the credit really should go to him."*

10   *"Sam. Sammy. Sam," a voice from the crowd outside the pyramid came. Sam fought to open his eyes to see who was calling his name.*

11   "Sam, it's time for bed," said Mr. Carmichael, gently shaking Sam's shoulder. "I know you really wanted to see the rest of the program, but it's late, and you've been sleeping for at least half an hour. I put in a tape, so we can watch the rest of it tomorrow, okay?"

12   Sam rubbed his eyes and sleepily looked up at his dad. "We have to make it to Egypt one of these days, Dad," he said, yawning as he headed up the stairs to bed.

Vocabulary Skills

Write the words from the story that have the meanings below.

1. stretched out; made longer

   _____
   Par. 3

2. something that makes sense

   _____
   Par. 3

3. started again; continued

   _____
   Par. 5

4. important; meaningful

   _____
   Par. 7

5. effect

   _____
   Par. 8

Circle the homophone that correctly completes each sentence below.

6. The popcorn bowl was made of _____. (metal, meddle)

7. Several popcorn _____ fell in between the couch cushions. (colonels, kernels)

Check the sentence in which *case* has the same meaning as it does in paragraph 7.

8. _____ The attorney won her case with almost no difficulty.

   _____ Please stop at the store for a case of bottled water.

In each row, circle the word that does not belong.

9. inquire   investigate   explore   incredible

10. discover   resume   find   locate

11. tomorrow   yawn   sleep   tired

Reading Skills

1. Is the part of the story in which Sam is being interviewed fantasy or reality? How can you tell?

   _____

   _____

2. What is something that Sam and his dad have in common?

   _____

3. Why does Sam say that his dad deserves part of the credit for his discovery?

   _____

4. In Sam's dream, who grants him permission to explore the hidden room?

   _____

5. Do you think that Sam and his dad will actually travel to Egypt one day? Explain your answer.

   _____

   _____

Study Skills

Check each word that could be found on a page having the guide words shown in dark print.

1. **sunshine—surgeon**

   _____ sunflower _____ suppose
   _____ surfboard

2. **paddle—pamphlet**

   _____ palate _____ pancake
   _____ papaya

3. **frustrate—furnish**

   _____ fumble _____ frog _____ funnel

Pyramid Power

What secrets of life long ago do the pyramids hold?

1   Although pyramid-shaped structures can be found all over the world, the most famous pyramids are located in Egypt. The remains of approximately 90 pyramid sites are scattered across the country, but the pyramids of the Giza plateau are by far the best known. Three giant stone structures tower over the desert floor and are visible for miles. But why are they there, and who built them?

2   Pyramids were used throughout ancient Egypt as extravagant tombs for pharaohs. Pharaohs ruled the kingdoms of ancient Egypt, but they were more than just ordinary kings. Ancient Egyptians believed that the pharaoh was a living god who they had to worship and obey. When the pharaoh died, it was only fitting to build such a huge monument in which to bury him.

3   Because the pyramids are so old, many of them are now just piles of stones, but the pyramids at Giza are still standing tall. The largest of the three, the tallest pyramid in the world, is the Great Pyramid of Giza. It was built for the pharaoh Khufu in 2570 B.C. For nearly 4,000 years, this pyramid was the tallest building on earth. It was originally 480 feet tall, but because of erosion, it now stands at 450 feet tall. Each side is 750 feet long.

4   Egyptologists, or people who study ancient Egyptian history, are amazed by how precisely this giant structure was built using the primitive technologies that would have been available. For example, despite how long the sides of the pyramid are, the builders were able to make each side the same length within half an inch. The pyramids' sides also face exactly north, south, east, and west.

5   Originally, Egyptologists thought that it took hundreds of thousands of slaves almost 30 years to build the Great Pyramid. Today, the most accepted theory is that farmers worked on the pyramid during the times of the year when they did not need to be in their fields. It is also now believed that only about 30,000 people were needed for the construction.

6   The Great Pyramid was built using giant stones that weighed as much as four tons each. The whole pyramid weighs almost eight million tons! Without cranes and trucks, how in the world did the ancient Egyptians move the stones into place? No one knows for certain, but most people believe that sleds were used to slide the stones over great distances. Scholars also think that ramps were built to move the stones up the side of the pyramid and into place. One problem with this theory is that the ramps would have needed to be almost as big as the pyramid itself.

Vocabulary Skills

1. Check the sentence in which *face* has the same meaning as it does in paragraph 4.

   _____ If you face our house, the driveway will be on your right.

   _____ Chris had a big smile on his face when Kimm walked in the door.

2. Check the sentence in which *cranes* has the same meaning as it does in paragraph 6.

   _____ Aunt Sheryl and Lilly used a bird guide to identify the cranes they saw.

   _____ There were three large cranes at the construction site.

Underline the word with a suffix in each sentence. Then, write the meaning of the word on the line.

3. The Egyptologist was amazed at the size of the pyramids.

   _____

4. People did not know whether the mystery of the pyramids would be solvable.

   _____

5. Some people were doubtful that the Egyptians could have built the pyramids without cranes and trucks.

   _____

Reading Skills

1. Why is the Great Pyramid only 450 feet tall today when it was originally 480 feet tall?

   _____

2. About how much does the Great Pyramid weigh?

   _____

3. How do scholars think the ancient Egyptians moved the stones they used to make the pyramids?

   _____

4. Who were the pharaohs of ancient Egypt?

   _____

5. What conclusion can you come to using the information that the sides of the pyramids faced exactly north, east, south, and west?

   _____

6. Check the phrase that best describes the author's purpose.

   _____ to inform

   _____ to persuade

   _____ to entertain

Study Skills

Egyptian Pyramid Statistics		
Pharaoh	Location	Height (ft.)
Userkaf	Saqqara	161
Khufu	Giza	480
Menkaure	Giza	213
Sahure	Abusir	154

1. For which pharaoh was the pyramid in Abusir built?

   _____

2. How tall is the pyramid in Saqqara?

   _____

3. Which two pyramids are closest in height?

   _____

4. Which two pyramids are located in the same place?

   _____

Ride Like the Wind!

What do you think transportation will be like 100 years in the future?

1 Finn sighed and tossed his windpack by the front door. He kicked off his shoes and walked into the kitchen.

2 "Finn, did you hang up your windpack like I asked you?" asked Mom, ruffling his hair. "I'm tired of tripping over it all the time. I wish you would take better care of your belongings."

3 "I had to walk the whole three miles home from school today!" said Finn, grabbing a few orange juice capsules from the basket on the kitchen counter.

4 "Why did you have to walk?" Grandpa asked. "What's wrong with your windpack?"

5 Finn sat down next to his grandpa. "The compressor is broken again."

6 "Finn," said Mom, "were you playing techball with your windpack on again?"

7 "Mom, I learned my lesson last time, I promise," said Finn. "I know the lasers aren't good for the charger in the windpack. My pack was full of air when I left for school, but on the way home I heard a buzzing sound."

8 Mom nodded. "Well, I won't have a chance to take a look at it until tomorrow morning. Dad is out of town until Friday, so you can use his windpack until we have yours fixed. Remember, though, no lasers!" she said as she headed upstairs.

9 "I know, Mom," sighed Finn. "Windpacks are so much work," he complained to Grandpa. "I wish they'd invent something that was easier to take care of."

10 Grandpa smiled. "Finn, you have no idea how easy and clean windpacks are compared to cars."

11 "You never actually had a car, did you Grandpa?" Finn asked. "I thought those were obsolete before you were old enough to have one of your own."

12 Grandpa pulled a small, thin photocard out of his wallet. He typed in a few numbers. "I think I have these organized by year," he said. "I bought my car around 2025."

13 "That's nearly 50 years ago!" exclaimed Finn.

14 Grandpa continued pushing buttons until he came to a color photo of himself as a young man. He stood proudly next to an enormous dark red vehicle. "This kind of car was a called a minivan," Grandpa told Finn.

15 "Tell me again what made them run," Finn said.

16 "Gasoline," answered Grandpa. "The world is a much cleaner place without it," he added. "In the last 50 years, pollution has been reduced by 75 percent. I guarantee that you and I will both live longer because of it."

17 Finn was quiet for a moment. "Grandpa, I guess windpacks aren't as much of a pain as I sometimes think they are."

18 Grandpa nodded as he put his photocard back in his wallet. "There's always room for improvement," he said, patting his grandson on the shoulder.

Vocabulary Skills

Write the words from the story that have the meanings below.

1. a machine that contracts or presses together to push out air or gases

   _____
   Par. 5

2. no longer in use

   _____
   Par. 11

Check the meaning of the underlined word in each sentence.

3. Grandpa showed Finn what was located under the minivan's <u>hood</u>.

   _____ a piece of metal on hinges that covers the engine of a vehicle

   _____ a cloth covering for the head, usually attached to a jacket or sweater

4. Grandpa said that the <u>kind</u> of car he owned was called a minivan.

   _____ nice; thoughtful

   _____ type or variety

Circle the homophone that correctly completes each sentence below.

5. Finn filled his pack with _____ at the windstation. (heir, air)

6. The car companies _____ that gasoline-powered cars were becoming outdated. (new, knew)

Fill in the blanks below with the possessive form of the word in parentheses.

7. _____ dad is out of town. (Finn)

8. There is a picture of _____ minivan on his photocard. (Grandpa)

9. The _____ advantage over cars is that they are cleaner and easier to maintain. (windpacks)

Reading Skills

1. Check the line beside the word or words that best describe what type of selection this is.

   _____ science fiction

   _____ fable

   _____ informational

2. Is this story a fantasy or does it take place in reality? How can you tell?

   _____

   _____

3. What does Grandpa persuade Finn to change his mind about, and how does he do it?

   _____

   _____

4. **Dialogue** is what a character says. The words in dialogue are always in quotation marks. On the line below, write the words that are dialogue in paragraph 13.

   _____

   _____

5. Name two elements of the story that tell you the story takes place in the future.

   _____

   _____

6. When was the picture with Grandpa and his minivan taken?

   _____

   _____

Wind Power: It's a Breeze

How do you think wind is used today?

1   Think about the different ways that people use the wind. You can use it to fly a kite or to sail a boat. Wind is also one of our cleanest and most abundant power sources, as well as one of the oldest. Historians have found proof of windmills being used in Persia, an ancient Iranian culture, as far back as the seventh century B.C. They were first introduced to Europe during the 1100s, when armies returned from the Middle East with knowledge of harnessing wind power.

2   Like a pinwheel, the blades of a windmill spin when the wind blows. The spinning blades turn wheels and gears inside the structure, which in turn run machinery or perform other tasks. The term *windmill* is commonly used to describe all of these power generators, but *wind turbine* is the more precise term. One of the original uses

of wind power was to mill, or grind, wheat into flour. People also used windmills to pump water from deep underground when there was not a water source available above ground.

3   When electricity was discovered in the late 1800s, a new use for wind turbines was found. People who lived in remote areas did not have access to the electrical power that was distributed in the cities. They attached wind turbines to equipment that would turn the energy from the spinning blades into electricity. This process allowed farmers and their families to have electric lights and radio.

4   By the 1940s, electricity was available to people in almost all areas of the United States, so windmills were rarely used. Even water pumps were run using electricity. However, during the 1970s, people started becoming concerned about the pollution that is created when coal and gas are burned to produce electricity. People also realized that these fossil fuels would not last forever. There is only a limited supply of coal and gas available.

5   Citizens who wanted to use cleaner, renewable energy sources rediscovered the wind. Today, there is a global movement to supply more and more of our electricity through the use of wind turbines. One windmill does not produce very much energy, so windmill "farms" are built. Dozens of windmills spin together and create a large amount of energy. The best places for windmills are those places with the most wind, like the open plains of the central United States, on the ocean, and on mountain ridges.

6   Europe is leading the way in wind power. Nearly 75% of all turbines are located there. The country that produces the most energy from wind is Germany. However, Germany uses a lot of energy, and wind only supplies about 5% of all its electrical needs. Denmark is the global leader by using wind to supply almost 20% of its energy usage.

Vocabulary Skills

Write the words from the passage that have the meanings below.

1. more than enough; plentiful

   _____
   Par. 1

2. controlling and putting to work

   _____
   Par. 1

3. machine that changes energy from one form into another

   _____
   Par. 2

4. exact

   _____
   Par. 2

5. far away and hard to access

   _____
   Par. 3

In each row, circle the word that does not belong.

6. power   energy   farm   electricity

7. turn   locate   rotate   spin

8. produced   concerned   worried   nervous

9. One word in paragraph 5 contains both a prefix and a suffix. Write the word and its meaning on the line below.

   _____

Reading Skills

1. Why are windmill farms built?

   _____

2. What is another name for windmills?

   _____

3. Name two types of fossil fuels.

   _____

4. What is one way in which fossil fuels and wind power are different?

   _____

5. Why are open plains, the ocean, and mountains all good places for windmills?

   _____

6. On the lines below, write a short sentence that is a summary of paragraph 3.

   _____

   _____

Circle the word that best completes each sentence.

7. By the 1940s, electricity was _____ to people in most parts of the country.

   removed   donated   available

8. One advantage to wind power is that it does not create _____.

   noise   pollution   energy

Study Skills

Use a dictionary to help you divide these words into syllables.

1. h i s t o r i a n

2. e l e c t r i c i t y

3. m a c h i n e r y

4. g e n e r a t o r

5. Number the words below in alphabetical order.

   _____ windshield

   _____ window

   _____ windmill

   _____ windstorm

Make Your Own Kite

Have you ever flown a kite before?

Materials You Will Need:

one 20-inch wooden dowel rod; one 24-inch wooden dowel rod; a pencil; a ruler; a craft knife; wood glue; fishing line; a piece of heavyweight paper, at least 26 inches square (can be found at crafts stores); scissors; tape; a sewing needle; string; ribbon

Optional Materials:

stickers, paint, markers, and rubber stamps

Directions:

1. Ask a parent or other adult to use the craft knife to make a notch across the flat end of each dowel rod.

2. Make a mark with a pencil 6 inches from the top of the large dowel rod and 10 inches from the top of the small dowel rod.

3. Place the smaller dowel rod on top of the larger one. Glue the two rods together at the places where you made a mark. Be sure that the notches at the ends of the rods are horizontal when your kite frame is lying flat on a table.

4. After the glue has dried, wind some fishing line around the intersection of the two rods to make sure they stay securely joined together. The fishing line should form an X at the intersection of the rods.

5. Now take the fishing line, which should still be attached to the X in the center of the frame, and thread it through the notch at each end of the dowel rods. Thread it through each notch a second time, and then return the fishing line to the center X. Make a few more loops around the X. Then knot the line and cut off the excess.

6. Place the kite frame on the piece of paper. Trace the shape of the kite, and then add two inches to the border. Cut out the larger shape. Center the frame over the paper, and then fold the edges over the frame. Tape the folded edges securely.

7. If you like, you may decorate your kite with the stickers, paint, markers, and stamps.

8. Use the needle to make a small hole in the paper at the top and bottom of the kite. From the frame side, push a piece of fishing line through each hole and knot it. Take the rest of the fishing line (which should still be wound on the spool), and tie the loose end of it about one-third of the way down the middle piece.

9. Attach a 6-foot-long piece of string to the base of the kite. This will be the kite's tail.

10. Use the ribbon to tie a bow every 10 or 12 inches along the kite's tail.

11. Your kite is complete. All you need to do is wait for a breezy day, take your kite to the park, and see how high it can soar!

Vocabulary Skills

Write the words from the passage that have the meanings below.

1. not required

   _____
   materials list

2. a v-shaped cut

   _____
   Step 1

3. parallel to, or level with, the horizon

   _____
   Step 3

4. the point where two things meet

   _____
   Step 4

5. an amount greater than needed

   _____
   Step 5

6. Check the sentence in which *form* has the same meaning as it does in step 4.

   _____ You must fill out this form to enroll in the program.

   _____ Form a ball with the dough in your hands.

7. Check the sentence in which *thread* has the same meaning as it does in step 5.

   _____ I bought some yellow thread to match the sweater I was trying to mend.

   _____ Thread the cord through the opening in the back of the TV stand.

Circle the homophone that correctly completes each sentence below.

8. The kitten's _____ was almost caught in the door. (tale, tail)

9. The morning after the race, all my muscles were _____. (sore, soar)

Reading Skills

1. Where can you find the heavyweight paper to make your kite?

   _____

2. Name two optional materials you can use to decorate your kite.

   _____

3. For which task will you need the help of a parent or other adult?

   _____

4. How much larger than the kite frame should your piece of paper be?

   _____

5. Check the line beside the word or words that best describe what type of selection this is.

   _____ fiction

   _____ how-to

   _____ persuasive

Study Skills

Use the facts from step 5 to complete Part I of the outline below.

I. Make the kite frame

   A. thread fishing line through notches

   B. _____

   C. _____

   D. knot the line and cut off excess

Born to Swim

How do you convince yourself to do something that makes you nervous or scared?

1   Molly sat in the backseat of the station wagon nervously biting her nails. Her mom and Uncle Connor were reminiscing about the days when they competed in school sports.

2   "Your mom was a great swimmer, Molly," said Uncle Connor, turning partly toward the backseat. "She wasn't anywhere near as fast as you are, but she was so graceful in the water. She couldn't hit a softball to save her life, and she couldn't even stand up on ice skates. But as soon as your mom hit the water, she was a fish. You could tell she was born to swim. I'm sure that's where you got your talent."

3   Molly smiled at the idea of her mom swimming as easily and gracefully as a fish. For a moment, she even forgot that they were on the way to her first swim meet of the season. "What about you, Uncle Connor?" she asked. "Were you a swimmer, too?"

4   Uncle Connor chuckled. "I'll let you answer that, Sophie," he said to Molly's mom.

5   "Your uncle sinks like a rock," said Molly's mom, smiling at her daughter in the rearview mirror. "He knows how to swim, because I taught him myself, but it isn't pretty to watch."

6   Before Molly knew it, they were pulling into the parking lot at the school. Her mom gave her a quick kiss on the head for luck, and Uncle Connor winked at her. "We'll see you after the meet, Miss Molly," he said. "Just do your best."

7   Molly took a deep breath as she headed over to her coach and teammates. As she waited her turn to swim, she sat on a bench and gave herself a pep talk. *You can do it. You've done it before. Just stay calm, and stay focused. Don't forget to breathe. You can do it.*

8   Finally, Molly heard the shrill sound of the whistle. She pushed off the starting block and felt a moment of shock as her body hit the cool water. Then, she was moving through the pool

with strong, sure strokes. Molly thought she could hear the voices of her mom and uncle in the crowd when she turned her head to breathe. She did a flip turn when she came to the end of the pool and pushed off the wall with all her strength. As Molly headed back, she could see the water churning in the lane beside her. She increased the speed of her strokes and finally felt her hand touch the blue tile on the wall.

9   Molly sucked in deep breaths of air as she pulled herself from the water and grabbed her towel from the bench. She searched for the faces of her mom and Uncle Connor in the crowd. When she found them they were both holding up a single finger in the air and laughing. Number one! Molly couldn't help grinning back and raising one arm in the air. Her hard work during the summer had paid off!

Vocabulary Skills

Write the words from the story that have the meanings below.

1. remembering; fondly looking back on old times

   _____
   Par. 1

2. moving with ease and beauty

   _____
   Par. 2

3. having a sharp, high-pitched sound

   _____
   Par. 8

4. moving forcefully or vigorously

   _____
   Par. 8

5. Find the simile in paragraph 5, and write it on the line below.

   _____

6. What two things were compared to each other in number 5?

   _____   _____

7. Choose one of the answers to number 6, and use it to create your own simile on the lines below.

   _____

   _____

Write a compound word using two words in each sentence.

8. Molly sat in the seat that was in the back of the station wagon.

   _____

9. Molly's mom could view her in the mirror that showed the rear of the car.

   _____

Reading Skills

Read the sentences below. Write **B** next to the sentence if it happened before Molly dove into the water. Write **A** if it happened after.

1. _____ Uncle Connor told Molly that her mom was a graceful swimmer.

2. _____ Molly grabbed her towel from the bench.

3. _____ Molly's mom and uncle were each holding up a single finger in the air.

4. _____ Molly's mom gave her a kiss on the top of her head.

5. _____ Molly heard the whistle blow.

6. On the lines below, write a short sentence that states the main idea of the story.

   _____

   _____

7. Do you think Molly will swim in future meets? Why?

   _____

   _____

Study Skills

Use the pronunciation key on the inside back cover of this book to write the words that match these pronunciations.

1. /grās′ fəl/ _____

2. /laf′ fing/ _____

3. /skül/ _____

4. /dŏ′ ter/ _____

Ederle Amazing!

Read on to learn more about this talented and determined woman.

1 Can you imagine doing one thing for more than 14 hours without stopping? In 1926, Gertrude Ederle (*ED er lee*) became the first woman to swim across the English Channel. It took her 14 hours and 39 minutes, and she broke the men's record at that time by almost two hours.

2 Before Ederle, only five people had managed to swim across the English Channel, a body of water that divides England and France. All five were men, and Ederle was determined to be the first woman to accomplish the same feat. Ederle had been a strong swimmer since she was a child. When she was only 17, she participated in the 1924 Olympics in Paris. She won two individual bronze medals and a gold medal as part of the American freestyle relay team.

3 In 1925, Ederle decided that she was ready to face the challenge of swimming the Channel. Well into the race, Ederle began coughing. Her trainer, who was traveling in a small boat alongside her, thought she was in trouble and reached out to help her. As soon as he touched her, Ederle was disqualified from the race.

4 A year later, Ederle again attempted to swim across the English Channel. This time, she was successful. She battled the cold temperature of the water, rough winds, and fog. She knew that she could encounter jellyfish, Portuguese man-of-wars, and even sharks. The English Channel was also a very busy shipping route, and swimmers had to be sure to stay out of the path of oncoming freighters.

5 In addition to these dangers, swimming for such a long period of time can become boring. In one of the boats that traveled alongside Ederle, there was a phonograph, which was an early version of the record player. Music from the records and from people singing in the boats helped keep Ederle occupied as she swam.

6 The weather was especially rough during Ederle's journey across the Channel. This is one reason why her record-setting time was so amazing. Because of the rough waters, Ederle ended up having to swim 35 miles to cross the Channel, instead of the 21-mile distance she had planned. Even with the extra 14 miles, Ederle's record stood for many years. In 1950, another American female swimmer, Florence Chadwick, was finally able to beat it.

7 When Gertrude Ederle returned home to the United States, a parade was held in her honor to help celebrate the victory. She met President Coolidge, and she even landed a role in a movie called *Swim, Girl, Swim.*

8 When Ederle was a child, her hearing was damaged when she had the measles. Swimming the English Channel caused more damage to her hearing, and by 1940, Ederle was deaf. Nothing stopped this determined woman, however. She settled in New York City where she taught swimming to deaf children. Ederle died in 2003 at the age of 98.

Vocabulary Skills

Circle the homophone that correctly completes each sentence below.

1. Gertrude Ederle _____ several medals in the 1924 Olympics. (won, one)

2. Ederle played a _____ in a movie about her life. (roll, role)

3. Ederle worked very hard to accomplish the _____ of swimming the English Channel. (feat, feet)

Write the idiom from paragraph 7 on the line next to its meaning.

4. earned a part _____

Find the compound words from the selection that contain the words below.

5. free _____
   Par. 2
6. side _____
   Par. 3
7. fish _____
   Par. 4

Reading Skills

1. Check the line beside the word or words that best describe what type of selection this is.

   _____ historical fiction

   _____ biography

   _____ myth

2. Check the words that describe Gertrude Ederle.

   _____ artistic   _____ nosy

   _____ courageous   _____ athletic

   _____ determined   _____ talkative

3. Find a phrase in the selection that shows the author admires Gertrude Ederle. Write it on the lines below.

   _____

   _____

4. Why was Ederle disqualified the first time she tried to swim the English Channel?

   _____

   _____

5. What are two dangers of swimming the English Channel?

   _____

   _____

Study Skills

Write the name of the reference source you could use to answer each question below.

| encyclopedia | dictionary |
| atlas | thesaurus |

1. Where is the English Channel located?

   _____

2. What is the plural form of *Portuguese man-of-war*?

   _____

3. How did Ederle get her start in swimming?

   _____

4. What happens if you get stung by a jellyfish?

   _____

5. What is another word for *determined*?

   _____

Floating on Air

What is the oldest form of air travel? Keep reading to learn more about it.

1   For most of human history, people could only dream of flying. It was not until the late 1700s that traveling through the air became a reality. In 1783, the Montgolfier brothers of France sent their first passengers, a sheep, a duck, and a rooster, aloft in a paper and silk balloon that had been filled with hot air.

2   Shortly after this event, on November 11, 1783, Pilâtre de Rozier and Marquis d'Arlandes took a ride above Paris in one of the Montgolfier brother's balloons. For half an hour, they floated high above the city and entered the history books as the first humans to fly.

3   Hot air balloons are able to fly because the heated air inside the balloon becomes lighter than the air outside. Helium and hydrogen are also used in balloons because these gases are naturally lighter than the air in earth's atmosphere.

4   After it was proven that balloons could carry people, the next step was to see how far they could go. Crossing the English Channel was seen as a major test. The first attempt was by Rozier in a balloon that used both hydrogen and hot air. This was not such a good idea. Hydrogen is very flammable. Rozier's balloon caught fire, and he did not survive. Despite such an early example of hydrogen's danger, people continued to use it for many years. On May 6, 1937, the gigantic German airship *Hindenburg*, filled with hydrogen, burst into flames. This disaster finally put an end to the use of hydrogen for air travel.

5   Soon after Rozier's fatal attempt, the first successful flight across the English Channel was completed. The French inventor Jean-Pierre Blanchard, accompanied by Boston physician John Jeffries, flew from England to France on January 7, 1785. Blanchard demonstrated the magic of hot air balloons all over the world, and in 1793 became the first person to fly in North America. President George Washington was present for this event, and gave Blanchard a message to carry on his flight from Pennsylvania to New Jersey. It was the first example of airmail.

6   By crossing the English Channel, Blanchard and Jeffries proved that hot air balloons could travel over long distances. However, it was still nearly two hundred years before someone crossed an ocean in a hot air balloon. In 1978, a team of three balloonists flew the *Double Eagle II* across the Atlantic Ocean. In 1981, the *Double Eagle V*, carrying two of the same pilots, crossed the Pacific.

7   The next big record to be set was a nonstop flight around the world. On March 21, 1999, Bertrand Piccard and Brian Jones completed a hot air balloon trip that took them all the way around earth. Three years later, after five unsuccessful attempts, Steve Fossett became the first balloonist to fly solo around the world!

Vocabulary Skills

Write the words from the passage that have the meanings below.

1. high aboveground

   _____
   Par. 1

2. easily burned or set fire to

   _____
   Par. 4

3. causing death

   _____
   Par. 5

4. went along with

   _____
   Par. 5

5. alone; by oneself

   _____
   Par. 7

Read each word below. Then, write the letter of its synonym on the line beside the word.

6. _____ enormous   **a.** effort

7. _____ attempt   **b.** trip

8. _____ disaster   **c.** tragedy

9. _____ journey   **d.** gigantic

Reading Skills

1. Check the phrase that best describes the author's purpose.

   _____ to entertain

   _____ to explain the history of hot air balloons

   _____ to persuade the reader to try traveling by hot air balloon

2. Who were the three passengers in the first hot air balloon trip?

   _____

3. What was Steve Fossett's accomplishment?

   _____

4. Why is hot air used in the balloons?

   _____

   _____

5. Between which two states did the first example of airmail travel?

   _____

6. Why do you think people were so excited by the Montgolfier brothers' accomplishment?

   _____

   _____

Study Skills

A library's reference system can help you find a book. Use the information below to answer the questions that follow.

Call No:	881.37 MO
Author:	Morales, Elia
Title:	Up, Up, and Away: Hot Air Ballooning Through the Years
Publisher:	Caswell & Fitz Publishing, 1999

1. What is the author's last name?

   _____

2. What year was the book published?

   _____

3. Which book would be located closer to the book with the call number above—the book with call number 881.37 RE or the book with call number 879.38 MA?

   _____

Capturing the Moon: A Retelling of a Jewish Tale

Will the citizens of Chelm be able to capture the moon for their own use?

1 In the small town of Chelm (*helm*), the leaves began to turn color and fall to the ground. The air became crisp during the sunny days, and at night the people of Chelm closed their windows and put an extra blanket on the bed. The days were getting shorter. The sky was already becoming dark as people made their way home from work. They complained that it was hard to see where they were going in the dim light. They tripped on the loose stones in the street. They had difficulty recognizing their own friends and neighbors on dark nights.

2 The wise elders of Chelm decided to call a town meeting to address the citizens' discontent. "We are busy people," said Isaac. "When night falls early, we cannot stay in our homes. We must continue to go about our business, just as we do during the rest of the year. The darkness makes this hard for everyone."

3 "It is true," agreed Abraham. "Just the other evening, I nearly ran into my own uncle on the street. I did not recognize him but for the sound of his voice."

4 "Why can't we have oil lamps on the street?" inquired one man. "My cousins who live in the city have told me that this is not uncommon."

5 The village elders looked at one another. They scratched their heads and pulled their beards. Finally, Moishe said, "It is just not possible. This is a small village. We are not wealthy people. Oil lamps may light the streets of cities, but we cannot afford them here."

6 "What about the light of the moon?" asked a man standing in the back of the room. "The moon belongs to everyone. There is no expense for using its light to see in the dark of night. When it is full, the moon is bright enough to light this entire village."

7 The elders nodded. "This is a wise man," they said, "to think of using something that is free for all. But how will we capture the moon?" they asked.

8 After much discussion, it was decided that the townspeople would wait for the next full moon. They would catch the moon when it was seen in the water of a bucket they would leave behind the town hall. They would keep it tightly covered until it was next needed.

9 During the next full moon, the elders waited until they could see the moon floating in the water of the bucket. They crept up to the bucket and quickly covered it with a thick piece of fabric. They tied a string around the rim of the bucket and triumphantly placed it in the shed.

10 Several weeks later, the elders noticed that it was once again becoming difficult to see as they walked home for their dinners. The townspeople gathered around as the elders prepared to uncover the moon and allow it to light the dark evening. They carefully untied the string and lifted the fabric from the bucket. The citizens of Chelm waited expectantly for the light of the full moon to fall across their faces, but nothing happened. They peered into the bucket, but all they could see was the dark water.

11 "The moon has been stolen!" declared Moishe.

12 The elders sadly shook their heads. "We should have kept it in a safer place," they said. "We should have guarded it carefully. We will know better next time."

Vocabulary Skills

Write the words from the story that have the meanings below.

1. the older people in a group who are wise and well-respected

   _____
   Par. 2

2. unhappiness; dissatisfaction

   _____
   Par. 2

3. cost

   _____
   Par. 6

4. celebrating a success or victory

   _____
   Par. 9

5. as though waiting for something to happen

   _____
   Par. 10

Fill in the blanks below with the possessive form of the word in parentheses.

6. The town elders decided to call a meeting to address the _____ unhappiness. (citizens)

7. The _____ decision was to capture the moon in a bucket. (elders)

8. The _____ light belongs to everyone. (moon)

Reading Skills

1. Check the line beside the word or words that best describe what type of selection this is.

   _____ folktale

   _____ historical fiction

   _____ informational

2. What problem did the people of Chelm have in the story?

   _____

3. Why didn't the elders want to place oil lamps on the streets?

   _____

4. Why was it becoming dark earlier?

   _____

5. Were the village elders wiser than the townspeople in the story? Explain.

   _____

   _____

6. If you had been one of the townspeople, how would you have explained why the plan to capture the moon wouldn't work?

   _____

   _____

Write **F** before the sentences that are facts. Write **O** before the sentences that are opinions.

7. _____ The townspeople were unhappy that they couldn't see well at night.

8. _____ The elders were smarter than the townspeople.

Study Skills

Check each word that could be found on a dictionary page having the guide words shown in dark print.

1. **antibody—appeal**

   _____ antonym _____ antler
   _____ approval

2. **confess—construct**

   _____ conductor _____ confetti
   _____ congratulate

3. **knead—koala**

   _____ kitchen _____ knight
   _____ knuckle

Moon Mystery

What are the phases of the moon?

1   On a clear night, go outside and look for the moon. Do the same thing again a week later, and the moon you see will look different. It is the same, familiar rocky sphere that has been circling Earth for millions of years, so why does it always seem to change shape?

2   Sometimes, the moon is a bright disk that illuminates, or lights up, the night sky. Other times, it is just a sliver of white. Sometimes, the moon can be seen during the day. Other times, it is not visible at all. These different amounts of visibility are called the phases of the moon. They occur because the sun, the moon, and Earth are always moving.

3   One thing that almost never changes, however, is that the sun illuminates one side of the moon. Because we live on the surface of Earth, the moon's appearance changes depending on how much of that illumination we can see. For example, a full moon occurs when the moon and the sun are on opposite sides of Earth and we are able to look directly at the lighted side of the moon.

4   A new, or dark, moon occurs when the moon and the sun are on the same side of Earth. In this case, we are looking directly at the unlit side of the moon that is facing away from the sun and is in shadow. The other phases occur as the moon orbits Earth and we see more or less of the illuminated half. A half-moon is when the moon is to the side of Earth, and you can see equal amounts of the lit and unlit halves.

5   A lunar eclipse is the only time the sun's light is prevented from reaching the moon. This occurs when the sun, the moon, and Earth are in a straight line with Earth in the middle. As the moon travels into the darkness of Earth's shadow, it seems as though all or part of it disappears.

6   A solar eclipse is slightly different. It occurs when the sun, the moon, and Earth are lined up but the moon is in the middle. Although the sun is many times larger than the moon, it is also much, much farther away. This makes the sun and the moon appear to be the same size. When the moon's path goes in front of the sun, it temporarily blocks the sun and causes a solar eclipse. A solar eclipse is much rarer than a lunar eclipse.

7   Although there is still some debate, many scientists believe that the moon was once part of Earth. Millions of years ago, something crashed into Earth and broke off a large section of the planet. Gravity kept this huge chunk from floating away into space, and it became our moon. One strong piece of evidence that supports this theory is that the moon is made of the same materials as Earth.

Vocabulary Skills

Write the words from the passage that have the meanings below.

1. different stages

   _____
   Par. 2

2. kept from happening

   _____
   Par. 5

3. for only a brief period of time

   _____
   Par. 6

4. a discussion in which there are different points of view

   _____
   Par. 7

5. information that helps one come to a conclusion

   _____
   Par. 7

Circle the homophone that correctly completes each sentence below.

6. A new moon occurs when the moon and the sun are on the same _____ of Earth. (sighed, side)

7. The moon is _____ of the same materials as Earth. (made, maid)

8. The light from the sun _____ on the moon. (shown, shone)

The prefix **un-** means *not* or *opposite of*. For example, *unfriendly* means *not friendly*. Add **un** to each word below. Then, use each new word in a sentence.

9. interested _____

   _____

10. prepared_____

   _____

11. lock _____

   _____

Reading Skills

1. What is one way that a lunar eclipse and a solar eclipse are similar?

   _____

   _____

2. What is one way that a lunar eclipse and a solar eclipse are different?

   _____

   _____

3. Why are there different phases of the moon?

   _____

   _____

Write **T** before the sentences that are true. Write **F** before the sentences that are false.

4. _____ Some scientists believe the moon was once part of Earth.

5. _____ A solar eclipse is the only time the sun's light is prevented from reaching the moon.

6. _____ During an eclipse, the sun, the moon, and Earth are in a straight line.

7. _____ A solar eclipse is more common than a lunar eclipse.

Study Skills

Number the words below in alphabetical order.

1. _____ moonlight   2. _____ lunch

   _____ moose   _____ luna moth

   _____ moonscape   _____ luminous

   _____ moody   _____ lunar

By the Light of the Moon

What do Pablo and Nita discover when they are camping out in their backyard?

1   "Pablo, did you hear that?" whispered Nita. She rolled over in her sleeping bag. She could see her brother's outline as he sat up in the tent.

2   "Did I hear what?" asked Pablo sleepily.

3   Nita waited a moment until she heard the sound again. "That!"

4   Pablo was suddenly wide-awake. "I heard it that time," he said. "What do you think it is?"

5   "It sounds like a kitten or another baby animal," said Nita, slipping on her tennis shoes. She slowly unzipped the door of the tent and stepped into the backyard. "Pablo, could you bring the flashlight?" asked Nita.

6   Nita could hear a rustling sound inside the tent, and then she heard her brother muttering to himself. "Nita, I think the battery in the flashlight is dead," said Pablo, emerging from the tent.

7   "Shhhh," said Nita. "I don't want to scare away whatever it is. Don't worry about the flashlight. Did you notice how bright it is all of a sudden?"

8   Pablo nodded, turning his face toward the sky. "It's a full moon," he said. "Those clouds must have just passed over it."

9   Suddenly, they heard a mewing sound coming from the bushes that made a border along the back porch of their house. "It's a kitten," whispered Pablo. In the dark bushes, the tiny black-and-white face of a kitten was illuminated by the light of the moon. "I'm going to go get Mom and Dad."

10   When Pablo returned a moment later with his sleepy parents wearing their bathrobes, Nita was cradling the tiny kitten in her arms. The kitten was purring and licking Nita's fingers with its tongue. Nita giggled. "Her tongue is as rough as sandpaper, but it still tickles," she said.

11   Pablo and Nita's parents sighed and looked at each other. "Okay, kids," said their mom, "let's get this little one inside and see if we can get her to eat anything."

12   "Can we keep her, Mom?" pleaded Nita as they walked into the kitchen.

13   "You said we could get a pet when we were old enough to help take care of it," added Pablo.

14   "First, we have to find out if she belongs to anyone," said Dad. "We can call the animal shelters tomorrow morning and put up some signs in the neighborhood."

15   "What if she doesn't belong to anyone?" asked Pablo.

16   "Then, I guess you better start thinking of a name for the kitten," said Mom, opening the refrigerator door.

17   "I already have one," said Nita, stroking the small black nose. "We wouldn't have found her without the light of the full moon tonight. I think her name should be Luna. It's the Latin word for *moon*."

18   "One thing at a time," said Mom, smiling as Luna hungrily drank the milk she had poured into a saucer. "One thing at a time."

Vocabulary Skills

Write the words from the story that have the meanings below.

1. a line that goes around the outer edge of something

   _____
   Par. 1

2. coming out of; appearing

   _____
   Par. 6

3. lit up

   _____
   Par. 9

4. holding as if in a cradle

   _____
   Par. 10

5. begged

   _____
   Par. 12

Find the simile in paragraph 10, and write it on the line below.

6. _____

Read each pair of words listed below. If the words are synonyms, write **S** on the line. If the words are antonyms, write **A** on the line.

7. _____ whispered   yelled

8. _____ bright   dim

9. _____ stroking   petting

Reading Skills

Mark each sentence below **F** if it is in first-person point of view and **T** if it is in third-person point of view.

1. _____ The kitten's face was illuminated by the light of the moon.

2. _____ I hope we get to keep the kitten.

3. _____ I heard a mewing sound coming from the bushes.

4. _____ Nita unzipped the door of the tent.

5. Where were Pablo and Nita camping?

   _____

6. What did Pablo and Nita's parents say they had to do before they could keep the kitten?

   _____

7. Why does Nita want to name the kitten Luna?

   _____

   _____

Study Skills

Use the information on the poster below to answer the questions that follow.

FOUND

Black-and-white kitten, about 9 weeks old

Has black tail with white tip and all black paws

Found on Bentley Street on the evening of June 18

Please call 555-4791 if you have any information.

1. About how old is the kitten?

   _____

2. What number should people call if they have any information about the kitten?

   _____

3. What is the date on which the kitten was found?

   _____

One Giant Leap for Mankind

What do your parents and grandparents remember about July 20, 1969?

1   In the early 1960s, the United States was in a race with the Soviet Union to develop new technologies. A nation's ability to travel in space was seen as the ultimate test, so President John F. Kennedy made a bold speech. He declared that the United States would land a human being on the moon by the end of the decade. On July 20, 1969, this mission was accomplished when two astronauts walked on the surface of the moon.

2   NASA's Apollo space program was developed with the specific goal of landing a man on the moon. The first six Apollo missions were unmanned space flights. *Apollo 7* through *Apollo 10* were flights that carried people into orbit around Earth and the moon but did not land anywhere until they returned to Earth. By July of 1969, *Apollo 11* was ready for takeoff. It would be the first flight whose mission was to land on the moon.

3   Launched from the Kennedy Space Center in Cape Canaveral, Florida, the *Columbia* spacecraft carried astronauts Neil Armstrong, Michael Collins, and Buzz Aldrin. After orbiting Earth one-and-a-half times, *Columbia* headed for the moon and orbited it once as well. After reaching a preplanned position on the dark side of the moon, Armstrong and Aldrin entered the lunar module *Eagle* and descended to the surface.

4   They were headed to an area of the moon called the *Sea of Tranquility*. However, the area where the *Eagle* was programmed to land was too rocky. Armstrong had to take control of the craft and steer it to a safer place. Because the small craft carried only a limited amount of fuel, this action worried the astronauts as well as the scientists back on Earth. Would there be enough fuel left for the *Eagle* to take off and return to the *Columbia*?

5   At least for a while, though, the excitement of having humans on the moon overshadowed their concerns. Neil Armstrong was first to leave the capsule. As he descended the *Eagle's* ladder, he turned on a camera so that people on Earth could watch this historic event. Watched by more than 600 million people, Armstrong stepped onto the moon and said these very famous words, "That's one small step for man, one giant leap for mankind." Armstrong became the first human to set foot on another object in space, followed soon after by Aldrin.

6   While they were on the moon, Armstrong and Aldrin collected soil and rock samples and left behind scientific instruments. They also planted a United States flag and took a phone call from President Richard Nixon. They left behind a plaque that said:

7

> Here Men From Planet Earth
>
> First Set Foot Upon the Moon
>
> July 1969 A.D.
>
> We Came In Peace for All Mankind

8   Everyone held their breath as the *Eagle* took off from the moon. There was just enough fuel for Armstrong and Aldrin to return to the *Columbia* where Michael Collins anxiously waited. All three astronauts returned to Earth safely and became instant heroes all over the world.

Vocabulary Skills

1. Check the sentence in which *steer* has the same meaning as it does in paragraph 4.

_____ The steer charged toward the gate, but the rancher closed it in time.

_____ It is hard to steer the car when it is so windy outside.

2. Check the sentence in which *craft* has the same meaning as it does in paragraph 4.

_____ It is dangerous for a small craft to be out on the ocean during a storm.

_____ We were allowed to take our craft projects home at the end of the day.

Fill in the blanks below with the possessive form of the word in parentheses.

3. People were worried about the _____ fuel level. (*Eagle*)

4. The _____ goal was to land on the moon. (astronauts)

5. _____ Apollo program was a success! (NASA)

Reading Skills

1. Check the words that describe Neil Armstrong.

_____ shy

_____ courageous

_____ ambitious

_____ funny

_____ strong-willed

2. Number the events below to show the order in which they happened.

_____ Armstrong and Aldrin entered the *Eagle*.

_____ The *Columbia* spacecraft was launched from the Kennedy Space Center.

_____ Armstrong and Aldrin planted a flag on the moon.

_____ Armstrong steered the *Eagle* to a less-rocky surface.

_____ President Kennedy said the United States would land a human being on the moon by the end of the decade.

3. What were Armstrong's first words on the moon?

_____

_____

4. What do you think Armstrong meant when he said this?

_____

_____

Study Skills

Write the name of the reference source you could use to find the information to answer each question below.

thesaurus	encyclopedia
dictionary	atlas

1. Where is Cape Canaveral, Florida?

_____

2. What is a synonym for *courageous*?

_____

3. What does the word *lunar* mean?

_____

4. What sort of space program did the Soviet Union have in the 1960s?

_____

A Backyard Discovery

What does Daniel find in his backyard when construction begins for an addition to his house?

1   Daniel sat at the breakfast table drinking his orange juice. Something seemed different that morning, but he just couldn't put his finger on it. He bit into a crisp slice of toast, when all of a sudden he realized what was missing. It was the sound of jackhammers and big pieces of machinery working in the backyard. During the past week, Daniel had become accustomed to the constant roar of engines as a crew of workers prepared the backyard for the addition to Daniel's house.

2   "Mom, did you notice something different this morning?" he asked.

3   Daniel's mom smiled. "Silence," she said. "I can actually hear birds chirping again. The construction crew was called away for a couple of days to work on another project. I'm anxious to have our addition finished, but I told the foreman that I wouldn't mind a couple of days of peace and quiet, even if it does delay our schedule a bit."

4   "Can we go outside and look around?" asked Daniel, finishing his last bite of toast. "I know you said it was dangerous to go out there with all the heavy equipment nearby, but I'd really like to take a look around."

5   "Sure," said Daniel's mom. "I'm pretty curious myself."

6   The Ivanovics' backyard looked completely unfamiliar to Daniel and his mom. Piles of rocks and dirt nearly obscured the garage. A backhoe was parked where the tulip bed used to be. Daniel was relieved to see that the chestnut tree he had helped plant when he was four years old had been spared.

7   While Daniel's mom worked to salvage a few plants from the edge of the construction site, Daniel walked around the perimeter of the gaping hole. Something caught his eye, and he stooped down to take a closer look. He gently blew away the rust-colored dirt that partially covered his find. Once the dust had settled, he was able to take a closer look.

8   "Mom, I think you're going to want to see this," said Daniel. A moment later, his mom crouched beside him, looking at the nearly perfect fossil he had found.

9   "This is amazing, Daniel!" said Mrs. Ivanovic, shaking her head. "If you weren't so observant, this fossil probably would have been destroyed in a couple of days and we would have never known it was here."

10   "What do you think it is, Mom?" asked Daniel, peering closer.

11   "I don't know," Mrs. Ivanovic answered. "It looks like a fish of some kind, but I suppose it could have been a reptile. We should call the Natural History Museum and ask if someone can help us remove it from these rocks without damaging it."

12   Daniel headed to the house to get the phone. He couldn't wait to find out what sort of prehistoric animal had once lived in his backyard. Whatever it turned out to be, Daniel knew he had made a discovery he wouldn't soon forget.

Vocabulary Skills

Write the words from the story that have the meanings below.

1. to cause something to happen at a later time

_____
Par. 3

2. made hard to see

_____
Par. 6

3. wide open

_____
Par. 7

Write the idiom from paragraph 1 on the line next to its meaning.

4. to be unable to identify something or figure it out

_____

Read each word below. Then, write the letter of its synonym on the line beside the word.

5. _____ appeared   **a.** almost

6. _____ unsafe   **b.** seemed

7. _____ nearly   **c.** destroyed

8. _____ demolished   **d.** dangerous

Find the compound words from the selection that contain the words below.

9. fast _____
Par. 1

10. hoe _____
Par. 6

Reading Skills

1. Check the phrase that best describes the author's purpose.

_____ to instruct

_____ to explain

_____ to entertain

Read the sentences below. Write **B** next to the sentence if it describes something that happened before Daniel went outside. Write **A** if it describes something that happened after.

2. _____ Daniel was glad his chestnut tree hadn't been damaged.

3. _____ Daniel drank his orange juice.

4. _____ Something caught Daniel's eye.

5. _____ Mrs. Ivanovic said that Daniel was observant.

6. _____ Mrs. Ivanovic explained why the construction crew wasn't working.

7. Do you think Daniel will be able to identify the fossil he found? Explain your answer.

_____

_____

Study Skills

Use the table of contents below to answer the questions.

Table of Contents

1. What is the title of Chapter 3?

_____

2. Which chapter contains information on identifying fossils?

_____

3. What page would you turn to for information on buying fossils?

_____

Digging Up History

How do scientists know so much about animals that no longer exist?

1 What is the oldest thing you have ever seen? Maybe it's a family photograph or piece of furniture that was passed down through the generations. It might be a tree in your town or a piece of artwork in a museum. If you've ever visited a natural history museum, then you have probably seen a fossil that might be thousands or even millions of years old. Did you ever wonder how that fossil was formed and why it was able to survive for such a long period of time?

2 The word *fossil* comes from a Latin word that means to *dig*. This is because digging is necessary to uncover most fossils. Fossils are the remains of prehistoric plants and animals that have been preserved for thousands of years. They allow paleontologists and other scientists to form an idea of what the conditions on earth were like long ago.

3 The soft parts of an organism, like skin or plant tissue, are not usually preserved. Fossils of the harder parts, like teeth, bones, or the skeleton of a leaf, are much more commonly found. When the remains of the plant or animal are slowly replaced by minerals over time, they become petrified. Some of the most famous examples of this type of fossil can be found in Petrified Forest National Park in eastern Arizona.

4 Under other conditions, a decomposed plant or animal may leave an imprint that fills with sand. Over time, the sand hardens and turns to stone. The stone will be a replica of the plant's or animal's remains.

5 Some of the most fascinating discoveries occur when an organism has been trapped and preserved in organic material such as ice, amber, or tar. Amazing specimens like the wooly mammoth have been found frozen in Siberia, where it is so cold that portions of the ground never thaw. Paleontologists believe that the animals may have slipped into crevices between rocks and been unable to make their way out.

These are rare cases in which every part of the animal has been preserved. Scientists have even been able to determine the diets of animals based on the contents of their stomachs.

6 Insects and other small animals are sometimes preserved in amber. They get caught in the thick, sticky sap of certain trees and are unable to free themselves. The resin, or sap, of the trees eventually hardens and turns to amber, perfectly preserving the tiny creatures inside.

7 Plants and animals can also be caught and preserved in tar, or natural asphalt. Scientists believe that when animals came to a drinking hole, they were sometimes caught in the tar that lay beneath the surface of the water. The most famous example of this can be found at the La Brea Tar Pits in Los Angeles, California. The bones and teeth of animals like saber-toothed tigers, wolves, mastodons, and horses have been found there.

8 Paleontologists have the interesting job of uncovering the mystery of life long ago. They may never have all the pieces to solve the puzzle, but each discovery brings them a little closer to understanding the history of the natural world.

Vocabulary Skills

Write the words from the passage that have the meanings below.

1. scientists who study prehistoric life

_____
Par. 2

2. an exact copy

_____
Par. 4

3. melt

_____
Par. 5

4. liquid that flows through plants

_____
Par. 6

Circle the homophone that correctly completes each sentence below.

5. Have you ever _____ a fossil before? (scene, seen)

6. Scientists were able to determine the mammoths' diet _____ on the contents of their stomachs. (baste, based)

Reading Skills

1. Where can you find a good example of petrified wood?

_____

2. Why is it so valuable for scientists to find animals that have been preserved in ice?

_____

_____

3. Name two types of animals that have been found in the La Brea Tar Pits.

_____

4. How do insects or small animals become preserved in amber?

_____

5. Why is the work of paleontologists important?

_____

6. On the lines below, write a summary of paragraph 5.

_____

_____

7. What is one way that plants and animals trapped in amber are similar to those trapped in ice?

_____

Circle the word that best completes each sentence.

8. The soft parts of a plant or an animal usually _____.

harden   decompose   uncover

9. In petrified wood, the soft tissues have been _____ by minerals.

determined   trapped   replaced

Study Skills

Use the pronunciation key on the inside back cover of this book to write the words that match these pronunciations.

1. /fō′ tə graf′/ _____

2. /kre′ vis/ _____

3. /bē nēth′/ _____

4. /ser′ ten/ _____

5. /fā məs/ _____

The Fossil Lady

What were Mary Anning's discoveries?

1   In 1799, in Lyme Regis, Great Britain, a little girl named Mary Anning was born. Mary was close to her father, who was a cabinetmaker. In his spare time, he collected fossils from the cliffs at Lyme Regis, one of the best places in the world for fossil collecting. Sometimes, Mr. Anning would take his small daughter with him on his expeditions. It was difficult for the family when Mr. Anning died in 1810, but he left them a valuable gift—his knowledge of fossils.

2   The Anning family was quite poor after the death of Mr. Anning. Both Mary and her brother did their best to contribute income. They collected fossils and were often able to sell their finds to local collectors or to tourists. One collector, Thomas Birch, came to be fond of the family. He was sympathetic to their poverty and decided to sell his own collection of fossils to help the Annings financially. The Annings were grateful for Mr. Birch's support, as it allowed them to live more comfortably.

3   One of the specimens that Mary is most well known for having discovered, with some help from her brother, is the fossilized skeleton of an Ichthyosaurus. It was not the first skeleton of this type to be discovered, but it is believed to be the first complete skeleton. What makes this even more remarkable is that Mary was only about 12 years old when her discovery took place!

4   Mary continued to have a great interest in fossils as she grew older. In 1821, she discovered the first skeleton of a Plesiosaur, which was probably her greatest contribution to science. This discovery gave Mary the respect of the scientific community. They had been hesitant to take her seriously in the past because she was young and she was a woman. After Mary's discovery of the Plesiosaur, they had no choice but to acknowledge her reputation as a serious fossilist.

5   Mary Anning died in 1847 at the age of 47. Although she had been a lover and collector of fossils her entire life, she was rarely given credit for her specimens when they ended up in museums or in private collections. In many ways, the society she lived in wasn't ready for someone like Mary. In recent years, however, more books and articles have been written about this dedicated and fascinating woman. The authors know that it is not too late to have Mary Anning remembered in history as "The Fossil Lady."

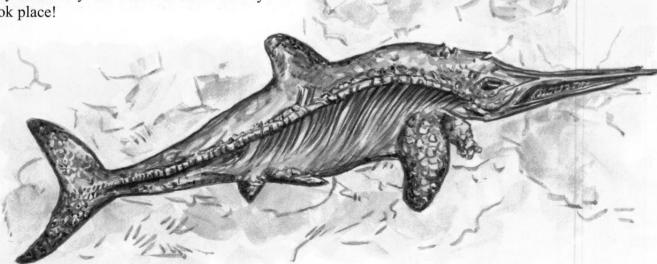

Vocabulary Skills

Write the words from the passage that have the meanings below.

1. to give or help bring about

   _____
   Par. 2

2. understanding of others' feelings

   _____
   Par. 2

3. the state of being poor; having little wealth

   _____
   Par. 2

4. uncertain or doubtful

   _____
   Par. 4

In each row, circle the word that does not belong.

5. collect   collector   discovery   collection

6. recognize   society   accept   acknowledge

7. remember   rare   uncommon   unusual

Reading Skills

1. Check the words that describe Mary Anning.

   _____ determined   _____ scientific

   _____ intelligent   _____ suspicious

   _____ outgoing

2. Check the word that best describes what type of selection this is.

   _____ fiction

   _____ legend

   _____ biography

3. Check the sentence that best states the main idea of the selection.

   _____ Mary Anning's father died while she was still a child, and she and her brother helped support the family.

   _____ Mary Anning was a fossil hunter from the 1800s whose contributions are still recognized today.

   _____ Mary Anning lived near the cliffs at Lyme Regis in Great Britain.

4. Who bought the fossils that Mary and her brother found?

   _____

Study Skills

Use the time line below to answer the questions that follow.

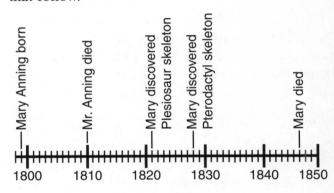

1. In what year did Mr. Anning die?

   _____

2. What happened in 1828?

   _____

3. How many years passed between Mary's discovery of the Plesiosaur and the Pterodactyl?

   _____

Earning Power

Will Jamila ever be able to buy the bike she wants?

1   Jamila sat on the front porch, bouncing a small rubber ball against the worn wood planks. Tyler sat in the rocker next to her. "What's wrong, Jamila?" he asked. "Did you ask your parents about the bike?"

2   Jamila nodded as she bounced the ball. "They said that I have a perfectly good bike. I tried to tell them that I need a racing bike with gears, but they just didn't understand."

3   "When is your birthday?" asked Tyler helpfully. "Maybe you could ask for a new bike for your birthday."

4   Jamila shook her head. "It was more than a month ago," she said. "I don't think I'm going to get this bicycle, Tyler. I have some of my birthday money left from my grandparents, but it won't be enough to buy the bike I want."

5   Jamila and Tyler sat quietly on the porch for a few minutes. The only sound was the steady thud of the rubber ball hitting the porch. Suddenly, Tyler jumped up. "How much do you want this bike?" he asked Jamila.

6   "I really want it," said Jamila. "I want to start training with the Green Ridge Cyclists. If I don't start training in the next month, I won't be ready to ride in the annual fundraiser."

7   "Have you asked your parents if they have any chores you can do around the house?" suggested Tyler. "When I was saving to buy my skateboard, my parents posted a list of things I could do. We agreed on an hourly rate, and every time I completed a chore, I logged it on the list with the amount of time it took me to get it done."

8   For the first time all afternoon, Jamila started to feel a bit hopeful. "That's a great idea, Tyler," said Jamila. "My parents are always saying that there just aren't enough hours in the day for everything they need to do."

9   A few days later, Tyler stopped over at Jamila's house. She and her mom were crouched over the flowerbeds in the front yard. "Hi, Tyler," they said in unison as they watched him walk up the path to the house.

10   "Tyler, I want to thank you for your creative thinking," said Mrs. Johnson, wiping her hands on her jeans. "We're almost done weeding all the flowerbeds, and with Jamila's help, it took me half the time. Yesterday, she painted the garage, wrapped birthday presents for her cousins, and helped her dad clean out the attic."

11   Jamila smiled. "At this rate, I'm going to have my bicycle in no time."

12   "And Jamila's dad and I are going to have a clean, organized house and some free time," added her mom.

13   Tyler grinned. "I'm glad I could help. I don't suppose that making cookies is on your list of things to do today, is it?"

14   Jamila and Mrs. Johnson laughed. "Maybe if we had a little more help with the rest of the weeding," Jamila said.

Vocabulary Skills

Check the meaning of the underlined word in each sentence.

1. Jamila shifted her bike into second <u>gear</u>.

    _____ equipment used for a specific activity

    _____ a mechanism that affects speed in a car or bicycle

2. Jamila wanted to <u>train</u> to ride in the fundraiser.

    _____ to practice and get into shape

    _____ a string of railroad cars

Compound words are divided into syllables between the two words that make the compound. For example, *play/ground*. Divide the words below into syllables using a slash *(/)*.

3. s k a t e b o a r d

4. b i r t h d a y

5. g r a n d p a r e n t

6. f u n d r a i s e r

7. a f t e r n o o n

8. f l o w e r b e d

Reading Skills

1. Check the phrase that best describes the author's purpose.

    _____ to entertain

    _____ to instruct

    _____ to explain

2. What problem does Jamila have at the beginning of the story?

    _____

3. How does Tyler help her solve the problem?

    _____

4. Why does Mrs. Johnson like Tyler's idea?

    _____

Write **F** before the sentences that are facts. Write **O** before the sentences that are opinions.

5. _____ Jamila wants to buy a new bike.

6. _____ Jamila helps her mom weed the garden.

7. _____ Tyler is a creative thinker.

8. _____ Tyler hopes that Jamila and her mother will make cookies.

9. _____ Jamila's parents should buy the bike for her.

Study Skills

Use the information below to answer the questions that follow.

Chores	Time Spent
Paint garage door	2 hours
Wrap presents	1 hour
Weed flowerbeds	1.5 hours
Clean attic	3 hours
Sort recycling	1.5 hours

1. How long did it take Jamila to weed the flowerbeds?

    _____

2. Which chore took Jamila the longest amount of time?

    _____

3. If Jamila earns three dollars an hour, how much money did she make painting the garage door?

    _____

Money Matters

Where does money come from?

1   Have you ever looked closely at a dollar bill? You might see one almost every day, but most people don't take the time to stop and examine the piece of currency that is probably more recognized than any other in the world.

2   Paper money is printed at the Bureau of Engraving and Printing, which is a division of the United States Treasury Department. Beginning in 1862, all U.S. currency was printed in Washington, D.C. Today, about half of our nation's currency is printed in a second location in Fort Worth, Texas. You might be surprised to learn that money is only printed in the following denominations, or amounts: $1, $2, $5, $10, $20, $50, and $100. Larger bills have not been printed since 1946.

3   You may receive a bill that looks worn and faded. Other bills may feel new and crisp. This is because new bills are constantly being put into circulation to replace bills that are damaged or worn out. Five-dollar bills are used frequently, so they have the shortest life span. On average, a five-dollar bill lasts only about 15 months. In comparison, a 50-dollar bill may last about five years. Coins have a much longer life span than most bills and last an average of 25 years.

4   One problem that the people at the Bureau of Engraving and Printing worry about is counterfeiting. Counterfeiting occurs when people duplicate currency. As technology becomes more advanced, it becomes more of a challenge to find ways to outwit counterfeiters.

5   Beginning with the 100-dollar bill in 1996, the Bureau of Engraving and Printing has been slowly redesigning and issuing new U.S. currency. The new bills make it harder to successfully copy money. Today's bills have a watermark that shows the same historical figure that appears on the bill. The watermark is visible when the bill is held up to the light.

6   There is also a security thread that can be seen in bright light. In very small letters on the thread, it says *USA* and the denomination of the bill. In the 20- and 50-dollar bill, the thread also has a tiny flag imprinted on it.

7   In addition, U.S. currency is printed on a special type of paper that is a blend of linen and cotton with tiny bits of red and blue thread in it. This paper can withstand a lot of use, and it is easy to recognize by touch. It is actually against the law to manufacture this type of paper without special permission!

8   The next time you receive your allowance or reach for a dollar to pay for something, take a close look at the bill in your hand. It's a little piece of American history and culture. See how many of its characteristics you can identify. You just might be surprised by how much you know.

Vocabulary Skills

Write the words from the passage that have the meanings below.

1. a country's form of money

   _____
   Par. 1

2. one of the parts into which something is divided

   _____
   Par. 2

3. the passage of something from person to person or place to place

   _____
   Par. 3

4. copy; reproduce

   _____
   Par. 4

5. outsmart or be more clever than someone

   _____
   Par. 4

Find an antonym in the selection for each of the words below.

6. new _____
   Par. 3

7. easier _____
   Par. 5

8. invisible _____
   Par. 5

9. dim _____
   Par. 6

Circle the homophone that correctly completes each sentence below.

10. A _____ bill will eventually be replaced. (worn, warn)

11. I received a crisp, _____ five-dollar bill from the bank. (knew, new)

12. A nickel is worth five _____. (sense, cents)

Reading Skills

Write **T** before the sentences that are true. Write **F** before the sentences that are false.

1. _____ On average, coins last about 50 years.

2. _____ U.S. currency is printed on a special type of paper.

3. _____ Today, all U.S. currency is printed in Washington, D.C.

4. _____ Two-dollar bills have not been printed since 1946.

5. _____ *USA* appears on the security thread of bills issued today.

6. What is one way in which a five dollar bill and 50-dollar bill are similar?

   _____

7. What is one way in which they are different?

   _____

8. Why does advanced technology make it more of a challenge for the government to outwit counterfeiters?

   _____

   _____

9. What are the seven denominations of bills?

   _____

   _____

10. What is a watermark?

    _____

    _____

Money in the Bank

Do you have a bank account?

1   "Jamila, I just found five dollars sitting on the coffee table," said Mrs. Johnson. "Is that your money?"

2   Jamila looked up from the book she was reading. "Oops. I emptied my jacket pockets before I left for soccer practice yesterday. I was running late, so I didn't have time to take the money up to my room." Jamila's mom handed her the bill and watched as her daughter folded it up and placed it neatly in the back of her book.

3   Jamila went back to reading. A moment later, she looked up when she heard her mother heave a deep sigh. "Jamila, you just tucked that money into the back of your book. I'm quite sure that you're not going to be able to find it when you need it. You are working so hard to save for a new bicycle. I don't want you to lose track of any of your hard-earned money. Didn't Grandpa buy you a piggybank for your birthday a few years ago?"

4   Jamila nodded. "I have one, but the key doesn't work anymore. I stopped putting money in it because I can't get it out. Some of the money I earned is in a jar on my desk. Some is in an envelope in the glove compartment of the car. I think I might also have a few dollars in my backpack."

5   Mrs. Johnson smiled fondly at Jamila. "It looks like it's time for you to get your own bank account," she said. "Do you want to go to the bank with me?" She glanced at her watch. "They'll still be open for another hour."

6   Jamila jumped up. "Will the account be in my own name?" she asked excitedly.

7   "Of course," answered her mom. "Why don't you go see if you can gather up the money you have stashed around the house. You might be surprised by how much you have when it's all in one place. At least you'll know where it all is," she added.

8   At the bank, Jamila and her mom opened a savings account. The banking specialist explained how the money in the savings account would earn interest. The longer the money stayed in the account, the more it would earn.

9   Jamila was surprised to learn that she could earn money just by keeping her money in a savings account. "I wish I had done this a long time ago," she told her mom. "Maybe I'd have already saved enough to buy my bike."

10   The banking specialist smiled. "I don't know that the interest would have added up that fast," she said, "but it's certainly better to be earning something than just having your money sit in a piggybank."

11   "Or in a jar, an envelope, or a backpack," added Jamila, grinning at her mom.

Vocabulary Skills

Read each word below. Then, write the letter of its synonym on the line beside the word.

1. _____ watched   **a.** amazed

2. _____ jumped   **b.** observed

3. _____ surprised   **c.** buy

4. _____ purchase   **d.** leaped

The suffix **-ment** means *the state or condition of being*. For example, *excitement* means *the state or condition of being excited*. Write a word using **ment** to match each definition below. Then, write a sentence using each word.

5. the state or condition of governing

_____

_____

6. the state or condition of placing

_____

_____

7. the state or condition of being improved

_____

_____

Reading Skills

1. The **protagonist** is the main character in a story, or the person the story is mostly about. Who is the protagonist in this story?

_____

2. What is Jamila saving her money to buy?

_____

3. What is one reason that a savings account would be a good idea for Jamila?

_____

4. If Jamila left her money in a savings account for a year, would it earn more or less interest than if she left it there for two years?

_____

Mark each sentence below **F** if it is in first-person point of view and **T** if it is in third-person point of view.

5. _____ The key to my piggybank doesn't work.

6. _____ Jamila and her mother went to the bank to open a savings account.

7. _____ The bank specialist smiled at Jamila.

Study Skills

Use the savings account form to answer the questions.

Savings Account Application		
last name	first name	middle initial
street address		
city	state	zip code
date of birth	parent's or guardian's name	

1. What are the first two pieces of information the application asks for on the third line?

_____

2. Whose name, other than your own, do you need to include on the application?

_____

3. What other information should the form ask?

_____

Collecting Change

What is the oldest coin in your piggybank?

1   Do you collect anything? Collecting is a popular hobby with people all around the world. Some people collect baseball cards, teapots, or seashells. Others collect matchbook covers, stamps, bottles, or dolls. There are almost as many types of collections as there are collectors.

2   Coin collecting, called *numismatics*, is one of the oldest and most popular types of collecting. People enjoy learning about coins and their history. They like the challenge of finding rare or unusual coins. Some see their collections as a valuable investment. Others just enjoy the beauty and variety of their coins.

3   There are many different types of coin collections. Some numismatists choose to collect foreign coins. They may focus on a particular country or a particular time period when they begin their collections. Another popular way to collect is to choose a theme and then look for coins that have pictures of the animals, people, or objects that fit into that theme. For example, a collector may search for coins with images of ships, birds, or even royalty.

4   In the past few years, many children have started collecting coins because of the United States Mint's 50 State Quarters Program. In 1999, the U.S. Mint began a program in which they would produce five new state quarters every year for 10 years. Each quarter has a picture that represents something unique or special about the state. For example, New York's quarter has a picture of the Statue of Liberty, Georgia's has a picture of a peach (the state symbol), and North Carolina's has the Wright brothers' airplane.

5   Some collections can become very valuable. This depends on several factors: the type of coin, the rarity of the coin, and the demand for the coin. If you owned a rare coin that few other people were interested in collecting, it would be worth much less than a rare coin that many other people would like to own.

6   Condition also plays an important role in determining a coin's worth. Serious collectors store their coins very carefully in special display cases. They handle their coins only by the edges or with special gloves. If you owned a Liberty Head nickel from 1913, which is worth about one million dollars, you would probably be willing to give it special treatment, too!

7   If you are interested in starting a coin collection, the best thing to do is to learn a little about it first. You can find books about coin collecting for kids at the library, or you can visit the Web site of the United States Mint for tips on getting started. You'll learn how to determine the worth of various coins, properly store your collection, and keep track of what you own. And the next time you look through the spare change in your pocket or the coins in your piggybank, you might just find that you have the beginnings of a very interesting hobby!

Vocabulary Skills

Write the words from the passage that have the meanings below.

1. a fun activity done in one's spare time

    _____
    Par. 1

2. putting money to use by buying something that will become more valuable in the future

    _____
    Par. 2

3. a specific subject or topic

    _____
    Par. 3

4. something that is rare or unusual

    _____
    Par. 5

5. value

    _____
    Par. 7

Write a compound word using two words in each sentence.

6. Shells that are found near the sea are

    _____.

7. A small book that contains more than one match is a _____.

8. Pots that are used to brew tea are

    _____.

9. A bank that is shaped like a piggy and used to store money is called a

    _____.

Reading Skills

1. What is a numismatist?

    _____

2. In the United States Mint's 50 State Quarters Program, how many new quarters are released every year?

    _____

3. Name two reasons that people like to collect coins.

    _____

    _____

4. How does the demand for a coin affect its value?

    _____

    _____

5. Where can you find more information about starting a coin collection?

    _____

6. Why do you think that serious collectors handle their valuable coins so carefully?

    _____

Study Skills

United States Mint 50 State Quarters Program		
State	Year Minted	# out of 50
Delaware	1999	1
Florida	2004	27
Kentucky	2001	5
Louisiana	2002	18
Missouri	2003	24

1. Which state's quarter was minted in 2002?

    _____

2. In what year was Kentucky's quarter released?

    _____

3. Which state's quarter was the first released in the U.S. Mint's program?

    _____

Visiting Wild Places

Where in the world would you most like to travel?

1   Raj and Malcolm sat at a table in the library with books spread out all around them. Malcolm was intently looking at a page in a volume of the encyclopedia when he heard Raj whispering his name. Malcolm looked up.

2   "Malcolm, we need to choose a topic," said Raj. "We've been here for more than two hours, and we still haven't agreed on something. We're running out of time."

3   Malcolm closed the encyclopedia and set it on the table with the other books. "Let's reread the assignment," he said. "Then, we'll each propose an idea and decide which one would make a better report."

4   Raj opened his notebook and began reading. "Work with a partner to choose a place that you would most like to visit. Prepare a presentation for the class that describes the place you've chosen. Be sure to provide reasons for your choice."

5   Raj thought for a moment. "I'd most like to visit the Amazon," he said finally. "That's where the largest rain forest in the world is located. The Amazon Basin encompasses more than a million square miles of rain forest. It is also home to the Amazon River, which is the second longest river in the world after the Nile."

6   "That sounds as though it could make a pretty interesting presentation," admitted Malcolm. "What would you say when Ms. Friedman asks you why you selected the Amazon?"

7   "Well," said Raj, "the Amazon is still very mysterious. It's one of the few parts of the world that hasn't been very well explored yet. People don't even know how many tributaries the Amazon has. They do know, though, that in Brazil alone there are at least 200. The Amazon rainforest also has many types of plants and animals that aren't found anywhere else in the world. In one day, entomologists found more than 400 species of butterflies in a small area."

8   Malcolm nodded. "That sounds a little like the Galápagos Islands," he said. "They are made up of 13 large islands and several hundred small islands that lie off the coast of Ecuador, along the equator. The islands are best known for all the unusual species of plants and animals that are found only there and nowhere else in the world. About 85 species of birds live on the islands," said Malcolm, shaking his head in amazement. "The British naturalist Charles Darwin spent a lot of time there studying the wildlife."

9   Raj grinned at Malcolm. "This was no help at all!" he exclaimed. "The Galápagos Islands sound just as interesting to me as the Amazon."

10   "Maybe we can ask Ms. Friedman if we can do both," suggested Malcolm. "There are a lot of similarities between the two places. We could each do a short presentation about the place we selected, and then we could do a joint presentation about their similarities and differences."

11   "Perfect!" said Raj, beginning to gather the books from the table. "I knew if we just brainstormed long enough we'd come up with a solution."

Vocabulary Skills

Read each sentence below. Then, write the word from the **-ight** word family that best completes the sentence.

| bright | sights | tonight | slight | right |

1. Raj and Malcolm feel that they have made the _____ choice.

2. Raj would most like to see the _____ in the Amazon.

3. Malcolm plans to take several books home with him _____.

Underline the word with a prefix or suffix in each sentence. Then, write the meaning of the word on the line.

4. Charles Darwin was a well-known naturalist from Great Britain.

_____

5. Malcolm suggests that he and Raj reread the assignment.

_____

_____

6. Malcolm shakes his head in amazement at all the different species of wildlife that live in the Galápagos Islands.

_____

Reading Skills

1. Do you think that Raj and Malcolm would choose to work on another project together in the future? Why or why not?

_____

_____

2. Does this story take place in reality, or is it a fantasy?

_____

3. What is one way in which the Galápagos Islands and the Amazon are similar?

_____

_____

4. What is one way in which the Galápagos Islands and the Amazon are different?

_____

_____

5. What does Raj find most interesting about the Amazon?

_____

_____

6. What is the longest river in the world?

_____

7. Check the words that describe Malcolm.

_____ enthusiastic   _____ intelligent

_____ lonely   _____ rude

Study Skills

1. Number the words below in alphabetical order.

_____ propose

_____ present

_____ proposal

_____ presentation

Check each word that could be found on a dictionary page having the guide words shown in dark print.

2. **trestle—triplet**

_____ troll   _____ trillion   _____ tributary

3. **mole—monsoon**

_____ money   _____ modern
_____ monkey wrench

River Dolphins

Have you ever heard of pink dolphins?

1   When most people think of dolphins, they imagine the gray, friendly-looking creatures that live in the ocean. Although these are the most well-known type of dolphins, more than 20 other species exist. Almost all dolphins live in the salty, warm waters of oceans around the world, but four species live in freshwater rivers. Of these four, the pink Amazon river dolphin, or *boto*, is the most unusual.

2   The colors of botos vary quite a bit. Some have only a slight pinkish tint to their skin, but others are as bright and vivid as flamingos. Scientists still have not determined why the botos' skin is pink or why there is so much variation. Some theories have to do with the amount of time the dolphin is in the sun or how physically active it is. The one thing scientists do know for sure is that the young botos are blue-gray in color and do not develop their pink coloring until they are adults.

3   The unusual coloring of pink dolphins is not the only thing that distinguishes them from their more common cousins. Botos also have long, thin, beaklike noses that help them catch fish in hard-to-reach places. Unlike other species of dolphins, they can turn their heads 180 degrees. This is because the vertebrae, the small bones of their neck, are not fused together. This allows botos great flexibility, which is another advantage when they are maneuvering in rivers.

4   In the low-lying river areas of South America, the forests frequently flood during the long rainy season. The water actually becomes deep enough that botos are able to swim through the forests, using their natural flexibility to make their way in between trees! The flooded forests make a good temporary home for the pink dolphins. There is a good supply of fish, and they are protected from fishermen's nets.

5   Conservation groups are worried about the future of botos in South America. People generally do not hunt the dolphins because there are many myths and legends surrounding these animals. However, the dolphins do compete with fishermen for food. Botos can become tangled in fishermen's nets and drown. There is also an increasing problem with pollution in the rivers where the dolphins live.

6   Botos are not currently an endangered species, but they are not far from becoming one. Scientists, conservationists, and concerned people are doing their best to make sure that these friendly pink creatures remain safe and protected in the warm waters of South American rivers.

Vocabulary Skills

Write the words from the passage that have the meanings below.

1. a light shade of a color

   _____
   Par. 2

2. very bright and strong

   _____
   Par. 2

3. difference

   _____
   Par. 2

4. sets apart or makes different

   _____
   Par. 3

5. blended or joined together

   _____
   Par. 3

Read each pair of words listed below. If the words are synonyms, write **S** on the line. If the words are antonyms, write **A** on the line.

6. _____ stiff   flexible

7. _____ safe   protected

8. _____ worried   concerned

9. _____ temporary   permanent

Fill in the blanks below with the possessive form of the word in parentheses.

10. Scientists are not sure why the
    _____ skin is pink. (botos)

11. The pink _____ nose is long
    and thin. (dolphin)

12. Botos can become tangled in
    _____ nets. (fishermen)

Reading Skills

1. Check the best summary for paragraph 5.

   _____ Myths and legends surround the pink dolphin.

   _____ Conservation groups have reason to be worried about pink dolphins.

   _____ Rivers where botos live are becoming more polluted.

Write **F** before the sentences that are facts. Write **O** before the sentences that are opinions.

2. _____ More than 20 species of dolphins exist.

3. _____ Dolphins tend to have friendly faces.

4. _____ Botos do not develop their pink coloring until they are adults.

5. _____ Because of their unusual coloring, botos are the most beautiful species of dolphin.

6. _____ More should be done to help protect botos.

7. Name two threats to the safety of botos.

   _____

Study Skills

Next to each topic below, write the letter you would use to find more information in an encyclopedia.

1. _____ pink dolphins

2. _____ rain forests

3. _____ the Amazon River

4. _____ South American rivers

5. _____ endangered species

Galápagos Giants

What efforts are being made to help protect these unique reptiles?

1   Imagine an animal that is naturally found only one place in the world. It may weigh as much as 600 pounds and can survive for an entire year without food or water. It can live more than 150 years—one of the longest life spans for any vertebrate, or animal with a backbone. This animal would seem almost invincible. That's why it might surprise you to learn that all 11 subspecies of Galápagos tortoises are in danger of becoming extinct.

2   The Galápagos Islands lie about 600 miles from the western coast of Ecuador in the waters of the Pacific Ocean. They are so far from any landmass that many of the animals living there are found nowhere else in the world. Two kinds of giant tortoises, each with a uniquely shaped shell, are among the diverse animals found there. The saddle-backed tortoise has a longer neck and legs than the domed tortoise. It lives on the hotter, drier islands. The shell of the domed tortoise is rounder, and its limbs are shorter and thicker. It lives on the cooler, wetter islands.

3   The first major threat to the giant tortoises occurred in the 18th and 19th centuries when whaling ships captured the animals to feed their crews. They discovered that the tortoises could live for long periods of time without food or water. They began capturing large numbers of tortoises to store in the ships and provide the crew with fresh meat on long trips. Scientists believe that between 100,000 and 200,000 tortoises were killed in this way.

4   People are no longer allowed to use the giant tortoises for meat, but another threat to their survival still exists. When travelers discovered the Galápagos Islands, they brought nonnative animals with them. Animals such as dogs, cats, rats, and goats did not live on the islands before humans introduced them. These animals eat the eggs that the giant tortoises lay and bury in the sand. Other animals feed on the same types of plants that the tortoises eat. This forces the tortoises to compete for food that was once plentiful.

5   It is not too late for these enormous creatures to be saved, however. Conservationists have been busy educating people about the giant tortoise. They have also been breeding the tortoise in captivity. Once the eggs have safely hatched and the babies have grown big enough to defend themselves, they are released into the wild. These efforts do not solve the problem of protecting tortoise eggs from predators, but they do help ensure that some giant tortoises will continue to exist in the wild.

Vocabulary Skills

Write the words from the passage that have the meanings below.

1. unable to be harmed

   _____
   Par. 1

2. a large area of land

   _____
   Par. 2

3. not originally from a particular place

   _____
   Par. 4

4. protect

   _____
   Par. 5

In each row, circle the word that does not belong.

5. damp   moist   dry   wet

6. cats   tortoises   rats   goats

7. destroy   save   protect   conserve

Reading Skills

1. Check the phrase that best describes the author's purpose.

   _____ to inform

   _____ to entertain

   _____ to instruct

Circle the word that best completes each sentence.

2. The eggs of the Galápagos tortoise are _____ by other animals.

   protected   threatened   ignored

3. Conservationists _____ the young tortoises when they can defend themselves.

   breed   feed   release

4. The Galápagos Islands are located in a _____ area.

   remote   urban   new

Read the descriptions below. Write **S** next to the phrase if it describes the saddle-backed tortoise. Write **D** if it describes the domed tortoise.

5. _____ lives on hotter, drier islands

6. _____ has longer legs and neck

7. _____ has a rounder shell

8. _____ lives on wetter, cooler islands

9. Why did the crews of whaling ships capture the giant tortoises?

   _____

10. What is the biggest threat to the survival of the Galápagos tortoise today?

    _____

Study Skills

Write the name of the reference source you could use to answer each question below.

atlas	dictionary
encyclopedia	thesaurus

1. How are the different species of turtles similar and different?

   _____

2. How is the word *Galápagos* pronounced?

   _____

3. What is a synonym for *defend*?

   _____

4. What country, other than Ecuador, are the Galápagos Islands closest to?

   _____

Body Language

How can you communicate without words?

1   Elena and David sat in the backseat of their parents' car. Their cousins, Raphael and Luis, sat beside them. It was the first time the cousins had all been together since they were babies. That was when Elena and David's family had returned to Mexico for a visit.

2   Mr. and Mrs. Rodriguez spoke Spanish at home sometimes, but Elena and David knew only a few words. They always meant to learn the language because they knew it was important to their parents, but somehow they never had. Now that they sat beside their cousins, they wondered how on earth they were all going to communicate during Raphael and Luis's week-long visit.

3   "Do you play baseball?" David asked his cousins.

4   His mom glanced at them in the rearview mirror and started to translate. Then, she stopped and shrugged her shoulders. "You're all going to have to come up with a way to make yourselves understood this week," she said. "Now is as good a time as any to get started, I suppose."

5   David thought for a moment, and then he pretended to swing a baseball bat. Elena looked up and then mimicked catching a ball in a glove. Raphael and Luis grinned. *"Béisbol,"* they said nodding. "Mark McGuire and Sammy Sosa."

6   David and Elena laughed. "Exactly!" they said. By the time the Rodriguez's car pulled in the driveway, it had been decided that David and Elena would gather a few of their friends for a quick game of softball before dinner.

7   As they walked home after the game, Elena glanced up at Luis. "You're really fast," she said. She moved her legs up and down in an exaggerated running motion. *"Rápido,"* she said, remembering what her dad always said when he was in a hurry to get the family out the door.

8   Luis smiled at her. "I am runner," he said shyly.

9   Raphael patted his brother on the back. *"Numero uno,"* he said to Elena and David, holding a single finger up in the air. Then, he clasped both hands above his head and shook them, first to one side and then the other.

10   "That's great," said David. He glanced at Elena. "I think he means that Luis is the fastest runner at school."

11   Elena gave her brother a look. "Of course that's what he means, David." She turned back to Luis. "I'm a runner, too," she told him. She made very quick running motions, pointed to herself, and then shook her head. *"No rápido,"* she said. Then, she made slower running motions, pointed to herself again, and pointed far off in the distance. She looked at Luis to see if he had understood. Luis gave Elena the thumbs-up sign as the four cousins walked in the house for dinner.

12   "How did it go?" asked Mr. Rodriguez, placing napkins on the table for dinner.

13   "Language is way overrated, Dad," joked David. "All the four of us need are some acting lessons, and there won't be a thing we can't tell each other!"

Vocabulary Skills

Write the words from the story that have the meanings below.

1. to express in another language

   _____
   Par. 4

2. imitated

   _____
   Par. 5

3. took hold of; grasped

   _____
   Par. 9

4. said to be better than it really is

   _____
   Par. 13

Compound words are divided into syllables between the two words that make the compound. For example, *play/ground*. Divide the words below into syllables using a slash (/).

5. b a c k s e a t

6. s o m e h o w

7. r e a r v i e w

8. y o u r s e l v e s

Reading Skills

1. What problem do the four cousins have at the beginning of the story?

   _____

   _____

2. How do they solve their problem?

   _____

   _____

3. Why does David tell his dad that "language is way overrated"?

   _____

   _____

4. What does Elena try to explain to Luis about her skills as a runner?

   _____

   _____

5. Why didn't Mrs. Rodriguez translate for the cousins?

   _____

   _____

6. Number the events below to show the order in which they happened.

   _____ Luis gives Elena the thumbs-up sign.

   _____ David asks his cousins if they play baseball.

   _____ Mr. Rodriguez sets the table for dinner.

   _____ Elena tells Luis that she is a runner, too.

   _____ Mrs. Rodriguez decides not to translate.

Read the descriptions below. Write **E** next to the phrase if it describes Elena. Write **D** if it describes David. Write **B** if it describes both David and Elena.

7. _____ don't speak much Spanish

8. _____ is a good runner

9. _____ says Luis is a fast runner

Study Skills

Use the pronunciation key on the inside back cover of this book to write the words that match these pronunciations.

1. /kə myū′ ni kāt′/ _____

2. /kəz′ inz/ _____

3. /stā shən/ _____

4. /bē sīd′/ _____

Talking in Code

Have you ever talked to friends using a secret code?

1   Before telephones came along, most people communicated over long distances by mail. However, another invention came just before the telephone that allowed long-distance messages to be sent just as quickly: the electrical telegraph. It was not able to transmit actual spoken words, but the telegraph could send coded signals along an electrical wire. These signals, called *Morse code* after one of the inventors of the telegraph, were then translated back into words at the receiving end.

2   Samuel Morse, a famous artist in the early 1800s, was also interested in electricity, one of the newest discoveries of that time. During the 1830s, Morse worked with another inventor, Alfred Vail, to develop a way of using electricity for communication.

3   They devised a simple system in which electricity was used to create short and long sounds that would travel through wires. These two sounds could be grouped in different ways to symbolize letters, numbers, and punctuation marks. For instance, three short sounds, or dots, would equal the letter *s*, and three long sounds, or dashes, would equal the letter *o*. The words *Morse code* would look like this when using the dot and dash system:

-- --- ·-· ··· ·   -·-· --- -·· ·
M   O   R   S E   C   O   D E

4   On May 24, 1844, Morse and Vail sent their first long-distance message. It was transmitted from Baltimore, Maryland, and received in Washington, D.C. This demonstration was a breakthrough for communication technology and caused telegraph wires to be run across the nation.

5   As more and more cities were connected with electrical wires, people were able to communicate instantly over great distances. Telegraph operators became very important people in the community because they were trained to write and translate Morse code messages. Using only dots, dashes, and pauses in between, the operator could tap out a message. The operator at the other end would interpret the signals and translate them back into written words.

6   Morse code is a versatile method of communication. Messages can be sent in Morse code using sound, light, and even radio signals. In fact, Morse code has been used for more than 160 years, longer than any other code in history. Although the military and other government agencies no longer use it, amateur radio operators still regularly communicate with Morse code. One of the main reasons is that dot and dash signals can be understood even when a signal is very weak due to interference or distance.

7   Another reason is that Morse code allows people who speak different languages to communicate. Many words and phrases in Morse code are abbreviated, similar to the way you might use shorthand like *LOL* (laughing out loud) or *BTW* (by the way) when you are online. For example, *CUL* stands for "see you later" and *TU* stands for "thank you." People from many different cultures learn these codes, regardless of their native language. All of a sudden, they have a common language to talk to the world!

Vocabulary Skills

Write the words from the passage that have the meanings below.

1. to send from one place to another

   _____
   Par. 1

2. created

   _____
   Par. 3

3. sudden progress

   _____
   Par. 4

4. able to be used in many ways

   _____
   Par. 6

5. something that gets in the way

   _____
   Par. 6

6. a shortened way to communicate something

   _____
   Par. 7

Read each word below. Then, write the letter of its antonym on the line beside the word.

7. _____ transmit   **a.** different

8. _____ weak   **b.** professional

9. _____ common   **c.** receive

10. _____ amateur   **d.** strong

The suffix **-ous** means *full of* or *having*. For example, *humorous* means *full of humor*. Write a word using **ous** to match each definition below. Then, write a sentence using each word.

11. full of joy _____

   _____

12. full of poison _____

   _____

Reading Skills

Write **F** before the sentences that are facts. Write **O** before the sentences that are opinions.

1. _____ Messages can be sent in Morse code using sound, light, and radio signals.

2. _____ Morse code allows people who speak different languages to communicate.

3. _____ More people should learn to use Morse code today.

4. _____ On May 24, 1844, Morse and Vail sent their first long-distance message.

5. _____ Morse code is a simple system to learn.

6. On the lines below, write the words *come see* in Morse code using the information from the selection.

   _____

   _____

Study Skills

Write the part of a book you would use to find the information to answer each question below.

table of contents   glossary index

1. On what page can you find information about Samuel Morse?

   _____

2. What part of speech is the word *telegraph*?

   _____

3. Which chapter explains how Morse code was invented?

   _____

Silent Communication

Do you know anyone who can communicate using sign language?

1   Do you have a friend or a relative who is deaf? If not, maybe you have seen people who are deaf at a restaurant or a mall communicating with their hands. This form of communication is known as American Sign Language, or ASL. Precise numbers are not available, but researchers have estimated that between 100,000 and 500,000 people in North America use sign language as their primary means of communication. It is an important part of the deaf community and serves as part of the cultural identity of being deaf.

2   If you have ever watched people sign to one another, you know that it can be quite impressive to see. Their hands and fingers fly through the motions. Like listening to someone speak a foreign language, it can be intimidating to watch someone communicate using sign language. However, once you begin to learn the different elements, you notice similarities with spoken language that make it seem more familiar.

3   Just like spoken language, there are different dialects of sign language. People from different regions of the country speak different dialects of ASL. In addition, there is also British Sign Language, or BSL. Although the English language is the basis for both forms of sign language, they are viewed as two separate languages. They contain as many differences as British English and American English do.

4   ASL is made of units that include four basic hand forms: hand shape, hand location, hand movement, and hand orientation, or the direction in which the hand faces. A particular sign might translate as a single word, like *dog* or *cat*. Some signs might translate to a whole phrase or sentence, such as *I stared at it for a long time*. Facial expressions can also be an important part of sign language. A sign may mean something different when it is done on its own than it does when it is accompanied by raised eyebrows or a tilt of the head.

5   Fingerspelling is another element of sign language in which each letter must be spelled out using a particular gesture. It is slower than using signs, but it is often an easy way for beginners to learn some basics of sign language.

6   Many hearing people know and use ASL on a daily basis to communicate with friends or family members who are deaf. If you are interested in learning how to sign, or fingerspell, the 26 letters of the alphabet, visit the Web site www.where.com/scott.net/asl/abc.html. It won't take you long to learn the letters. Then, you can say anything you'd like without uttering a single word!

Vocabulary Skills

Write the words from the passage that have the meanings below.

1. guessed; calculated roughly

   _____
   Par. 1

2. first in order of importance

   _____
   Par. 1

3. varieties of a language that change based on the group or part of the country

   _____
   Par. 3

4. large areas

   _____
   Par. 3

5. saying out loud

   _____
   Par. 6

6. What do the abbreviations *ASL* and *BSL* stand for?

   _____

Write the idiom from paragraph 2 on the line next to its meaning.

7. do something quickly _____

Write **S** if the possessive word is singular. Write **P** if it is plural.

8. _____ the girl's signs

9. _____ the deaf community's identity

10. _____ the dialects' differences

Reading Skills

1. What is fingerspelling?

   _____

2. What are the four basic hand forms of ASL?

   _____

   _____

3. Why do some hearing people know and use sign language?

   _____

4. Why do you think that sign language might be part of the cultural identity of being deaf?

   _____

   _____

5. Why are ASL and BSL viewed as two separate languages?

   _____

   _____

Write **T** before the sentences that are true. Write **F** before the sentences that are false.

6. _____ Only deaf people use sign language.

7. _____ Fingerspelling is slower than using other signs.

8. _____ There is only one dialect of ASL.

9. _____ Some signs may translate to an entire phrase or sentence.

10. _____ About two million people in North America use ASL.

Study Skills

Use the key below to read the sentence in sign language. Then, write the sentence on the line.

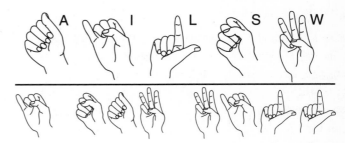

1. _____

A New Start

Do you make New Year's resolutions every year? What have some of your resolutions been?

1 Nate and Sierra sat at the kitchen table in Nate's kitchen. An empty pizza box lay on the table beside a plate of half-eaten broccoli and carrot sticks. It was 11 o'clock on New Year's Eve, and Nate and Sierra were in the middle of a heated game. With one move, Sierra won and collected her pieces.

2 "I've either got to find a new partner, or I need to improve my game," said Nate gloomily. "I can't remember the last time we played a game that I won," he added, nibbling on a piece of limp broccoli.

3 Sierra rolled her eyes. "Nate, that is just not true," she said. "I think you won a game of cards a year or two ago," she joked.

4 Nate tossed the piece of broccoli in her direction, and Sierra laughed as she ducked. "So, what should we do for the next hour?" Nate asked.

5 "Have you ever made New Year's resolutions?" asked Sierra.

6 "Not really," replied Nate. "My parents make them, and they ask my sister and me what ours are. Casey always has a list a mile long, but I've never really taken it seriously."

7 "Do you want to make real resolutions this year?" asked Sierra. "We could each choose three things that are important to us and remind each other about them during the next year."

8 "I know what my first one would be," said Nate. He grabbed a pad of paper and wrote his name on one side. Below it, he wrote, *learn how to ski.*

9 "I didn't know you were interested in skiing," said Sierra.

10 Nate looked a bit embarrassed. "My entire family, even my cousins and grandparents, are great skiers. I haven't gone on a family ski trip in years because I had a bad fall when I was

little. I've been nervous about skiing since then. I'd like to give it another try."

11 "You're good at everything you try, Nate," said Sierra. "I know you can do it."

12 "What are you going to put on your list?" Nate asked.

13 Sierra thought for a moment. "My sister and I argue too much," she said. "Everyone thinks that twins will be each other's best friend. In some ways we are, but I wish we got along better."

14 "I have another one," said Nate suddenly. "My grandpa and I volunteered at a food bank at Thanksgiving. It felt good to help people who were going through a rough time. I'd like to do something like that regularly."

15 Sierra nodded. "I'm going to put that one on my list, too," she said. "Okay, we each need one more." She looked down at her hands and sighed. "I suppose I should stop biting my nails," she said. "It's been a bad habit I've had since I was little."

16 "We're going to have a fantastic year!" said Nate enthusiastically.

17 "But you still need to think of one more resolution," said Sierra.

18 Nate threw a handful of confetti in the air as the announcer on the TV in the next room exclaimed "Happy New Year!"

19 "That's easy," said Nate. "I need to improve my game skills enough to beat you at a game once in a while!"

Vocabulary Skills

Write the words from the story that have the meanings below.

1. unhappily; with discouragement

   _____
   Par. 2

2. not stiff or crisp

   _____
   Par. 2

3. vows or pledges to do something

   _____
   Par. 5

4. with strong positive feelings

   _____
   Par. 16

5. Find the pair of homophones in paragraph 1, and write them on the lines below.

   _____ _____

Find a homophone in the story for each word below.

6. duct _____
   Par. 4

7. our _____
   Par. 4

Read each pair of words listed below. If the words are synonyms, write **S** on the line. If the words are antonyms, write **A** on the line.

9. _____ empty   full

10. _____ fantastic   wonderful

11. _____ tossed   threw

12. _____ won   lost

Reading Skills

1. Who is Casey?

   _____

   _____

2. Why do you think Nate wants to give skiing another try?

   _____

3. What bad habit does Sierra resolve to break?

   _____

4. Check the words that describe Sierra.

   _____ supportive

   _____ timid

   _____ competitive

   _____ kind

   _____ nervous

5. **Hyperbole** is an exaggerated statement that is used to make a point. Find the hyperbole in paragraph 6, and write it on the line below.

   _____

Study Skills

Use the pie graph below to answer the questions that follow.

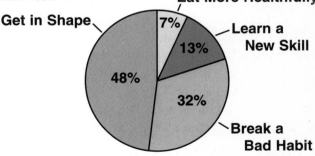

1. Which resolution was the most popular?

   _____

2. What percentage of people chose *learn a new skill*?

   _____

3. Which resolution received 32% of the votes?

   _____

Happy New Year!

How does your family welcome in the New Year?

1   New Year's celebrations are a little bit different all around the world. They are celebrated with different customs, traditions, and special foods. They may even be observed at different times of the year. One similarity is that they are all marked by a celebration and a symbolic welcoming of the new year while saying farewell to the old.

2   In the United States, we use the Julian calendar, created by Emperor Julius Caesar. Celebrations usually begin on December 31, or New Year's Eve, and continue on into January 1, the first day of the new year.

3   Probably the most famous American celebration takes place in New York City's Times Square. A large crowd gathers below the 1,070-pound crystal ball that measures six feet in diameter. At 11:59 P.M. the ball is lowered. It reaches the bottom of the tower at the stroke of midnight, and the crowd erupts into cheers and exclamations of good wishes. Many people watch the ball drop on television during their own New Year's celebrations. It is common for people to count down to the new year as they watch the ball drop.

4   Making New Year's resolutions is another popular American tradition. Many people see the beginning of a new year as the time to make changes or have a fresh start. New Year's resolutions can serve as promises or reminders to oneself of changes and improvements to be made over the course of the upcoming year.

5   Black-eyed peas, ham, and cabbage are traditional dishes to serve on New Year's Day. They are symbols of good luck and prosperity for the coming year. People in other countries also have New Year's traditions surrounding food. For example, the Dutch often eat doughnuts to welcome in the New Year. Because doughnuts are shaped like a circle, they are thought to symbolize the completion of a cycle—the beginning of a new year and ending of the previous year.

6   In Japan, people eat long soba noodles in celebration. Eating these noodles without breaking them symbolizes long life. In Spain, there is the tradition of eating 12 grapes at midnight. This marks successful grape harvests of the past and the hope for more in the future.

7   One of the most colorful New Year's celebrations takes place in China and at Chinese festivals around the world. The Chinese New Year is determined by the lunar calendar, and falls between January 21 and February 19. The festival lasts about two weeks. During this time, towns are decorated with colorful lanterns and flowers. People thoroughly clean their homes to symbolize getting rid of the misfortunes of the previous year. Parades and fireworks mark the festivities, and seafood and dumplings are traditionally eaten.

8   The next time January 1 approaches, take some time to consider the events of the previous year. Think about your goals and hopes for the next year. Maybe you can even start a new tradition with your family and friends to welcome in each new year!

Vocabulary Skills

Write the words from the passage that have the meanings below.

1. good-bye

   _____
   Par. 1

2. the length of a circle from one side to the other

   _____
   Par. 3

3. approaching; next

   _____
   Par. 4

4. condition of being lucky and successful

   _____
   Par. 5

5. bad luck

   _____
   Par. 7

Read each word or phrase below. Then, write the letter of its abbreviation in the space beside it.

6. _____ post-meridian   a. Jan.

7. _____ feet   b. P.M.

8. _____ January   c. NY

9. _____ New York   d. Dec.

10. _____ December   e. ft.

Reading Skills

1. Check the line beside the word that best describes what type of selection this is.

   _____ fiction

   _____ informational

   _____ folktale

2. How do people celebrate New Year's Eve in Times Square?

   _____

   _____

3. Name two foods that people traditionally eat on New Year's Day.

   _____

   _____

4. Why does the Chinese New Year fall on a different day than the American New Year?

   _____

   _____

Circle the word that best completes each sentence.

5. New Year's customs and traditions _____ from country to country.

   vary   decline   exist

6. The foods people eat in celebration of the New Year often _____ their wishes for the coming year.

   cancel   explain   symbolize

7. Many people see the beginning of a new year as a time to make a _____ start.

   special   fresh   careful

Study Skills

Join Us for a New Year's Eve Party!

When: **December 31, 8:00 P.M.**

Where: **The DeJohns' House**
       1548 Nicholson Ave.

Who: **Bring your family, bring your friends!**

We will provide snacks, noisemakers, and party hats.

1. Will the hosts provide food?

   _____

2. At which address will the party be held?

   _____

3. What time will the party begin?

   _____

Answer Key

Page 3

Vocabulary Skills

Write the words from the story that have the meanings below.

1. just before the present time
   recently _Par. 1_

2. one half of Earth when divided by the equator
   hemisphere _Par. 6_

3. opposite
   reverse _Par. 7_

4. specific words or phrases
   expressions _Par. 10_

In each row, circle the word that does not belong.

5. (Australia) Texas Massachusetts Ohio

6. freezing winter sledding (tropical)

7. brolly bonza (idea) mate

Find the compound words from the selection that contain the words below.

8. north _____ northeast _Par. 3_

9. summer _____ summertime _Par. 6_

10. man _____ snowman _Par. 6_

When you add an apostrophe (') and the letter s to a singular noun, it shows that a person or thing owns something. Fill in the blanks below with the possessive form of the word in parentheses.

11. Ms. __Dimitri's__ class is interested in learning about Australia. (Dimitri)

12. __Australia's__ seasons are different than the seasons in the United States. (Australia)

13. __Gemma's__ family lived in Queensland. (Gemma)

Reading Skills

A **fact** is something that is known to be true. An **opinion** is what a person believes. It may or may not be true. Write **F** before the sentences that are facts. Write **O** before the sentences that are opinions.

1. _F_ Gemma moved to the United States from Australia.

2. _F_ Queensland is more than twice as big as Texas.

3. _O_ It would be exciting to visit Australia.

4. _O_ The weather in Australia is more enjoyable than it is in Massachusetts.

5. _F_ Australia is in the Southern Hemisphere.

6. What is the Great Barrier Reef?
   the largest coral reef in the world

7. What does *fair dinkum* mean?
   honest

Study Skills

Guide words are printed at the top of each page in a dictionary. The guide word at the left is the first word on the page. The guide word at the right is the last word on the page. Check each word that could be found on a page having the guide words shown in dark print.

1. **gown—grateful**
   _✓_ grape _✓_ grasp ____ going

2. **mallet—mansion**
   _✓_ manage ____ mall ____ maple

3. **reflect—relax**
   ____ reef _✓_ reindeer _✓_ rehearse

3

Page 5

Vocabulary Skills

Write the words from the passage that have the meanings below.

1. originally from a particular place
   native _Par. 1_

2. in danger
   threatened _Par. 3_

3. to produce a liquid or other substance
   secrete _Par. 3_

4. the number of people, plants, or animals in a specific place
   population _Par. 4_

5. patient; accepting
   tolerant _Par. 4_

A **synonym** is a word that means the same, or almost the same, as another word. Find a synonym in the story for each of the words below.

6. irritating _annoying_

7. grow up _mature_

8. quickly _rapidly_

The suffix **-ist** means *someone who does something*. For example, a *biologist is someone who studies biology*. Add **ist** to each base word below. Then, use each new word in a sentence.

9. art _artist_
   Answers will vary.

10. violin _violinist_
    Answers will vary.

11. novel _novelist_
    Answers will vary.

Reading Skills

1. Do you think cane toads will continue to be a problem in Australia? Explain your answer.
   Answers will vary.

2. Why were cane toads first brought to Australia?
   to eat the beetles that were destroying the sugar cane crops

3. Why are there so many cane toads in Australia if only one hundred or so were originally released?
   They lay many eggs and have almost no natural predators.

4. Check the sentence that best states the main idea of the selection.
   ____ Cane toads can weigh as much as four pounds.
   ____ Cane toads do not have any natural predators in Australia.
   _✓_ Cane toads were brought to Australia to eat sugar cane beetles, but they ended up becoming a dangerous pest.

Study Skills

1. If you wanted to learn more about the cane toads in Australia, check the subjects below you could use to find information in an encyclopedia.
   _✓_ amphibians ____ Australia
   ____ sugar cane ____ mammals
   _✓_ nonnative species _✓_ toads

5

Page 7

Vocabulary Skills

Write the words from the story that have the meanings below.

1. an area next to a building that is often used for eating outdoors
   patio _Par. 1_

2. feeding on grass
   grazing _Par. 1_

3. a type of mammal that carries its young in a pouch
   marsupials _Par. 9_

4. look like
   resemble _Par. 9_

Words that are opposite in meaning are called **antonyms**. Read each word below. Then, write the letter of its antonym on the line beside the word.

5. _d_ true   a. shrink
6. _a_ grow   b. always
7. _c_ similar c. different
8. _b_ never   d. false

Underline the compound word in each sentence. Then, write the two words that make up each compound.

9. The babies of marsupials live in their mothers' pouches until they can take care of themselves.
   them _____ selves

10. The wombat makes its nest underground.
    under _____ ground

11. The wombat looks like a groundhog or a beaver.
    ground _____ hog

Reading Skills

1. What are baby kangaroos called in Australia?
   joeys

2. Why do koalas spend so much of their time sleeping?
   They don't get much energy from the leaves of the eucalyptus tree.

3. What kind of pet is Gillian?
   a wombat

4. Why do you think a baby kangaroo lives in its mother's pouch for a while after it is born?
   so it has time to grow a bit larger in order to take care of itself and keep up with the others in the group

Study Skills

Write the name of the reference source you could use to find out the information in each question below.

encyclopedia	dictionary
atlas	

1. Where could you look to find the location of a particular city in Australia?
   atlas

2. Where could you look to find the meaning of the word *burrows*?
   dictionary

3. Where could you look to find information about what kangaroos eat?
   encyclopedia

7

Page 9

Vocabulary Skills

Write the words from the passage that have the meanings below.

1. people who live in a particular place
   inhabitants _Par. 1_

2. scientists who study past cultures
   archaeologists _Par. 1_

3. for a long time
   permanently _Par. 2_

4. has an effect on
   influences _Par. 2_

5. left open to harm without protection
   exposed _Par. 3_

6. a period of 100 years
   century _Par. 4_

In each row, circle the word that does not belong.

7. hunt fish (settle) gather

8. fight struggle (improve) conflict

9. (hollow) trumpet didgeridoo instrument

10. Find the word with the suffix **-ist** in paragraph 1. Then, write the meaning of the word.
    archaeologists: people who study archaeology

The suffix **-able** means *able to*. Add the suffix to the verbs below to form adjectives. Then, write a sentence with each adjective.

11. comfort _comfortable_
    Answers will vary.

12. break _breakable_
    Answers will vary.

Reading Skills

1. Why did Aboriginal people move around instead of staying in one place?
   They moved around when they needed a new supply of food.

2. What influences almost every part of the Aboriginal culture?
   nature

Study Skills

Use the map of Australia's six states and two territories to answer the questions that follow.

1. Which state is directly south of the Northern Territory?
   South Australia

2. Which state is east of the Northern Territory?
   Queensland

3. What is the name of the state that is the furthest south?
   Tasmania

4. Which state is larger—Western Australia or New South Wales?
   Western Australia

9

Answer Key

Page 11

Write the words from the story that have the meanings below.

1. walked slowly, dragging the feet
   shuffled

2. the main or most important part in a performance
   lead

3. the lowest balcony in a theater
   mezzanine

4. decorated in a very detailed, complex way
   ornate

Words that have two middle consonants are divided into syllables between the consonants. For example, pic/ture or bas/ket. Divide the words below into syllables using a slash (/).

5. per/form
6. tan/go
7. or/nate
8. cen/ter

Read each word below. Then, write the letter of its synonym on the line beside the word.

9. b walked   a. beat
10. c began   b. strolled
11. a rhythm   c. started
12. d chuckle   d. laugh

Reading Skills

1. Find one sentence that shows Gavin was not looking forward to going to the dance performance. Write it on the line below.
   Possible answer: "I don't even like ballet," Gavin complained.

2. What problem did Gavin have at the beginning of the story?
   He did not want to go to the dance performance.

3. How did Gavin feel about the performance once it began?
   He thought it was interesting.

Write F before the sentences that are facts. Write O before the sentences that are opinions.

4. O Modern dance is interesting to watch.
5. F Joseph has one of the lead roles in the performance.
6. F The Capshaws took the subway to get to the theater.
7. O Gavin will be a good dancer.

Study Skills

A table of contents shows the chapters in a book and the page each chapter begins on. Use the table of contents below to answer the questions.

Table of Contents

Chapter 1 History of Dance in America........2
Chapter 2 Types of Dance.......................21
Chapter 3 Stars of the Stage....................39
Chapter 4 Most Popular Shows.................52

1. What is the title of Chapter 2?
   Types of Dance

2. Which chapter contains information about the history of dance?
   Chapter 1

3. What is the title of the chapter that begins on page 39?
   Stars of the Stage

Page 13

Vocabulary Skills

Write the words from the passage that have the meanings below.

1. hitting things together to create a sound
   percussion

2. passing down ideas or ways of doing something
   tradition

3. tempting
   enticing

4. the first time something is seen; an introduction
   debut

5. a period of ten years
   decade

Check the meaning of the underlined word in each sentence.

6. STOMP is a hit all over the world.
   ___ to strike or beat
   ✓ something very popular

7. The group called Pookiesnackenburger had their own television show.
   ✓ a performance
   ___ to display or allow to be seen

8. STOMP continues to draw large crowds.
   ___ to make a picture of
   ✓ to attract

Find the compound words from the selection that contain the words below.

9. balls ___ basketballs
10. day ___ everyday
11. lamp ___ lampposts

Reading Skills

Write T before the sentences that are true. Write F before the sentences that are false.

1. T The performers in STOMP use common objects and turn them into instruments.
2. F Luke Cresswell, one of the founders of STOMP, played the trumpet.
3. T There is a street called STOMP Avenue in New York City.
4. T STOMP's first performance was at London's Bloomsbury Theatre.
5. F STOMP was formed by two Latin American musicians.
6. In Britain, what does the word busker mean?
   street performer
7. Why couldn't Luke Cresswell use a traditional drum set when he was performing?
   because he played on the sidewalk

Study Skills

1. Use the numbers 1-5 to put the words below in alphabetical order.
   2 rhythm
   3 rib
   1 rhinoceros
   4 ribbon
   5 riddle

Page 15

Vocabulary Skills

Write the words from the passage that have the meanings below.

1. someone who directs the movements of a dance performance
   choreographer

2. experts
   masters

3. was a part of
   participated

Write the words from the selection that match the abbreviations below.

4. Jr. Junior
5. NY New York
6. NJ New Jersey

A word that sounds the same as another word but has a different spelling and meaning is a homophone. Circle the homophone that correctly completes each sentence below.

7. Savion's family could not afford a (pair) of special tap dancing shoes. (pear pair)
8. Savion wore cowboy boots to his first tap dancing (lesson). (lesson lessen)
9. One movie Savion (made) was with director Spike Lee. (made maid)

Reading Skills

1. Check the words that describe Savion Glover.
   ✓ energetic   ✓ motivated
   ___ nosy   ___ quiet
   ✓ enthusiastic

2. In what show was Savion's first professional performance?
   The Tap Dance Kid

3. What story did Bring in 'Da Noise, Bring in 'Da Funk tell?
   history of African Americans

4. Who did Savion study to become better at tap dancing?
   Possible answers: Sammy Davis, Jr., Gregory Hines, masters of tap dancing

Study Skills

Use the poster below to answer the questions that follow.

The Alden Theater presents . . .
Savion Glover's Improvography
Wednesday, August 16th
at 8:00 P.M.
Tickets go on sale August 2—
Call 814-555-SHOW
Tickets $22-35

1. What is the price range for tickets to see Improvography?
   $22-35

2. What is the name of the theater that is hosting the performance?
   The Alden Theater

3. What date do tickets go on sale?
   August 2

Page 17

Vocabulary Skills

Write the words from the story that have the meanings below.

1. makes a lasting feeling or image
   impressive

2. areas of land that are each equal to 4,840 square yards
   acres

3. goal; purpose
   mission

4. people who sell things
   vendors

5. to move around in a busy manner
   bustle

A simile compares two things using the words like or as. Find the simile in paragraph 1, and write it on the line below.

6. windows that glittered like jewels

Compound words are divided into syllables between the two words that make the compound. For example, play/ground. Divide the words below into syllables using a slash (/).

7. farm/house
8. back/yard
9. home/sick

Reading Skills

Read the descriptions below. Write F next to the phrase if it describes Fiona. Write N if it describes Nora.

1. F says she can't see anything green from the window

2. F feels like everything is made of steel, stone, and glass

3. N points out several green things on the street below

4. F says she misses their old farmhouse

5. N says they found their piece of green in the city

6. What do you think "green space" is?
   Answers will vary.

7. What problem do Fiona and Nora have in this story?
   Possible answer: They are not used to living in a big city.

8. Where do you think Fiona and Nora used to live before they moved to the city?
   Possible answer: on a farm in the country

9. Nora points out three green things she can see from the window. What does Fiona mean when she says, "You know that's not what I'm talking about," to her sister?
   Fiona uses "green" to mean trees, grass, and other plants, not just the color green.

Study Skills

The word you look up in a dictionary is called an entry word. An entry word is usually a base word. For example, if you want to find the meaning of happier, you would look up the base word happy. Write the entry word you would look for in a dictionary next to each word below.

1. glittered glitter
2. honking honk
3. libraries library
4. exploring explore

Answer Key

Page 19

Vocabulary Skills

Write the words from the story that have the meanings below.

1. used to or familiar with
   accustomed Par. 1

2. choice
   selection Par. 2

3. the area around something
   perimeter Par. 4

4. received from a relative
   inherited Par. 4

5. a structure that supports climbing plants
   trellis Par. 6

6. the landlord or manager of a building
   superintendent Par. 9

An **idiom** is a group of words that has a special meaning. For example, the idiom *hit the hay* means *go to bed*. Write the idiom from paragraph 3 on the line under its meaning.

7. a talent for growing plants
   green thumb

Read each word below. Then, write the letter of its antonym on the line beside the word.

8. b enormous   a. different
9. d exciting   b. tiny
10. a same   c. summer
11. c winter   d. boring

Fill in the blanks below with the possessive form of the word in parentheses.

12. The librarian's friendship made the girls feel at home. (librarian)
13. Mom's talent for gardening had been passed on to Nora and Fiona. (Mom)

Reading Skills

1. Check the phrase that best describes the author's purpose.
   ✓ to tell a story about two sisters discovering rooftop gardens
   ___ to persuade the reader to start a rooftop garden
   ___ to share information about the best type of plants to use in a rooftop garden

Dialogue is what a character says. The words in dialogue are always in quotation marks.

2. On the line below, write the words that are dialogue in paragraph 5.
   That looks like a tree on the roof!

3. Check the word or words that best describe what type of selection this is.
   ___ historical nonfiction
   ___ folktale
   ✓ fiction

4. Do you think Mom will help the girls start a rooftop garden of their own? Why or why not?
   Answers will vary.

Study Skills

Use a dictionary to help you divide these words into syllables.

1. apartment a/part/ment
2. enormous e/nor/mous
3. spaghetti spa/ghet/ti

19

Page 21

Vocabulary Skills

Write the words from the passage that have the meanings below.

1. take in or soak up
   absorb Par. 1

2. related to life in the country
   rural Par. 1

3. change from one thing to another
   convert Par. 2

4. makes less
   reduces Par. 2

5. a quick look
   glimpse Par. 9

Write a compound word using two words in each sentence.

6. The pond contains fish that have a gold color.
   goldfish

7. The garden is located on the top of the roof.
   rooftop

8. A house for a bird can be placed in the garden.
   birdhouse

Reading Skills

1. Why do the rooftops of buildings get so hot?
   Possible answer: They absorb sunlight, especially when covered with tar.
2. How big is the rooftop garden at the Children's Hospital in St. Louis, Missouri?
   7,500 square feet

3. Do you think that more buildings will begin to convert their roofs to green spaces? Explain your answer.
   Answers will vary.

4. What is planted in the rooftop garden of the Royal York Hotel?
   a large herb garden

5. A **summary** is a short sentence that tells the most important facts about a topic. Check the sentence below that is the best summary for paragraph 2.
   ___ Cities are warmer than rural areas.
   ✓ Rooftop gardens can cool the air in cities and reduce the amount of energy used.
   ___ Buildings with rooftop gardens use less air conditioning.

Study Skills

An **outline** is used to put ideas in order. It shows the important facts in a story. Use the facts from paragraph 2 to complete Part I. Use the facts from paragraph 4 to complete Part II.

I. Often warmer in the city than in the country
   A. green roofs help cool air
   B. cooler buildings use less air conditioning
   C. reduces energy buildings use
II. Rooftop garden at Children's Hospital in St. Louis
   A. 7,500 square feet
   B. Children and their parents can be near nature without leaving the hospital.
   C. has flowers, fountains, and pond
   D. garden paths for children to walk on in slippers or bare feet

21

Page 23

Vocabulary Skills

Write the words from the passage that have the meanings below.

1. people who are guilty of something
   offenders Par. 1

2. working on its own; without being controlled
   automatically Par. 3

3. covered with a material that keeps warmth or sound from passing through it
   insulated Par. 3

Check the meaning of the underlined word in each sentence.

4. One way to help the environment is to save energy.
   ___ rescue
   ✓ conserve

5. Turn off the light when you leave a room.
   ✓ something bright that allows you to see
   ___ not heavy

6. Even an old tire can be recycled and put to good use.
   ✓ a rubber circle that surrounds a wheel
   ___ to become sleepy or weary

The prefix **mid-** means *the middle part*. For example, *midday* means *middle of the day*. Add the prefix **mid-** to each word below. Then, use each new word in a sentence.

7. night midnight
   Answers will vary.
8. summer midsummer
   Answers will vary.

Reading Skills

1. How do solar panels work?
   Energy from the sun is turned into electricity.
2. What types of recycled materials can tile and floors be made of?
   Possible answers: glass, tires
3. Name two things you can do at home or at school to help the environment.
   Answers will vary.

Study Skills

Use the brochure below to answer the questions that follow.

Celebrate Earth Day!
Who: You, your friends, and your family
How: By cleaning up the litter at McDougal Park (and staying for a free cook-out party)
When: Saturday, April 24 from 10:00 A.M. until 1:00 P.M.
Where: Meet at the baseball diamond at McDougal Park
Why: To keep our neighborhood clean and green!

1. Who can attend the Earth Day celebration?
   you, your friends, and your family
2. What time are people meeting on Saturday?
   10:00 A.M.
3. What service will the volunteers be performing?
   picking up litter at the park

23

Page 25

Vocabulary Skills

Write the words from the story that have the meanings below.

1. variety; different types
   diversity Par. 6

2. to speak or present
   deliver Par. 9

3. the amount something can vary or be different
   range Par. 9

4. spoken aloud
   oral Par. 11

5. particular ways of viewing something
   perspectives Par. 13

Read each word below. Then, write the letter of its synonym on the line beside the word.

6. c responded   a. select
7. d often   b. varied
8. a choose   c. replied
9. b different   d. frequent

A **word family** is a group of words that have the same letter combinations. For example, the words *could*, *would*, and *should* are in the same word family, because they all contain the **-ould** combination. Circle the words in each row that are part of the word family in parentheses.

10. (-ight) bring (bright) (tonight) tomorrow
11. (-ought) (fought) thin (thought) then
12. (-ight) midday (light) linger (midnight)

Reading Skills

Write **F** before the sentences that are facts. Write **O** before the sentences that are opinions.

1. O Poetry can be exciting.
2. F Ms. Jorge's class will be going on a field trip to a poetry slam.
3. O Poetry slams can be interesting to attend.
4. F Poetry has been a part of the oral tradition throughout history.
5. F Ms. Jorge enjoys poetry.
6. Do you think any of Ms. Jorge's students will participate in the poetry slam? Explain your answer.
   Answers will vary.

7. What is a poetry slam?
   a competition in which poets have three minutes to perform and are scored by a panel of audience members
8. Why do you think Taylor says that a poetry slam sounds like an Olympic event?
   because ten is also a perfect score in the Olympics, and judges also give the scores
9. Name two things that Ms. Jorge says kids enjoy about poetry slams.
   Possible answers: They get a chance to share their feelings; they get new perspectives

25

Answer Key

Page 27

Rewrite the following address without using the abbreviations.

1. Dr. Hannah Tyrrell
19052 Inglewood Dr.
Lincoln, NE 68512

   Doctor Hannah Tyrrell
   19052 Inglewood Drive
   Lincoln, Nebraska 68512

Fill in the blanks below with the possessive form of the word in parentheses.

2. Shel Silverstein is best known for his __children's__ literature. (children)

3. One of Shel __Silverstein's__ books is called *Falling Up*. (Silverstein)

4. The __character's__ name in one poem is Sarah Cynthia Sylvia Stout. (character)

Reading Skills

1. Number the events below to show the order in which they happened.

   __3__ Shel's first book was published.

   __5__ Shel died in 1999.

   __2__ Shel began his career as a cartoonist.

   __1__ Shel Silverstein was born in Chicago.

   __4__ *Where the Sidewalk Ends* was published.

2. What does it mean when the author says that Shel Silverstein illustrated all his children's books himself?

   He drew all of the pictures in them

3. About how many copies of Shel's books have been sold?

   20 million

4. Write your own example of alliteration.

   Answers will vary.

5. Check the words that describe Shel Silverstein.

   ✓ funny

   ___ lazy

   ✓ talkative

   ✓ artistic

   ___ clever

Study Skills

A **time line** shows the order in which things happened. Use the time line below to answer the questions that follow.

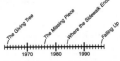

1. What was the most recent book published?

   Falling Up

2. Which book was published in 1984?

   Where the Sidewalk Ends

3. In what year was *The Giving Tree* published?

   1963

27

Page 29

Vocabulary Skills

Write the words from the story that have the meanings below.

1. having very strong feelings

   passionate

2. very important; worth a great deal

   valuable

3. memories

   reminiscences

4. brothers and sisters

   siblings

In each row, circle the word that does not belong.

5. book (desk) newspaper magazine

6. (vacation) poem story essay

7. friend companion (vehicle) pal

Read each pair of words listed below. If the words are synonyms, write **S** on the line. If the words are antonyms, write **A** on the line.

8. __A__ remember   forget

9. __S__ smiled   grinned

10. __A__ often   infrequently

11. __A__ brief   long

12. __S__ leave   depart

Reading Skills

1. Find one sentence that shows Ms. Donnelly is happy to be a poet. Write it on the lines below.

   Possible answer: I can't think of a single job I'd rather have instead.

2. Check the phrase that best describes the author's purpose.

   ✓ to tell a story about a poet who visits a classroom

   ___ to tell the reader about the lives of famous poets

   ___ to explain how to write a poem

Circle the word that best completes each sentence.

3. Ms. Donnelly felt __strongly__ about her best friend moving away.

   (strongly) excited joyful

4. Ms. Donnelly is eager to share her __experiences__ with the class.

   worries (experiences) confusion

Study Skills

A library's reference system can help you find a book. Use the information below to answer the questions that follow.

Call No:	455.62 SU
Author:	Sullivan-Todd, Kathy
Title:	My Life in Poetry
Publisher:	Darby House Publishing, 2004

1. What is the title of the book?

   My Life in Poetry

2. What year was the book published?

   2004

3. Which book would be located closer to the book with the call number above—the book with call number 455.62 VO or the book with call number 455.62 DA?

   455.62 VO

29

Page 31

Vocabulary Skills

Write the words from the passage that have the meanings below.

1. collections of writing by different authors

   anthologies

2. someone who watches and pays attention

   observer

3. to bring to people's attention

   promote

An **idiom** is a group of words that has a special meaning. Write the idiom from paragraph 4 on the line below its meaning.

4. things people can agree on

   common ground

A word that sounds the same as another word but has a different spelling and meaning is a **homophone**. Circle the homophone that correctly completes each sentence below.

5. Naomi was __raised__ by parents of different nationalities. (raised) razed)

6. Naomi __writes__ for children and for adults. (rights, (writes)

Reading Skills

1. Check the line beside the word or words that best describe what type of nonfiction selection this is.

   ___ historical nonfiction

   ✓ biography

   ___ how-to

2. A **summary** is a short sentence that tells the most important facts about a topic. Check the sentence below that is the best summary for paragraph 3.

   ___ Naomi uses descriptive language in her work.

   ___ Naomi grew up in St. Louis, Jerusalem, and San Antonio.

   ✓ Naomi's poetry is influenced by the places she has lived.

3. The author says that each of the places Naomi has visited or lived has its own "unique flavors." What does this mean?

   Answers will vary.

Study Skills

Use the table below to answer the questions that follow.

Title	Type of Book	Date Published
Sitti's Secrets	picture book	1994
Habibi	novel	1996
Come With Me: Poems for a Journey	poetry	2000
19 Varieties of Gazelle: Poems of the Middle East	poetry	2002

1. What type of book is *Habibi*?

   novel

2. Which book was published in 2000?

   Come With Me: Poems for a Journey

3. In what year was *Sitti's Secrets* published?

   1994

31

Page 33

Vocabulary Skills

Write the words from the story that have the meanings below.

1. not paying attention to what one is doing

   absently

2. repeat something from memory

   recite

3. a talent or natural ability

   aptitude

4. A **simile** compares two things using the words *like* or *as*. Find the simile in paragraph 4, and write it on the line below.

   my heart beats so fast that it feels like popcorn popping in my chest

5. What were the two things compared to each other in question 4?

   heartbeat, popcorn popping

6. Choose one item in question 5 and use it to create your own simile on the lines below.

   Answers will vary.

Reading Skills

Read the descriptions below. Write **N** next to the phrase if it describes Noah. Write **D** if it describes Daniel. Write **B** if it describes both Noah and Daniel.

1. __D__ is the older brother

2. __D__ is on a basketball team

3. __N__ is nervous about a spelling bee

4. __B__ gets stage fright sometimes

5. __D__ gives his brother good advice

6. What problem does Noah have in this story?

   stage fright

7. Name two times Daniel has experienced stage fright.

   fourth grade play, basketball games

8. What was Noah thinking about when Daniel was calling him at the beginning of the story?

   the spelling bee finals

9. Why does Noah feel less nervous by the end of the story?

   Possible answers: His brother will help him practice; his brother has given him advice about stage fright.

Study Skills

An **outline** is used to put ideas in order. It shows the important facts in a story. Use the facts from paragraph 4 to complete Part I. Use the facts from paragraph 9 to complete Part II.

I. Daniel describes his experiences with stage fright

   A. stage fright for 4th grade play

   B. stage fright before basketball games

   C. not nervous at practice

II. Daniel explains relaxation exercise

   A. close your eyes

   B. imagine doing the thing you are nervous about

   C. sounds strange but works

33

Answer Key

Page 35

Vocabulary Skills

Write the words from the passage that have the meanings below.

1. important and highly respected
   prestigious
2. people or companies who provide financial support
   sponsors
3. original source; beginning
   origin
4. know about in advance
   predict

Check the sentence in which the underlined word has the same meaning as it does in the story.

5. _____ Dominic was careful not to be stung by a <u>bee</u> when he walked across the lawn.
   _✓_ My aunt is going to a quilting <u>bee</u> next Saturday.
6. _✓_ Do you have time to play a <u>round</u> of golf with me today?
   _____ The baby played with the <u>round</u> rubber ball.

Fill in the blanks below with the possessive form of the word in parentheses.

7. The **winners'** words are often hard for even adults to spell. (winners)
8. Each **contestant's** goal is to become the new spelling champ. (contestant)
9. A contestant may ask for a **word's** definition. (word)

Reading Skills

1. Why wasn't a national bee held in 1943, 1944, or 1945?
   because of World War II
2. Name two words that winners of the national bee have spelled.
   Possible answers: chlorophyll, crustaceology, insouciant, chihuahua, sarcophagus, logorrhea, esquamulose, and milieu
3. What is one technique contestants use to spell unfamiliar words?
   Possible answer: studying word patterns
4. Check the sentence that best states the main idea of the selection.
   _____ Spellers cannot predict what words they will be asked to spell.
   _____ A contestant in the Scripps Howard National Spelling Bee can ask for a word's pronunciation, definition, and language of origin.
   _✓_ The Scripps Howard National Spelling Bee in Washington, D.C. is a time for the best spellers to compete for a grand prize.

Write **T** before the sentences that are true. Write **F** before the sentences that are false.

5. _T_ During the first round, contestants take a written test.
6. _F_ The Scripps Howard National Spelling Bee is held in the state of Washington.
7. _F_ Contestants must be older than 16.
8. _T_ The first national bee was held in 1925.

35

Page 37

Vocabulary Skills

Write the words from the story that have the meanings below.

1. a pleasant scent or smell
   aroma
2. get used to
   adjust
3. not very bright
   dim
4. decorated with designs made by needle and thread
   embroidered

Circle the homophone that correctly completes each sentence below.

5. Marco and Alicia **ducked** inside the tent. (ducked/duct)
6. *Empanadas* are made with pastry **dough** that is stuffed with filling and then baked or fried. (doe/dough)
7. Alicia and Marco took in all the **sights** and sounds at the *Cinco de Mayo fiesta*. (sights/sites)

Write a compound word using two words in each sentence.

8. An area on which you can walk by the side of the road is a **sidewalk**.
9. Marco wiped his hands on a towel used to dry a dish, or a **dishtowel**.
10. To cook their meal, Alicia and Marco used a book with recipes, or a **cookbook**.

Reading Skills

1. What do you think Mrs. Juarez means when she says she uses a jalapeño pepper for zing?
   Answers will vary.
2. Why wasn't anyone else in Alicia and Marco's cooking class?
   Alicia and Marco were the only people to register.
3. Do you think that Alicia and Marco will cook anything for their parents? Why or why not?
   Answers will vary.

Read the descriptions below. Write **A** next to the phrase if it describes Alicia. Write **M** if it describes Marco.

4. _M_ wants to learn how to make *gazpacho*
5. _A_ loves *empanadas*
6. _A_ enjoys watching the dancers at the *fiesta*

Study Skills

Write the name of the reference source you could use to find out the information in each question below.

| encyclopedia | dictionary |
| atlas | |

1. Where could you find out how to pronounce the word *mariachi*?
   dictionary
2. Where could you find out more information about *Cinco de Mayo*?
   encyclopedia
3. Where could you look to find out how far Mexico City is from Houston, Texas?
   atlas

37

Page 39

Vocabulary Skills

Write the words from the recipe that have the meanings below.

1. a kitchen tool used for draining liquid
   colander
2. to allow the liquid to flow away
   drain

Check the meaning of the underlined word in each sentence.

3. <u>Spread</u> part of the bean mixture in the dish.
   _____ a blanket or covering for a bed
   _✓_ to place a layer over a surface
4. The <u>foil</u> keeps the casserole from becoming too dry while it is baking.
   _✓_ a thin sheet of aluminum
   _____ to keep from being successful

Reading Skills

1. Number the steps below to show the order in which they happen.
   _3_ Add the beans to the tomato mixture.
   _2_ Sauté the vegetables in the skillet.
   _4_ Coat the baking dish with cooking spray.
   _1_ Preheat the oven.
   _5_ Bake the casserole until the cheese on top is bubbly.
2. Check the line beside the word or words that best describe what type of nonfiction selection this is.
   _✓_ how-to
   _____ biography
   _____ persuasive text

3. Check the phrase that best describes the author's purpose.
   _____ to tell a story about a family who makes a tortilla casserole
   _✓_ to explain how to make tortilla casserole
   _____ to show the history of casseroles in American cooking
4. What are the two types of cheeses that are used in this recipe?
   Monterey Jack and cheddar

Study Skills

An **index** is located at the end of many nonfiction books. It is an alphabetical listing of all the topics in a book. You can look in the index to find out where to look for information about a particular topic. Use the index below to answer the questions.

Index

Enchiladas 18
Flan 56
Guacamole 4
Refried Beans 32
Rice and Beans 26
Salsa
 Salsa Verde 7
 Tomato Salsa 6
Tortilla Casserole 20

1. On which page can you find a recipe for flan?
   56
2. Which entry in the index has two recipes listed below it?
   Salsa
3. What recipe would you find on page 32?
   Refried Beans

39

Page 41

Vocabulary Skills

A **word family** is a group of words that have the same letter combinations. Circle the words in each row that are part of the word family in parentheses.

1. (-*ight*) (blight) (delight) blink (tonight)
2. (-*ould*) (should) shelter counter (could)

The prefix **re-** means *again*. The prefix **pre-** means *before*. Add **re** or **pre** to each underlined word below to form a word that matches the definition.

3. to <u>enact</u> again **reenact**
4. to <u>arrange</u> before **prearrange**
5. to <u>fill</u> again **refill**

Circle the homophone that correctly completes each sentence below.

6. The types of celebration **vary** from place to place. (vary/very)
7. Children **break** open the *piñata* with a stick to get to the treats inside. (brake/break)

Reading Skills

1. What happens during a reenactment of a battle?
   People dress up in uniforms and have a pretend battle.
2. What is a *piñata*?
   a colorful, papier-mâché object that is filled with toys and candy and then broken open
3. Why is *Cinco de Mayo* such an important celebration even though the French returned a year later and took power?
   Winning the battle was a powerful example of the spirit and determination of the Mexican people.

4. Check the sentence below that is the best summary for paragraph 2.
   _✓_ The French were surprised to be defeated by the Mexican army in 1862.
   _____ The French wanted Emperor Maximilian to become the new ruler of Mexico.
   _____ The Mexican army was smaller than the invading French army.

Study Skills

Fiesta! Celebrate Cinco de Mayo on Saturday morning, May 5!

Sample the best Mexican food north of the border all day long!

Don't forget to bring your blanket and stay for the fireworks at dusk.

11:00 Parade begins
12:00 Speech by Mayor Gutierrez
1:00 Mariachi band contest
2:00 Make-your-own piñata party
3:00 Reenactment of the Battle of Puebla begins

1. Who is giving a speech at noon?
   Mayor Gutierrez
2. What happens at 1:00?
   mariachi band contest
3. When will the fireworks begin?
   at dusk

41

Answer Key

Page 43

Write the words from the story that have the meanings below.

1. different subject areas
   __categories__
   Par. 1

2. to produce a clear picture or image
   __focus__
   Par. 4

3. jobs; uses
   __functions__
   Par. 5

4. something that allows the body to use more oxygen and helps the heart get stronger
   __aerobic__
   Par. 6

Find an antonym in the story for each of the words below.

5. above __beneath__
   Par. 5

6. shallow __deep__
   Par. 3

7. backward __forward__
   Par. 4

8. relax __contract__
   Par. 5

Words that have a single middle consonant are usually divided into syllables before the consonant. For example, *e/vil* or *o/pen*. Divide the words below into syllables using a slash (/).

9. f o/c u s

10. e/v e r

11. r e/l a x

12. a/b o u t

Reading Skills

1. In paragraph 2, Kwame lists several different activities. How are these activities similar?
   __They all use muscles.__

---

2. How are voluntary and involuntary muscles different?
   __We can choose how and when to use voluntary muscles. Involuntary muscles move automatically as needed.__

3. What idea are Eva and Kwame trying to persuade their classmates into doing?
   __to exercise 30 minutes each day__

4. Name two types of aerobic exercise that are not mentioned in the story.
   __Answers will vary.__

5. Do you think that Kwame and Eva will get their pictures in the Santa Rosita newspaper? Explain your answer.
   __Answers will vary.__

Study Skills

A library's reference system can help you find a book. Use the information below to answer the questions that follow.

Call No.:	331.68 RE
Author(s):	Redwing, Jake and Alice
Title:	The Kids' Guide to Fitness and the Body
Publisher:	Body and Mind Publishing, Inc.

1. Who are the authors of the book?
   __Jake and Alice Redwing__

2. What is the name of the publisher?
   __Body and Mind Publishing, Inc.__

3. Which book would be located closer to the book with the call number above—the book with call number 331.52 RA or the book with call number 331.68 RA
   __331.68 RA__

43

Page 45

Vocabulary Skills

Write the words from the passage that have the meanings below.

1. arms, legs, wings, or flippers
   __limbs__
   Par. 1

2. the ability to move from one place to another
   __locomotion__
   Par. 2

3. let go; loosen or relax
   __release__
   Par. 3

4. used for a specific purpose
   __specialized__
   Par. 4

5. Check the sentence in which *roots* has the same meaning as it does in paragraph 5.
   ✓ The roots of the large tree extend deep underground.
   __ June's father helped her research their family's roots.

6. Check the sentence in which *pound* has the same meaning as it does in paragraph 3.
   __ Please do not pound so loudly at my door.
   ✓ The chef will need a pound of flour to make enough bread for dinner.

Reading Skills

1. Why do a snake's neck muscles need to be strong?
   __so it can swallow large prey__

2. About how far can a lion leap?
   __35 feet__

---

3. According to the selection, what is one way snakes and lions are similar?
   __Possible answer: They both use their muscles to hunt prey.__

Circle the word that best completes each sentence.

4. A lion's strength is important for its __survival__.
   interest (survival) body

5. An elephant can __accomplish__ many types of tasks with its trunk.
   (accomplish) forget create

Study Skills

Animal	# of Miles Per Hour It Can Run
crocodile	
mouse	
squirrel	
elephant	
coyote	
antelope	
cheetah	

1. Which is the fastest animal listed above?
   __cheetah__

2. Which two animals run at about the same speed?
   __crocodile and mouse__

3. About how fast can a coyote run?
   __about 43 m.p.h.__

4. Which animal runs about 12 miles per hour?
   __squirrel__

45

Page 47

Vocabulary Skills

Write the words from the passage that have the meanings below.

1. carry; transport
   __haul__
   Par. 2

2. looked at; considered
   __regarded__
   Par. 3

3. create; establish
   __found__
   Par. 3

4. places where art is displayed
   __galleries__
   Par. 5

5. not resembling anything real
   __abstract__
   Par. 6

Find an antonym in the story for each of the words below.

6. rapidly __slowly__
   Par. 2

7. temporarily __forever__
   Par. 3

8. depressing __cheerful__
   Par. 6

Reading Skills

1. Check the phrase that best describes the author's purpose.
   ✓ to share information about the elephant artists of Thailand
   __ to persuade the reader to buy a piece of elephant artwork
   __ to inform the reader about the different types of animals living in Thailand

2. What problem were the elephants of Thailand having before Komar and Melamid stepped in?
   __They did not have any work, and they were being abused.__

---

3. About how many elephants are there in Thailand today?
   __less than 5000__

4. Name one artist whose work some people believe resembles the elephant artwork.
   __Possible answers: Jackson Pollack, Vasily Kandinsky__

5. What is the name for the elephants' style of painting?
   __abstract__

Study Skills

1. What body of water lies south of the majority of Thailand?
   __the Gulf of Thailand__

2. Which country can be found along the western edge of Thailand?
   __Burma__

3. What direction would you go from Bangkok to get to China?
   __north__

4. Which country lies along most of the northern and eastern borders of Thailand?
   __Laos__

47

Page 49

Vocabulary Skills

Write the words from the passage that have the meanings below.

1. a possibility that hasn't yet become real
   __potential__
   Par. 2

2. a large painting that is done directly on a wall
   __mural__
   Par. 2

3. a sudden advance that allows one to continue
   __breakthrough__
   Par. 3

4. able to be known or remembered
   __recognizable__
   Par. 4

5. interested; curious about
   __intrigued__
   Par. 5

6. causing great surprise
   __shocking__
   Par. 6

Find the simile in paragraph 4, and write it on the line below.

7. __like music for the eyes__

Find a synonym in the story for each of the words below.

8. altered __changed__
   Par. 1

9. respected __admired__
   Par. 4

10. completed __finished__
    Par. 5

Underline the compound word in each sentence. Then, write the two words that make up each compound.

11. Creating a mural for Peggy Guggenheim was a breakthrough for Pollack.
    __break__ __through__

---

12. Pollack's footprints can be seen in some of his pieces.
    __foot__ __prints__

13. In the past, nobody had attempted to make art like Jackson Pollack's.
    __no__ __body__

Reading Skills

1. What has Pollack's technique been called?
   __action painting__

2. Name two artists whom Pollack admired.
   __Possible answers: Pablo Picasso, Joan Miro; Diego Rivera; Thomas Hart Benton__

3. Is this passage a fantasy, or does it take place in reality?
   __It takes place in reality.__

4. How did Pollack change painting forever?
   __He changed people's ideas of what art was.__

5. Why did critics think that Pollack's style of painting was more similar to music than to realistic painting?
   __Possible answer: In the same way that music is about sound, Pollack's paintings were about paint and did not represent something else.__

Study Skills

Use a dictionary to help you divide these words into syllables.

1. d e s/p e r/a t e/l y

2. p o/t e n/t i a l

3. r e/a l i s/t i c

4. p h o/t o/g r a p h s

5. t r a/d i/t i o n/a l

6. l i b/e r/a t/e d

49

Answer Key

Page 51

Vocabulary Skills

Write the words from the story that have the meanings below.

1. artwork made by gluing different materials onto a surface
   collages
2. made to feel timid or frightened
   intimidated
3. persuaded to do or believe something
   convinced
4. understanding or seeing something in a certain way
   interpretation

Circle the homophone that correctly completes each sentence below.

5. There were small ____ flecks ____ of paint on the table. (flecks/flex)
6. Ms. Kaye arranged a ____ scene ____ on the platform. (seen/scene)
7. Each ____ piece ____ of art is unique. (piece/peace)

Write **S** if the possessive word is singular. Write **P** if it is plural.

8. __P__ boys' artwork
9. __S__ Ms. Kaye's comments
10. __S__ Samir's painting
11. __P__ students' conversations

Reading Skills

1. What kind of earrings was Ms. Kaye wearing?
   They spelled art.

2. Why was Samir's painting unusual?
   He used unusual colors.
3. What do you think a still life is?
   Answers will vary.
4. What problem did Matthew and Samir have at the beginning of the story?
   They were intimidated by artwork that previous students had done.
5. What is one way in which Mathew and Samir are different?
   Possible answer: Samir prefers to paint, and Matthew prefers to draw.
6. Write a summary of paragraph 6 on the lines below.
   Answers will vary.

Study Skills

Maple Springs Community Summer Art Program

Classes begin on June 24.
Sign up online or in person.

Beginning Art	Tues. 1–3
Sculpture	Mon. and Wed. 10–12
Printmaking	Thurs. 6–9
Photography	Tues. and Thurs. 1–3

1. How can you sign up for classes?
   either online or in person
2. When does the sculpture class meet?
   Monday and Wednesday from 10–12
3. Which classes meet only one day a week?
   Beginning Art and Printmaking
4. Which class meets in the evening?
   Printmaking

51

Page 53

Vocabulary Skills

Write the words from the passage that have the meanings below.

1. trying out different things
   experimentation
2. more than one; several
   multiple
3. like an adult
   mature
4. a feeling of being content and fulfilled
   satisfaction

Read each pair of words listed below. If the words are synonyms, write **S** on the line. If the words are antonyms, write **A** on the line.

5. __A__ unique   common
6. __S__ amazed   astonished
7. __S__ joy   happiness
8. __A__ public   private

The prefix **ir-** means *not*. Add **ir** to each word below. Then, use each new word in a sentence.

9. responsible irresponsible
   Answers will vary.
10. replaceable irreplaceable
    Answers will vary.

Reading Skills

1. Why was it so unusual that Alexandra painted in the style of Cubists when she was small?
   She had not seen any of their paintings before.

2. Find on sentence in the passage that shows Alexandra loves what she does. Write it below.
   Possible answer: She cannot imagine doing anything else that would bring her such joy and satisfaction.
3. Check the line beside the word or words that best describe what type of selection this is.
   __✓__ biography
   ____ fiction
   ____ how-to
4. Check the words that describe Alexandra.
   __✓__ creative   ____ ambitious
   __✓__ generous   ____ scientific
   ____ impatient
5. Number the events below to show the order in which they happened.
   __4__ Alexandra had her first public show.
   __5__ Alexandra's works were shown in galleries and museums around the world.
   __2__ Alexandra's parents thought she should spend less time coloring.
   __3__ Alexandra began painting with acrylic and oil paints.
   __1__ Alexandra was born in Romania.

Study Skills

Write the entry word you would look for in a dictionary next to each word below.

1. coloring color
2. worried worry
3. continued continue
4. internationally international

53

Page 55

Vocabulary Skills

Write the words from the story that have the meanings below.

1. made of
   composed
2. be greater than
   exceed
3. respected and wise
   distinguished
4. worked toward
   strived

Compound words are divided into syllables between the two words that make the compound. For example, *play/ground*. Divide the words below into syllables using a slash (/).

5. n i g h t / s t a n d
6. s w e a t / s h i r t
7. s u n / l i g h t
8. s p a c e / s u i t

Fill in the blanks below with the possessive form of the word in parentheses.

9. Lena can see ___ Saturn's ___ rings through the telescope. (Saturn)
10. ___ Lena's ___ dad knows a lot about the planets. (Lena)
11. The ___ scientists' ___ discovery of 31 moons surprised Lena. (scientists)

Reading Skills

1. Do you think Lena will be a scientist one day? Explain your answer.
   Answers will vary.
2. What is one reason why Lena's dad thinks people will never be able to visit Saturn?
   Possible answers: It is made mostly of gases; it is too windy.
3. What part of the story is a fantasy for Lena? What part takes place in reality?
   When she accepts the award, it is fantasy. When she looks at Saturn with her father, it is reality.
4. The **protagonist** is the main character in a story. Who is the protagonist in this story?
   Lena

Study Skills

Write the name of the reference source you could use to find out the information in each question below.

encyclopedia	dictionary
thesaurus	

1. Where could you find the definition of the word *interplanetary*?
   dictionary
2. Where could you learn more about the conditions on Saturn?
   encyclopedia
3. Where could you find a synonym for the word *incredible*?
   thesaurus

55

Page 57

Vocabulary Skills

Write the words from the passage that have the meanings below.

1. came to a decision
   concluded
2. the place something or someone is going
   destination
3. sent by one person or thing to another
   transmitted
4. carefully moving or guiding
   maneuvering
5. remains; leftovers
   remnants

Compound words are divided into syllables between the two words that make the compound. For example, *play/ground*. Divide the words below into syllables using a slash (/).

6. s p a c e / c r a f t
7. s o m e / h o w
8. t a k e / o f f

In each row, circle the word that does not belong.

9. Galileo Cassini Huygens (Jupiter)
10. Jupiter (meteor) Saturn Earth
11. (sun) moon Titan Phoebe
12. amaze astonish (disappoint) surprise

Reading Skills

1. Check the line beside the word that best describes what type of passage this is.
   __✓__ informational
   ____ fiction
   ____ myth
2. What did Galileo think the bulges on either side of Saturn were caused by?
   He thought the bulges were other planets.
3. How long did it take the Cassini-Huygens spacecraft to travel from Earth to Saturn?
   seven years
4. How do scientists think the rings of Saturn were created?
   They are the remains of a moon that was destroyed.

Study Skills

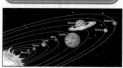

1. Which planet is closest to the sun?
   Mercury
2. Between which two planets is Earth located?
   Venus and Mars
3. What is the name of the fifth planet from the sun?
   Jupiter

57

Answer Key

Page 59

Vocabulary Skills

Write the words from the passage that have the meanings below.

1. places; locations
   sites
2. guided or directed
   conducted
3. possible
   potential
4. buildings that are used for a specific purpose
   facilities
5. words that describe something
   descriptive

Write the words from the passage that match the abbreviations below.

6. HI Hawaii
7. AZ Arizona
8. NM New Mexico

Read each sentence below. Then, write the word from the –ight word family that best completes the sentence.

9. Kitt Peak offers a special _____night_____ program where you can use powerful telescopes to view the universe.
10. You _____might_____ be able to see a meteor or a comet.
11. The words site and _____sight_____ are homophones, or words that sound the same but are spelled differently and have different meanings.

Reading Skills

1. Check the line beside the word that best describes what type of nonfiction selection this is.
   ___ biography
   _✓_ informational
   ___ persuasive
2. On the lines below, write a sentence that summarizes paragraph 1.
   Answers will vary.
3. In which mountain range is Kitt Peak located?
   Quinlan Mountains

Study Skills

Rates for Guided Tours at Kitt Peak

Adults:	$2.00 per person
Children (ages 6–12):	$1.00 per person
Children under 6:	free
Tohono O'odham Members:	free

1. Who can get a free guided tour at Kitt Peak?
   children under six and Tohono O'odham members
2. How much would it cost for two adults to take the tour?
   $4.00
3. How much would it cost for two 10-year-olds and one 5-year-old to take the tour?
   $2.00

59

Page 61

Vocabulary Skills

Write the words from the story that have the meanings below.

1. a landing area for ships and boats
   dock
2. into or onto a vehicle
   aboard
3. one of the floors on a ship or boat
   deck
4. things that don't follow the standard rules
   exceptions

Check the sentence in which moved has the same meaning as it does in paragraph 3.

5. ___ My aunt was moved to tears by the letter you wrote her.
   _✓_ Ivan moved to Tallahassee, Florida, last year.

Find the simile in paragraph 2, and write it on the line below.

6. The sky was as blue as the bottom of a swimming pool.

Check the correct meaning of the underlined word.

7. Mr. Roma rearranged the supplies on the boat.
   _✓_ arranged again
   ___ able to arrange
   ___ someone who arranges
8. None of the dishes on the boat were breakable.
   ___ before breaking
   ___ breaking again
   _✓_ able to break

9. The midday sun was hot on Sarah's dark hair.
   ___ before day
   _✓_ middle part of the day
   ___ not day

Reading Skills

1. Check the sentence that best states the main idea of the selection.
   ___ Pilar asks her grandpa what the flashlight, mirror, and whistle are for.
   ___ Sarah moved to Ohio from Iowa a couple of years before.
   _✓_ Sarah and Pilar go on a sailing trip with Pilar's grandparents and learn some safety tips about boating.

Write F before the sentences that are facts. Write O before the sentences that are opinions.

2. _F_ Sarah and Pilar helped load supplies on the boat.
3. _O_ Sailing is a good way to relax.
4. _F_ PFD stands for personal flotation device.
5. _O_ Mrs. Roma is a better sailor than Mr. Roma.
6. _F_ The characters in this story all live in Ohio.
7. How do you signal SOS?
   Using a light, make three quick flashes, three longer flashes, and then three more quick flashes.
8. Do you think that Sarah and Pilar will go sailing with Pilar's grandparents again? Why or why not?
   Answers will vary.

61

Page 63

Vocabulary Skills

Write the words from the passage that have the meanings below.

1. bringing about a result without wasting time or energy
   efficient
2. to cause something to move
   propel
3. hung; attached from above
   suspended
4. turn
   rotate
5. able to be seen; obvious
   visible

Read each word below. Then, write the letter of its antonym on the line beside the reader word.

6. _e_ forward   a. pulling
7. _a_ pushing   b. different
8. _d_ creates   c. insignificant
9. _b_ similar   d. destroys
10. _c_ important   e. backward

Write S if the possessive word is singular. Write P if it is plural.

11. _S_ the boat's sails
12. _P_ the sailors' skills
13. _P_ the sailboats' course
14. _S_ the wind's power

Reading Skills

1. What does it mean to sail before the wind?
   The wind is behind you.
2. Why does a sail need to be able to rotate?
   to be able to use the wind regardless of the direction it is blowing
3. When does a sailor need to travel in a zigzag pattern?
   when the sailor needs to travel directly into the wind
4. What purpose does a sailboat's keel serve?
   It keeps the boat traveling straight ahead.
5. Check the phrase that best describes the author's purpose.
   _✓_ to share information about how a sailboat works
   ___ to entertain the reader with a story about funny experiences with sailing
   ___ to inform the reader about great sailors of the past century
6. Check the line beside the word that best describes what type of selection this is.
   _✓_ informational
   ___ fiction
   ___ autobiography

Study Skills

Use a dictionary to help you divide these words into syllables.

1. e/ffi/cient
2. va/cuum
3. o/ppo/site
4. na/tu/ra/lly
5. de/sti/na/tion

63

Page 65

Vocabulary Skills

Write the words from the passage that have the meanings below.

1. the condition of being or existing
   existence
2. coming before in time
   previous
3. difficult; needing a lot of care and effort
   painstaking
4. unchanging
   constant

5. Check the sentence in which race has the same meaning as it does in paragraph 1.
   ___ People of many races attended the international festival in my town.
   _✓_ Habib and I will run the race downtown on Saturday.
6. Check the sentence in which streak has the same meaning as it does in paragraph 2.
   _✓_ My school soccer team has been on a winning streak this entire season.
   ___ There was a large streak on the mirror where Jess had wiped it with a towel.

Reading Skills

Circle the word that best completes each sentence below.

1. The challenger _____competes_____ against the defender.
   (competes) rebels supports
2. In the Louis Vuitton Cup, boats compete to see who will challenge the _____current_____ champion.
   original future (current)

3. The _____trophy_____ is passed from one winning team to the next.
   tradition (trophy) competition
4. Name one thing that was similar about all America's Cup races before 1983.
   Possible answer: The United States always won.
5. Name two countries that you think have the best chance of winning the America's Cup in 2007.
   Answers will vary.
6. Where did the first America's Cup take place?
   Possible answers: Isle of Wight; English Channel; England

Study Skills

Year	Name of Winning Boat	Country
1983	Australia II	Australia
1987	Stars & Stripes	United States
1988	Stars & Stripes	United States
1992	America³	United States
1995	Black Magic	New Zealand
2000	New Zealand	New Zealand
2003	Alinghi	Switzerland

1. Which country listed in the table above has the most wins?
   United States
2. What is the name of the winning boat from 1992?
   America³
3. Which country owns the Alinghi?
   Switzerland

65

Answer Key

Page 67

Vocabulary Skills

Write the words from the story that have the meanings below.

1. got closer to
   approached *Par. 2*

2. old; well-used
   worn *Par. 3*

3. gave to a cause
   contributed *Par. 4*

4. response; way of acting or behaving
   reaction *Par. 10*

5. glad; not worried
   relieved *Par. 11*

Words that have a single middle consonant are usually divided into syllables before the consonant. For example, a/bove or o/pen. Divide the words below into syllables using a slash (/).

6. w a/t e r

7. a/l o n g

8. m o/m e n t

Write a compound word using two words in each sentence.

9. Pilar watched a beautiful boat with a large white sail glide past.
   sailboat

10. Sarah had a sting from a bee on her arm.
    beesting

11. Pilar's grandparents read a paper that contained the news.
    newspaper

Reading Skills

1. What is the name of the island where they had their picnic?
   Kelleys Island

2. Why was Pilar's grandma a good person to have nearby when Sarah was stung by a bee?
   She used to be a nurse.

Read the sentences below. Write **B** next to the sentence if it tells about something that happened before Sarah was stung. Write **A** if it tells about something that happened after.

3. **B** Pilar and Sarah began playing Frisbee.

4. **B** The girls helped Mrs. Roma unpack the lunch.

5. **A** Sarah looked at the red welt on her arm.

Study Skills

Use the table below to answer the questions that follow.

Sailboats Docked at the Lake Erie Sailing Club

Name	Length	Dock Number
Annabelle Lee	26 feet	6
Windswept	44 feet	18
The Castaway	28 feet	55
Clementine	34 feet	119

1. Which boat listed above is the smallest?
   Annabelle Lee

2. How long is *The Castaway*?
   28 feet

3. Which boat is docked at Dock 18?
   Windswept

67

Page 69

Vocabulary Skills

Write the words from the passage that have the meanings below.

1. hard to understand
   complex *Par. 2*

2. over and over again
   repeatedly *Par. 3*

3. a group of animals that live together
   colony *Par. 4*

4. to crowd closely together
   huddle *Par. 6*

5. very interesting and appealing
   fascinating *Par. 9*

Circle the homophone that correctly completes each sentence below.

6. Each type of honey bee has a different **role** in the colony. (roll, (role))

7. The queen's body **weight** is about the same as that of the eggs she carries. ((weight), wait)

8. A queen bee can **lay** an enormous number of eggs. (lei, (lay))

Write **S** if the possessive word is singular. Write **P** if it is plural.

9. **S** the queen's eggs

10. **P** bees' colony

11. **S** the hive's temperature

12. **P** the workers' jobs

13. **S** the flower's nectar

Reading Skills

Read the descriptions below. Write **Q** next to the phrase if it describes queen bees. Write **W** if it describes worker bees.

1. **W** dies after stinging

2. **W** builds the nest

3. **Q** has a smooth, curved stinger

4. **Q** lays more than a thousand eggs a day

5. **W** cools eggs by fanning their wings

6. What is one place in the world where honey bees cannot be found?
   Antarctica

7. How long can a queen bee live?
   one to three years

Study Skills

Use the facts from paragraph 6 to complete Part I of the outline. Use the facts from paragraph 8 to complete Part II.

I. Worker bees
   A. make up most of the colony
   B. build and maintain the nest
   C. **gather nectar and pollen**
   D. **make honey**
   E. monitor the temperature for the young bees

II. Bee communication
   A. give directions to food through dancing
   B. **dances tell how far away the food is**
   C. scientists can follow the clear directions

69

Page 71

Vocabulary Skills

Write the words from the story that have the meanings below.

1. a set of straps used to attach a person or an animal to something
   harness *Par. 2*

2. feeling sure
   confident *Par. 11*

3. came down
   descended *Par. 13*

Read each pair of words listed below. If the words are synonyms, write **S** on the line. If the words are antonyms, write **A** on the line.

4. **A** properly   incorrectly

5. **S** try   attempt

6. **A** ascended   descended

Write the idiom from paragraph 12 on the line next to its meaning.

7. to enjoy and get used to something unexpected **gets under your skin**

Check the correct meaning of the underlined word.

8. Ask a dependable person to belay you.
   ___ depend again
   ✓ able to depend on
   ___ someone who depends

9. The climber will reattempt to climb the tallest wall.
   ___ attempt before
   ___ able to attempt
   ✓ attempt again

Reading Skills

1. Do you think this story takes place in reality, or is it a fantasy? Why?
   Answers will vary.

2. Do you think that Dante and Ethan will want to go rock climbing again? Why or why not?
   Answers will vary.

3. What is the purpose of a carabiner?
   To join things together; in climbing it attaches the belay device to the harness.

4. **Hyperbole** is an exaggerated statement. For example, *I am so hungry, I could eat a horse.* Find the hyperbole in paragraph 1, and write it on the line.
   Dante and Ethan had asked him a million questions about it.

Study Skills

Guide words are printed at the top of each page in a dictionary. The guide word at the left is the first word on the page. The guide word at the right is the last word on the page. Check each word that could be found on a page having the guide words shown in dark print.

1. bawl–beeswax
   ___ beginner   ✓ beautiful
   ✓ bayou

2. immigrant–impressive
   ___ incapable   ___ illustrate
   ✓ imposter

3. reflection–relish
   ✓ reflex   ✓ relative   ___ recline

71

Page 73

Vocabulary Skills

Write the words from the passage that have the meanings below.

1. to go up
   ascend *Par. 1*

2. an action that is taken to protect against danger or mistakes
   precaution *Par. 3*

3. climbing up to the top
   scaling *Par. 5*

4. planned movements
   maneuvers *Par. 5*

5. exactly the same
   identical *Par. 6*

Words that have two middle consonants are divided into syllables between the consonants. For example, pic/ture or bas/ket. Divide the words below into syllables using a slash (/).

6. p r a c/t i c e

7. c l i m/b e r

8. m i s/t a k e

9. a l/p i n e

Reading Skills

1. Check the sentence that best states the main idea of paragraph 2.
   ✓ Alpine climbing, ice climbing, and rock climbing are the three main types of climbing.
   ___ Alpine and ice climbing are usually done in teams.
   ___ Rock climbers look for walls or cliffs to climb almost anywhere.

Write **F** before the sentences that are facts. Write **O** before the sentences that are opinions.

2. **F** Free climbers use chalk and tape to keep their hands dry.

3. **O** People who enjoy rock climbing are adventurous and brave.

4. **F** Bouldering is one way new climbers can practice somewhere safe.

5. **F** In aid climbing, a person can use different types of tools.

6. **O** Rock climbing competitions are very interesting to watch.

7. Why do you think rock climbing competitions are usually held indoors?
   Answers will vary.

Study Skills

Use the index below to answer the questions.

Index

Best outdoor climbs (also listed by state) 14–15, 16, 17, 18–20, 21, 22–25
Climbing safety 2–9
Climbing with kids 51–63
Equipment 26–33
Indoor facilities 64–68, 75
Tips for beginners 10

1. What is another way the best outdoor climbs are listed?
   by state

2. Which pages have information about climbing with kids?
   51–63

3. What type of information would you find on page 10?
   tips for beginners

73

Answer Key

Page 75

Vocabulary Skills

Write the words from the passage that have the meanings below.

1. to get in the way of
   __obstruct__
2. the top or highest point
   __summit__
3. to overcome or get control of
   __conquer__

Read each word or phrase below. Then, write the letter of the abbreviation that matches in the space beside it.

4. __b__ feet   **a.** Mt.
5. __d__ miles per hour **b.** ft.
6. __a__ Mount   **c.** cm.
7. __c__ millimeters   **d.** m.p.h.

Find a synonym in the selection for each of the words below.

8. freezing __frigid__
9. hazardous __dangerous__
10. trip; journey __expedition__
11. daring __adventurous__

Reading Skills

1. On the lines below, write one sentence from the selection that shows the author was trying to persuade you that climbing Mount Everest is a dangerous goal.

   __Possible answer: Something is so__
   __intriguing about Mount Everest that__
   __people are still willing to risk their lives__
   __to climb it.__

Circle the word that best completes each sentence below.

2. The height of Mount Everest is __increasing__ slightly every year.
   decreasing (increasing) moving
3. Every year, many people __attempt__ to reach the summit of the mountain.
   regret pretend (attempt)
4. The __threat__ of an avalanche is always on the minds of the climbers.
   (threat) awareness belief

Study Skills

Use the graph below to answer the questions that follow.

1. In which year did the greatest number of people reach the summit?
   __2001__
2. How many people reached the summit in 1998?
   __120__
3. In which year did only 85 people reach the summit?
   __1997__

Page 77

Vocabulary Skills

Write the words from the story that have the meanings below.

1. a short phrase that describes a person's or group's ideas or beliefs
   __slogan__
2. covering a wide range
   __extensive__
3. objects or tools used for a specific purpose
   __utensils__

Write the idiom from paragraph 5 on the line next to its meaning.

4. sounds good __It's got a nice ring to it.__

Circle the homophone that correctly completes each sentence below.

5. Olivia thinks that her ideas will make the school year __great__. (grate (great)
6. The students are __allowed__ to post their signs on the bulletin boards in the hallways. (aloud (allowed)

Underline the compound word in each sentence. Then, write the two words that make up each compound.

7. Ahmad's classmates are eager to help him run his campaign.
   __class__   __mates__
8. Olivia has a background in school politics.
   __back__   __ground__

Reading Skills

1. Check the words that describe Olivia.
   __✓__ confident   __✓__ thoughtful
   ____ lazy   __✓__ ambitious

2. What does Ahmad think his strength as president would be?
   __He can bring some fresh ideas to__
   __school politics.__
3. What does Jenna think Olivia should emphasize in her campaign?
   __her experience__
4. **Alliteration** is the use of words that begin with the same sound. Find the alliteration in paragraph 4, and write it on the line.
   __Articulate, Authentic, and__
   __Approachable: Always Ahmad__

Study Skills

Use the map of Ahmad's and Olivia's school to answer the questions that follow.

1. What two rooms is the library located between?
   __an office and a classroom__
2. How many classrooms are there?
   __5__
3. Is the cafeteria closer to an office or to a classroom?
   __a classroom__

Page 79

Vocabulary Skills

Write the words from the story that have the meanings below.

1. changes that make things better
   __improvements__
2. to supervise a group of young people
   __chaperone__
3. to provide a service without getting paid for it
   __volunteer__
4. to affect in a positive way
   __benefit__

Find an antonym in the story for each of the words below.

5. problem __solution__
6. unwilling __willing__
7. noisy __quiet__
8. unjust __fair__

Write **S** if the possessive word is singular. Write **P** if it is plural.

9. __S__ Olivia's plans
10. __S__ this year's election
11. __P__ students' votes
12. __S__ Ahmad's ideas
13. __P__ parents' opinions

Reading Skills

1. Number the events below to show the order in which they happened.
   __2__ Ms. Pond read the names of the different class officers.

   __1__ Ms. Pond told the class she had the election results.
   __4__ Ahmad said he would like to create a volunteering club.
   __5__ Li Chen suggested that Ahmad and Olivia be co-presidents.
   __3__ Ahmad and Olivia waited in the hallway.

In **first-person point of view**, the reader knows the thoughts and feelings of the person telling the story. In **third-person point of view**, the reader only knows what an outsider knows about a character. Mark each sentence below **F** for first-person and **T** for third-person.

2. __F__ I wonder if Ahmad and Olivia would mind being co-presidents?
3. __T__ Olivia walked to the front of the room.
4. __T__ Ahmad said he would do his best to be a good president.
5. __F__ I can't believe that I am going to be class secretary!

Study Skills

Check each word that could be found on a dictionary page having the guide words shown in dark print.

1. acquaint—adhesive
   ____ achieve __✓__ acute ____ admiral
2. meander—mellow
   ____ merry ____ measure
   __✓__ meditate
3. urgent—utter
   __✓__ us ____ uproar __✓__ utilize

Page 81

Vocabulary Skills

Write the words from the passage that have the meanings below.

1. a public event or issue about which two sides have different views
   __controversy__
2. the least
   __minimum__
3. feeling nervous and uncertain
   __anxiously__
4. gave up or gave in
   __conceded__
5. lived in; occupied by
   __populated__
6. makes sure
   __ensures__

Read each word below. Then, write the letter of its abbreviation in the space beside it.

7. __d__ Wyoming   **a.** CA
8. __e__ Florida   **b.** D.C.
9. __a__ California   **c.** TX
10. __c__ Texas   **d.** WY
11. __b__ District of Columbia **e.** FL

12. Check the sentence in which *swing* has the same meaning as it does in paragraph 4.
    ____ Dad installed a new swing in the backyard.
    __✓__ The candidate hoped to swing the crowd's opinion.

Reading Skills

1. Check the line beside the word that best describes what type of selection this is.
   __✓__ informational
   ____ persuasive
   ____ fiction
2. What is the smallest number of electoral votes a candidate must receive to win the presidency?
   __270__
3. Why do some states have more electoral votes than others?
   __Some states have larger__
   __populations than others.__
4. Why do some people feel that the Electoral College is not a fair way to elect the president?
   __They feel that when a candidate wins the__
   __election in a state, the votes for the other__
   __candidate do not count because the__
   __winner receives all of the electoral votes.__
5. Why do some people believe that the Electoral College is a good system to elect the president?
   __They think it helps smaller, less__
   __populated states have a voice in__
   __the election.__
6. Why did people want the votes in Florida to be recounted?
   __It was a close race, and the__
   __election results in Florida could__
   __make a difference in the__
   __outcome.__

Answer Key

Page 83

Vocabulary Skills

Write the words from the story that have the meanings below.

1. hand out
   distribute

2. the act of paying careful attention
   observation

3. separated or in many directions
   scattered

4. a meeting to discuss a specific topic
   conference

5. nervous
   tense

The suffix **-ation** means *state, condition, act, or process of*. For example, the word *expectation* means *the act of expecting*. Add **ation** to each word, and write the new word on the line. Then, use the new word in a sentence. Remember that you may have to drop the final **e** before adding the suffix.

6. prepare preparation
   Answers will vary.

7. inspire inspiration
   Answers will vary.

8. imagine imagination
   Answers will vary.

9. Write the idiom in paragraph 9 on the line below its meaning.
   waited anxiously
   held their breath

Reading Skills

1. Check the sentence below that is the best summary for paragraph 3.
   ____ Mr. Chandler handed out the list to the students.
   ✓ Mr. Chandler gave the students tips about being careful during the scavenger hunt.
   ____ Mr. Chandler said, "May the best team win!"

2. What does each team have to do during the scavenger hunt?
   find every item on the list

3. Name three items that are on the list Mr. Chandler distributes.
   Answers will vary.

4. What does Alex offer to exchange for a yellow highlighter?
   a large paper clip and an extra cap eraser

Study Skills

Write the entry word you would look for in a dictionary next to each word below.

1. continued continue
2. announced announce
3. carrying carry
4. standing stand
5. heavier heavy

83

Page 85

Vocabulary Skills

Write the words from the passage that have the meanings below.

1. having a reason to do something
   motivated

2. reasonable or acceptable
   valid

3. an agreement reached by two opposing sides, each of which had to give up part of what they wanted
   compromise

4. receivers
   receptors

5. very strong
   intense

Words that end in **le** are usually divided into syllables before the consonant that precedes the **le**. For example, *ta/ble* or *han/dle*. Divide the words below into syllables using a slash (/).

6. peo/ple   8. dan/gle
7. no/ble   9. ram/ble

Reading Skills

1. Check the phrase that best describes the author's purpose.
   ✓ to inform
   ____ to persuade
   ____ to entertain

2. How are archaeologists and treasure hunters similar?
   They both search for undersea treasures.

3. How are they different?
   Archaeologists study shipwrecks as a piece of history, and treasure hunters hope to profit from the wrecks.

4. In the opinion of archaeologists, what is valuable about shipwrecks?
   They see the wrecks as a valuable snapshot of how citizens from past cultures lived and traveled.

5. How have archaeologists and treasure hunters compromised?
   Treasure hunters allow scientists to spend as much time as they need to study the wreck, and scientists have provided better equipment and resources for exploration.

6. In paragraph 6, the word *see* is set in quotation marks. What was the author's purpose for doing that?
   The sonar doesn't actually see things, but it can identify where they are.

Write **F** before the sentences that are facts. Write **O** before the sentences that are opinions.

7. O Treasure hunters have the right to use the contents of a shipwreck in any way they like.

8. F Dr. Robert Ballard discovered the *Titanic*.

9. O Both the treasure hunters and the archaeologists have a good point.

Study Skills

A **pronunciation key** is a list of sound symbols and key words. They show how to pronounce words. Use the pronunciation key on the inside back cover of this book to write the words that match these pronunciations.

1. /tre′ zher/ treasure
2. /sī′ en tist/ scientist
3. /rē sôr′ sez/ resources
4. /əth′ er/ other

85

Page 87

Vocabulary Skills

Write the words from the passage that have the meanings below.

1. to uncover something by digging
   excavate

2. a journey for a specific purpose
   expedition

3. placed something in position
   installed

4. things created by humans during a certain period of history
   artifacts

5. to protect something for the future
   preserve

In each row, circle the word that does not belong.

6. (explore) preserve protect save
7. expedition (hull) trip journey
8. history artifact (sailed) archaeologist

Find the compound words from the selection that contain the words below.

9. water underwater
10. thing everything
11. for forever

Reading Skills

1. How did the cofferdam make the work of the archaeologists easier?
   It allowed them to work in a dry area instead of deep underwater.

2. Why were the archaeologists pleased that a layer of mud covered the bottom of the boat?
   It helped preserve things.

3. Name three things that were found in the wreckage of the *Belle*.
   Answers will vary.

4. Where were the four boats in the French expedition supposed to be headed?
   the mouth of the Mississippi River

Write **T** before the sentences that are true. Write **F** before the sentences that are false.

5. F The *Belle* sank in 1656.
6. T The explorer La Salle led the French expedition.
7. F The *Belle* was an Italian ship.
8. F Almost everything in the wreckage of the boat had decayed and was no longer recognizable.
9. T A marine archaeologist discovered the wreckage of the *Belle*.

Study Skills

Write the number of the encyclopedia volume that would have the most information for each of these topics.

1. 5 La Salle
2. 9 shipwrecks
3. 1 archaeology
4. 6 Mississippi River

87

Page 89

Vocabulary Skills

Write the words from the passage that have the meanings below.

1. having great weight or meaning
   substantial

2. native; having always lived in a certain area
   indigenous

3. acknowledgment
   recognition

4. enlisted or enrolled new members
   recruited

5. took part in a rebellion against a leader
   mutinied

Circle the homophone that correctly completes each sentence below.

6. For some time, La Salle worked as a fur _____ trader. (fir (fur))

7. La Salle was the first to _____ sail the Great Lakes. ((sail) sale)

8. It took about _____ four years for La Salle to realize that he had not landed at the mouth of the Mississippi. ((four) for)

Underline the word with a prefix in each sentence. Then, write the meaning of the word on the line.

9. La Salle hoped that some friends could help him relocate the colony.
   locate again

10. Midway through his last journey, La Salle was killed.
    the middle part of the way

Reading Skills

1. Check the words that best describe La Salle.
   ✓ adventurous
   ____ unfriendly
   ✓ courageous
   ____ funny
   ✓ determined

Read the sentences below. If the event described happened before La Salle returned to France in 1683, write **B** on the line. If it happened after, write **A**.

2. A La Salle and his crew landed at Matagorda Bay.
3. B La Salle established himself as a fur trader.
4. A La Salle was killed when his men mutinied.
5. B La Salle named Louisiana after King Louis XIV.

6. Where was La Salle when he thought he had reached the mouth of the Mississippi?
   Matagorda Bay in Texas

7. What was the name of the first ship to sail the Great Lakes?
   Le Griffon

8. How did the state of Louisiana get its name?
   La Salle named the region Louisiana after King Louis XIV of France.

9. What group of people used the Mississippi for many years before the European explorers arrived?
   the indigenous people of the area or Native Americans

89

Answer Key

Page 91

Vocabulary Skills

Circle the homophone that correctly completes each sentence below.

1. Zookeepers have to work in all kinds of __weather__. (whether, (weather))
2. Annette finished cleaning the __bear's__ cage at two o'clock. ((bear's,) bare's)
3. The zookeeper __threw__ some meat to the lions. (through, (threw))

Write **S** if the possessive word is singular. Write **P** if it is plural.

4. __P__ zookeepers' duties
5. __S__ Miki's questions
6. __S__ Annette's opinion
7. __P__ animals' behavior

Reading Skills

Mark each sentence below **F** if it is in first-person point of view and **T** if it is in third-person point of view.

1. __T__ Annette enjoys her job.
2. __F__ I have to remind myself that the zoo animals are still wild creatures.
3. __T__ Takashi thinks Miki should start changing the litter box at home.
4. __F__ I would love having a job where I could work with animals every day.
5. Do you think Miki will continue to look for more information about becoming a zookeeper? Why or why not?
   __Answers will vary.__

6. On the lines below, write one sentence from the story that shows that Miki might enjoy a job as a zookeeper.
   __Possible answer: I don't think I'd__
   __ever get tired of seeing the animals.__
7. Why does Mr. Yamamoto tell Miki she should talk to the zookeeper?
   __so Miki can learn more about__
   __what it's like to be a zookeeper.__
8. Why don't zookeepers usually teach the zoo animals to do tricks?
   __They don't want the animals to__
   __do tricks just to entertain people.__

Study Skills

Use the information below to answer the questions that follow.

Green Valley Zoo

Hours of Operation

Monday	Closed
Tuesday–Friday	10–6
Saturday	9–6
Sunday	12–5

Admission:

Adults	$8
Children 3–12	$4
Children under 3	Free

1. Which day of the week is the zoo closed?
   __Monday__
2. What are the zoo's hours on Sunday?
   __12–5__
3. How much is admission for one adult and one 10-year-old child?
   __$12__

91

Page 93

Vocabulary Skills

Write the words from the selection that are homophones for the words below.

1. pear __pair__
2. billed __build__
3. paste __paced__
4. fourth __forth__

The suffix **-ness** means *the condition or quality of being*. For example, *lateness* means the *condition or quality of being late*. Write a word to match each definition below. Then, write a sentence using each word.

5. the condition or quality of being gentle
   __gentleness__
   __Answers will vary.__
6. the condition or quality of being tender
   __tenderness__
   __Answers will vary.__
7. the condition or quality of being kind
   __kindness__
   __Answers will vary.__

Reading Skills

1. What do Muschi and Maeuschen mean?
   __Muschi means pussycat and__
   __Maeuschen means little mouse.__
2. What is humorous about the names Muschi and Maeuschen?
   __Maeuschen is a large bear, not a__
   __small mouse. Also, cats and__
   __mice are not known for being__
   __friends.__

3. Why were Muschi and Maeuschen separated?
   __The zoo was building a new,__
   __larger cage for Maeuschen.__
4. How did Francine Patterson and Koko communicate with one another?
   __using American Sign Language__
5. How did Koko treat All Ball?
   __with gentleness and tenderness__
6. Check the sentence that best states the main idea of the selection.
   ____ Koko showed a great deal of interest in stories about cats.
   __✓__ Some animals can occasionally form strong friendships with animals from other species.
   ____ Muschi and Maeuschen live at the Berlin Zoo in Berlin, Germany.

Study Skills

Write the name of the reference source you could use to answer each question below.

encyclopedia	dictionary
atlas	

1. What are the eating habits of the Asiatic black bear?
   __encyclopedia__
2. Where is Berlin, Germany?
   __atlas__
3. How would you divide the word *temporary* into syllables?
   __dictionary__

93

Page 95

Vocabulary Skills

Find an antonym in the passage for each of the words below.

1. dull __sharp__
2. clumsy __agile__
3. thin __thick__
4. hard __soft__

Write **S** if the possessive word is singular. Write **P** if it is plural.

5. __S__ the breed's characteristics
6. __P__ cats' muscles
7. __S__ Russian blue's fur
8. __P__ humans' bones

Reading Skills

Circle the word that best completes each sentence below.

1. Cats use their tails for __balance__. running ((balance)) protection
2. There are many __variations__ in the colors and patterns of cats' fur. characteristics coats ((variations))
3. Some people think that cats are __independent__ creatures. ((independent)) wild lonely
4. Name two ways in which domestic cats and wild cats are similar.
   __Possible answers: Both types of cats__
   __have claws they can retract, sharp__
   __senses of hearing and smell,__
   __excellent night vision, and muscular__
   __and flexible bodies.__

5. How is the Manx cat different from other cats?
   __It has a very small stub of a tail__
   __or no tail at all and its front legs__
   __are shorter than its back legs.__
6. What is the legend surrounding the name of the Maine coon cat?
   __According to legend, it is part__
   __raccoon.__
7. In paragraph 8, what is the author trying to persuade the reader of?
   __to adopt a cat from a shelter__
   __instead of buying a purebred cat__
8. On the lines below, write a summary sentence for paragraph 8.
   __Adopting a cat from a shelter is__
   __a good idea because there are__
   __many homeless cats.__

Study Skills

Write the part of a book you would use to find the information to answer each question below.

table of contents	glossary
index	

1. On what page does chapter 7 begin?
   __table of contents__
2. How is the word *Persian* pronounced?
   __glossary__
3. On what page could you find information about litter box training?
   __index__
4. Does the book include a chapter about choosing the right cat for your lifestyle?
   __table of contents__

95

Page 97

Vocabulary Skills

Write the words from the passage that have the meanings below.

1. ways that something can be viewed
   __aspects__
2. enjoyed; was thankful for
   __appreciated__
3. facts that help one come to a conclusion
   __evidence__
4. bring back
   __retrieve__
5. representing or standing for
   __depicting__

Circle the pair of synonyms in each set of words below.

6. encourage control (grateful) (appreciative)
7. ancient (importance) statue (significance)
8. rewarding (smart) (intelligent) sculpture

The nouns below have base words that are verbs. Fill in the blanks to show the verb and suffix that combine to form each noun.

Noun	Verb	Suffix
9. replacement	replace	ment
10. breakable	break	able
11. enjoyment	enjoy	ment
12. washable	wash	able
13. arrangement	arrange	ment

Reading Skills

Write **F** before the sentences that are facts. Write **O** before the sentences that are opinions.

1. __O__ Cats are excellent companions.
2. __F__ Ancient Egyptians appreciated that cats kept the number of rodents under control.
3. __O__ The artwork on the inside of Egyptian tombs is beautiful.
4. __F__ Archaeologists have found mummified cats in Egyptian tombs.
5. __F__ The Egyptian goddess Bast is often shown to have the body of a woman and the head of a cat.
6. Why did the ancient Egyptians first form relationships with cats?
   __Wild cats were helping the Egyptians__
   __by keeping animals like mice and rats__
   __away from their supplies of grain.__
7. How have archaeologists learned so much about cats and the ancient Egyptians?
   __through clues that have been found__
   __in the tombs of Egyptians and in__
   __Egyptian artwork__

Study Skills

Read the dictionary entry below and answer the questions that follow.

companion /kəm pan′ yən/ *n.* a friend; one that keeps another company

1. What part of speech is *companion*?
   __a noun__
2. On the line below, write the word *companion* with slash marks to show where the syllable breaks are.
   __com/pan/ion__
3. Which syllable is stressed in *companion*?
   __the second syllable__

97

Answer Key

Page 99

Vocabulary Skills

Write the words from the story that have the meanings below.

1. stretched out; made longer
   extended

2. something that makes sense
   logical

3. started again; continued
   resumed

4. important; meaningful
   significant

5. effect
   impact

Circle the homophone that correctly completes each sentence below.

6. The popcorn bowl was made of _____. (**metal**, meddle)

7. Several popcorn **kernels** fell in between the couch cushions. (colonels, **kernels**)

Check the sentence in which *case* has the same meaning as it does in paragraph 7.

8. **✓** The attorney won her case with almost no difficulty.

   _____ Please stop at the store for a case of bottled water.

In each row, circle the word that does not belong.

9. inquire   investigate   explore   (**incredible**)

10. discover   (**resume**)   find   locate

11. (**tomorrow**)   yawn   sleep   tired

Reading Skills

1. Is the part of the story in which Sam is being interviewed fantasy or reality? How can you tell?

   It is fantasy. Possible answers: He is an adult. He is in Egypt. He has made an important discovery in the pyramids. His father wakes him up from a dream.

2. What is something that Sam and his dad have in common?

   They are both interested in archaeology and Egyptian pyramids.

3. Why does Sam say that his dad deserves part of the credit for his discovery?

   because his dad was supportive and encouraged his interest

4. In Sam's dream, who grants him permission to explore the hidden room?

   the Egyptian Supreme Council of Antiquities

5. Do you think that Sam and his dad will actually travel to Egypt one day? Explain your answer.

   Answers will vary.

Study Skills

Check each word that could be found on a page having the guide words shown in dark print.

1. **sunshine—surgeon**
   _____ sunflower   **✓** suppose
   ✓ surfboard

2. **paddle—pamphlet**
   ✓ palate   _____ pancake
   _____ papaya

3. **frustrate—furnish**
   ✓ fumble   _____ frog   **✓** funnel

99

Page 101

Vocabulary Skills

1. Check the sentence in which *face* has the same meaning as it does in paragraph 4.

   ✓ If you face our house, the driveway will be on your right.

   _____ Chris had a big smile on his face when Kimm walked in the door.

2. Check the sentence in which *cranes* has the same meaning as it does in paragraph 6.

   _____ Aunt Sheryl and Lilly used a bird guide to identify the cranes they saw.

   ✓ There were three large cranes at the construction site.

Underline the word with a suffix in each sentence. Then, write the meaning of the word on the line.

3. The Egyptologist was amazed at the size of the pyramids.

   someone who studies ancient Egypt

4. People did not know whether the mystery of the pyramids would be solvable.

   able to be solved

5. Some people were doubtful that the Egyptians could have built the pyramids without cranes and trucks.

   full of doubt

Reading Skills

1. Why is the Great Pyramid only 450 feet tall today when it was originally 480 feet tall?

   because of erosion

2. About how much does the Great Pyramid weigh?

   8 million tons

3. How do scholars think the ancient Egyptians moved the stones they used to make the pyramids?

   with sleds and ramps

4. Who were the pharaohs of ancient Egypt?

   the rulers of ancient Egyptian kingdoms

5. What conclusion can you come to using the information that the sides of the pyramids faced exactly north, east, south, and west?

   that the ancient Egyptians had some way of determining direction

6. Check the phrase that best describes the author's purpose.

   ✓ to inform
   _____ to persuade
   _____ to entertain

Study Skills

Egyptian Pyramid Statistics

Pharaoh	Location	Height (ft.)
Userkaf	Saqqara	161
Khufu	Giza	480
Menkaure	Giza	213
Sahure	Abusir	154

1. For which pharaoh was the pyramid in Abusir built?

   Sahure

2. How tall is the pyramid in Saqqara?

   161 feet

3. Which two pyramids are closest in height?

   Userkaf and Sahure

4. Which two pyramids are located in the same place?

   Khufu and Menkaure

101

Page 103

Vocabulary Skills

Write the words from the story that have the meanings below.

1. a machine that contracts or presses together to push out air or gases
   compressor

2. no longer in use
   obsolete

Check the meaning of the underlined word in each sentence.

3. Grandpa showed Finn what was located under the minivan's hood.

   ✓ a piece of metal on hinges that covers the engine of a vehicle

   _____ a cloth covering for the head, usually attached to a jacket or sweater

4. Grandpa said that the kind of car he owned was called a minivan.

   _____ nice; thoughtful
   ✓ type or variety

Circle the homophone that correctly completes each sentence below.

5. Finn filled his pack with _____ air at the windstation. (heir, **air**)

6. The car companies **knew** that gasoline-powered cars were becoming outdated. (new, **knew**)

Fill in the blanks below with the possessive form of the word in parentheses.

7. **Finn's** dad is out of town. (Finn)

8. There is a picture of **Grandpa's** minivan on his photocard. (Grandpa)

9. The **windpacks'** advantage over cars is that they are cleaner and easier to maintain. (windpacks)

Reading Skills

1. Check the line beside the word or words that best describe what type of selection this is.

   ✓ science fiction
   _____ fable
   _____ informational

2. Is this story a fantasy or does it take place in reality? How can you tell?

   It is a fantasy. It contains things that do not exist.

3. What does Grandpa persuade Finn to change his mind about, and how does he do it?

   Grandpa persuades Finn to appreciate the benefits of windpacks. He explains how they are cleaner and easier to care for than cars.

4. Dialogue is what a character says. The words in dialogue are always in quotation marks. On the line below, write the words that are dialogue in paragraph 13.

   "That's nearly 50 years ago!"

5. Name two elements of the story that tell you the story takes place in the future.

   Answers will vary.

6. When was the picture with Grandpa and his minivan taken?

   2025

103

Page 105

Vocabulary Skills

Write the words from the passage that have the meanings below.

1. more than enough; plentiful
   abundant

2. controlling and putting to work
   harnessing

3. machine that changes energy from one form into another
   generators

4. exact
   precise

5. far away and hard to access
   remote

In each row, circle the word that does not belong.

6. power   energy   (**farm**)   electricity

7. turn   (**locate**)   rotate   spin

8. (**produced**)   concerned   worried   nervous

9. One word in paragraph 5 contains both a prefix and a suffix. Write the word and its meaning on the line below.

   renewable; capable of being made new again

Reading Skills

1. Why are windmill farms built?

   to create large amounts of energy

2. What is another name for windmills?

   wind turbines

3. Name two types of fossil fuels.

   coal and gas

4. What is one way in which fossil fuels and wind power are different?

   Possible answers: There is an endless supply of wind, and wind power is cleaner.

5. Why are open plains, the ocean, and mountains all good places for windmills?

   They are the windiest places.

6. On the lines below, write a short sentence that is a summary of paragraph 3.

   Possible answer: Wind power allowed people in remote areas to have electricity when it was still new.

Circle the word that best completes each sentence.

7. By the 1940s, electricity was _____ to people in most parts of the country.

   removed   donated   (**available**)

8. One advantage to wind power is that it does not create _____ pollution.

   noise   (**pollution**)   energy

Study Skills

Use a dictionary to help you divide these words into syllables.

1. h i/s t o r/i/a n

2. e/l e c/t r i c/i/t y

3. m a/c h i/n e/r y

4. g e n/e/r a/t o r

5. Number the words below in alphabetical order.

   3 windshield
   2 window
   1 windmill
   4 windstorm

105

Answer Key

Page 107

Vocabulary Skills

Write the words from the passage that have the meanings below.

1. not required
   optional _(materials list)_

2. a v-shaped cut
   notch _(Step 1)_

3. parallel to, or level with, the horizon
   horizontal _(Step 2)_

4. the point where two things meet
   intersection _(Step 4)_

5. an amount greater than needed
   excess _(Step 5)_

6. Check the sentence in which *form* has the same meaning as it does in step 4.
   _____ You must fill out this form to enroll in the program.
   _✓_ Form a ball with the dough in your hands.

7. Check the sentence in which *thread* has the same meaning as it does in step 5.
   _____ I bought some yellow thread to match the sweater I was trying to mend.
   _✓_ Thread the cord through the opening in the back of the TV stand.

Circle the homophone that correctly completes each sentence below.

8. The kitten's _____ tail _____ was almost caught in the door. (tale / (tail))

9. The morning after the race, all my muscles were _____ sore _____ ((sore) / soar)

Reading Skills

1. Where can you find the heavyweight paper to make your kite?
   at a crafts store

2. Name two optional materials you can use to decorate your kite.
   Answers will vary.

3. For which task will you need the help of a parent or other adult?
   to cut the notches in the dowel rods

4. How much larger than the kite frame should your piece of paper be?
   2 inches all the way around

5. Check the line beside the word or words that best describe what type of selection this is.
   _____ fiction
   _✓_ how-to
   _____ persuasive

Study Skills

Use the facts from step 5 to complete Part I of the outline below.

I. Make the kite frame
   A. thread fishing line through notches
   B. thread it through again
   C. make a few more loops around the X
   D. knot the line and cut off excess

107

Page 109

Vocabulary Skills

Write the words from the story that have the meanings below.

1. remembering; fondly looking back on old times
   reminiscing _(Par. 1)_

2. moving with ease and beauty
   graceful _(Par. 2)_

3. having a sharp, high-pitched sound
   shrill _(Par. 5)_

4. moving forcefully or vigorously
   churning _(Par. 6)_

5. Find the simile in paragraph 5, and write it on the line below.
   Your uncle sinks like a rock.

6. What two things were compared to each other in number 5?
   uncle   rock

7. Choose one of the answers to number 6, and use it to create your own simile on the lines below.
   Answers will vary.

Write a compound word using two words in each sentence.

8. Molly sat in the seat that was in the back of the station wagon.
   backseat

9. Molly's mom could view her in the mirror that showed the rear of the car.
   rearview

Reading Skills

Read the sentences below. Write **B** next to the sentence if it happened before Molly dove into the water. Write **A** if it happened after.

1. _B_ Uncle Connor told Molly that her mom was a graceful swimmer.

2. _A_ Molly grabbed her towel from the bench.

3. _A_ Molly's mom and uncle were each holding up a single finger in the air.

4. _B_ Molly's mom gave her a kiss on the top of her head.

5. _B_ Molly heard the whistle blow.

6. On the lines below, write a short sentence that states the main idea of the story.
   Answers will vary.

7. Do you think Molly will swim in future meets? Why?
   Answers will vary.

Study Skills

Use the pronunciation key on the inside back cover of this book to write the words that match these pronunciations.

1. /grās' fəl/ graceful
2. /laf' fing/ laughing
3. /skül/ school
4. /dô' ter/ daughter

109

Page 111

Vocabulary Skills

Circle the homophone that correctly completes each sentence below.

1. Gertrude Ederle _____ won _____ several medals in the 1924 Olympics. ((won) / one)

2. Ederle played a _____ role _____ in a movie about her life. (roll / (role))

3. Ederle worked very hard to accomplish the _____ feat _____ of swimming the English Channel. ((feat) / feet)

Write the idiom from paragraph 7 on the line next to its meaning.

4. earned a part   landed a role

Find the compound words from the selection that contain the words below.

5. free _____ freestyle _____ _(Par. 2)_
6. side _____ alongside _____ _(Par. 2)_
7. fish _____ jellyfish _____ _(Par. 5)_

Reading Skills

1. Check the line beside the word or words that best describe what type of selection this is.
   _____ historical fiction
   _✓_ biography
   _____ myth

2. Check the words that describe Gertrude Ederle.
   _____ artistic   _____ nosy
   _✓_ courageous   _✓_ athletic
   _✓_ determined   _____ talkative

3. Find a phrase in the selection that shows the author admires Gertrude Ederle. Write it on the lines below.
   Answers will vary.

4. Why was Ederle disqualified the first time she tried to swim the English Channel?
   Her trainer reached out to help her because she was coughing.

5. What are two dangers of swimming the English Channel?
   Answers will vary.

Study Skills

Write the name of the reference source you could use to answer each question below.

| encyclopedia | dictionary |
| atlas | thesaurus |

1. Where is the English Channel located?
   atlas

2. What is the plural form of *Portuguese man-of-war*?
   dictionary

3. How did Ederle get her start in swimming?
   encyclopedia

4. What happens if you get stung by a jellyfish?
   encyclopedia

5. What is another word for *determined*?
   thesaurus

111

Page 113

Vocabulary Skills

Write the words from the passage that have the meanings below.

1. high aboveground
   aloft _(Par. 1)_

2. easily burned or set fire to
   flammable _(Par. 4)_

3. causing death
   fatal _(Par. 4)_

4. went along with
   accompanied _(Par. 5)_

5. alone; by oneself
   solo _(Par. 7)_

Read each word below. Then, write the letter of its synonym on the line beside the word.

6. _d_ enormous   a. effort
7. _a_ attempt   b. trip
8. _c_ disaster   c. tragedy
9. _b_ journey   d. gigantic

Reading Skills

1. Check the phrase that best describes the author's purpose.
   _____ to entertain
   _✓_ to explain the history of hot air balloons
   _____ to persuade the reader to try traveling by hot air balloon

2. Who were the three passengers in the first hot air balloon trip?
   a sheep, a duck, and a rooster

3. What was Steve Fossett's accomplishment?
   He became the first balloonist to fly solo around the world.

4. Why is hot air used in the balloons?
   It is lighter than the air outside the balloon.

5. Between which two states did the first example of airmail travel?
   Pennsylvania and New Jersey

6. Why do you think people were so excited by the Montgolfier brothers' accomplishment?
   because it was the first time they saw that people might be able to fly one day

Study Skills

A library's reference system can help you find a book. Use the information below to answer the questions that follow.

Call No:	881.37 MO
Author:	Morales, Elia
Title:	Up, Up, and Away: Hot Air Ballooning Through the Years
Publisher:	Caswell & Fitz Publishing, 1999

1. What is the author's last name?
   Morales

2. What year was the book published?
   1999

3. Which book would be located closer to the book with the call number above—the book with call number 881.37 RE or the book with call number 879.38 MA?
   the book with call number 881.37 RE

113

Answer Key

Page 115

Vocabulary Skills

Write the words from the story that have the meanings below.

1. the older people in a group who are wise and well-respected

   elders

2. unhappiness; dissatisfaction

   discontent

3. cost

   expense

4. celebrating a success or victory

   triumphantly

5. as though waiting for something to happen

   expectantly

Fill in the blanks below with the possessive form of the word in parentheses.

6. The town elders decided to call a meeting to address the ___citizens'___ unhappiness. (citizens)

7. The ___elders'___ decision was to capture the moon in a bucket. (elders)

8. The ___moon's___ light belongs to everyone. (moon)

Reading Skills

1. Check the line beside the word or words that best describe what type of selection this is.

   ___✓___ folktale

   _____ historical fiction

   _____ informational

2. What problem did the people of Chelm have in the story?

   They had difficulty seeing at night when there wasn't a full moon.

3. Why didn't the elders want to place oil lamps on the streets?

   It was too expensive.

4. Why was it becoming dark earlier?

   The seasons were changing.

5. Were the village elders wiser than the townspeople in the story? Explain.

   Answers will vary.

6. If you had been one of the townspeople, how would you have explained why the plan to capture the moon wouldn't work?

   Answers will vary.

Write **F** before the sentences that are facts. Write **O** before the sentences that are opinions.

7. ___F___ The townspeople were unhappy that they couldn't see well at night.

8. ___O___ The elders were smarter than the townspeople.

Study Skills

Check each word that could be found on a dictionary page having the guide words shown in dark print.

1. **antibody—appeal**

   ___✓___ antonym   ___✓___ antler

   _____ approval

2. **confess—construct**

   _____ conductor   ___✓___ confetti

   ___✓___ congratulate

3. **knead—koala**

   _____ kitchen   ___✓___ knight

   ___✓___ knuckle

115

Page 117

Vocabulary Skills

Write the words from the passage that have the meanings below.

1. different stages

   phases

2. kept from happening

   prevented

3. for only a brief period of time

   temporarily

4. a discussion in which there are different points of view

   debate

5. information that helps one come to a conclusion

   evidence

Circle the homophone that correctly completes each sentence below.

6. A new moon occurs when the moon and the sun are on the same ___side___ of Earth. (sighed, (side))

7. The moon is ___made___ of the same materials as Earth. ((made,) maid)

8. The light from the sun ___shone___ on the moon. (shown, (shone))

The prefix **un-** means *not* or *opposite of*. For example, *unfriendly* means *not friendly*. Add **un** to each word below. Then, use each new word in a sentence.

9. interested   uninterested

   Answers will vary.

10. prepared   unprepared

   Answers will vary.

11. lock   unlock

   Answers will vary.

Reading Skills

1. What is one way that a lunar eclipse and a solar eclipse are similar?

   They both occur when the sun, the moon, and Earth are in a line.

2. What is one way that a lunar eclipse and a solar eclipse are different?

   Answers will vary.

3. Why are there different phases of the moon?

   because the sun, the moon, and Earth are always moving

Write **T** before the sentences that are true. Write **F** before the sentences that are false.

4. ___T___ Some scientists believe the moon was once part of Earth.

5. ___F___ A solar eclipse is the only time the sun's light is prevented from reaching the moon.

6. ___T___ During an eclipse, the sun, the moon, and Earth are in a straight line.

7. ___T___ A solar eclipse is more common than a lunar eclipse.

Study Skills

Number the words below in alphabetical order.

1. ___2___ moonlight   2. ___4___ lunch

   ___4___ moose   ___2___ luna moth

   ___3___ moonscape   ___1___ luminous

   ___1___ moody   ___3___ lunar

117

Page 119

Vocabulary Skills

Write the words from the story that have the meanings below.

1. a line that goes around the outer edge of something

   outline

2. coming out of; appearing

   emerging

3. lit up

   illuminated

4. holding as if in a cradle

   cradling

5. begged

   pleaded

Find the simile in paragraph 10, and write it on the line below.

6. Her tongue is as rough as sandpaper.

Read each pair of words listed below. If the words are synonyms, write **S** on the line. If the words are antonyms, write **A** on the line.

7. ___A___ whispered   yelled

8. ___A___ bright   dim

9. ___S___ stroking   petting

Reading Skills

Mark each sentence below **F** if it is in first-person point of view and **T** if it is in third-person point of view.

1. ___T___ The kitten's face was illuminated by the light of the moon.

2. ___F___ I hope we get to keep the kitten.

3. ___F___ I heard a mewing sound coming from the bushes.

4. ___T___ Nita unzipped the door of the tent.

5. Where were Pablo and Nita camping?

   in their backyard

6. What did Pablo and Nita's parents say they had to do before they could keep the kitten?

   find out if she belongs to anyone

7. Why does Nita want to name the kitten Luna?

   They found her by the light of the moon.

Study Skills

Use the information on the poster below to answer the questions that follow.

> ### FOUND
> **Black-and-white kitten, about 9 weeks old**
> Has black tail with white tip and all black paws
> Found on Bentley Street on the evening of June 18
> Please call 555-4791 if you have any information.

1. About how old is the kitten?

   about 9 weeks old

2. What number should people call if they have any information about the kitten?

   555-4791

3. What is the date on which the kitten was found?

   June 18

119

Page 121

Vocabulary Skills

1. Check the sentence in which *steer* has the same meaning as it does in paragraph 4.

   _____ The steer charged toward the gate, but the rancher closed it in time.

   ___✓___ It is hard to steer the car when it is so windy outside.

2. Check the sentence in which *craft* has the same meaning as it does in paragraph 4.

   ___✓___ It is dangerous for a small craft to be out on the ocean during a storm.

   _____ We were allowed to take our craft projects home at the end of the day.

Fill in the blanks below with the possessive form of the word in parentheses.

3. People were worried about the ___Eagle's___ fuel level. (*Eagle*)

4. The ___astronauts'___ goal was to land on the moon. (astronauts)

5. ___NASA's___ Apollo program was a success! (NASA)

Reading Skills

1. Check the words that describe Neil Armstrong.

   _____ shy

   ___✓___ courageous

   ___✓___ ambitious

   _____ funny

   ___✓___ strong-willed

2. Number the events below to show the order in which they happened.

   ___3___ Armstrong and Aldrin entered the *Eagle*.

   ___2___ The *Columbia* spacecraft was launched from the Kennedy Space Center.

   ___5___ Armstrong and Aldrin planted a flag on the moon.

   ___4___ Armstrong steered the *Eagle* to a less-rocky surface.

   ___1___ President Kennedy said the United States would land a human being on the moon by the end of the decade.

3. What were Armstrong's first words on the moon?

   "That's one small step for man, one giant leap for mankind."

4. What do you think Armstrong meant when he said this?

   Armstrong was physically taking a single step onto the planet, but what he was doing was important for all humans.

Study Skills

Write the name of the reference source you could use to find the information to answer each question below.

| thesaurus | encyclopedia |
| dictionary | atlas |

1. Where is Cape Canaveral, Florida?

   atlas

2. What is a synonym for *courageous*?

   thesaurus

3. What does the word *lunar* mean?

   dictionary

4. What sort of space program did the Soviet Union have in the 1960s?

   encyclopedia

121

Answer Key

Page 123

Vocabulary Skills

Write the words from the story that have the meanings below.

1. to cause something to happen at a later time
   delay

2. made hard to see
   obscured

3. wide open
   gaping

Write the idiom from paragraph 1 on the line next to its meaning.

4. to be unable to identify something or figure it out
   couldn't put his finger on it

Read each word below. Then, write the letter of its synonym on the line beside the word.

5. __h__ appeared   a. almost
6. __d__ unsafe   b. seemed
7. __a__ nearly   c. destroyed
8. __c__ demolished   d. dangerous

Find the compound words from the selection that contain the words below.

9. fast   breakfast
10. hoe   backhoe

Reading Skills

1. Check the phrase that best describes the author's purpose.
   ___ to instruct
   ___ to explain
   _✓_ to entertain

Read the sentences below. Write **B** next to the sentence if it describes something that happened before Daniel went outside. Write **A** if it describes something that happened after.

2. __A__ Daniel was glad his chestnut tree hadn't been damaged.
3. __B__ Daniel drank his orange juice.
4. __A__ Something caught Daniel's eye.
5. __A__ Mrs. Ivanovic said that Daniel was observant.
6. __B__ Mrs. Ivanovic explained why the construction crew wasn't working.
7. Do you think Daniel will be able to identify the fossil he found? Explain your answer.
   Answers will vary.

Study Skills

Use the table of contents below to answer the questions.

Table of Contents

1. What is the title of Chapter 3?
   Storing and Caring for Your Fossils

2. Which chapter contains information on identifying fossils?
   Chapter 2

3. What page would you turn to for information on buying fossils?
   53

123

Page 125

Vocabulary Skills

Write the words from the passage that have the meanings below.

1. scientists who study prehistoric life
   paleontologists

2. an exact copy
   replica

3. melt
   thaw

4. liquid that flows through plants
   sap

Circle the homophone that correctly completes each sentence below.

5. Have you ever ___seen___ a fossil before? (scene (seen))

6. Scientists were able to determine the mammoths' diet ___based___ on the contents of their stomachs. (baste (based))

Reading Skills

1. Where can you find a good example of petrified wood?
   in Petrified Forest National Park in eastern Arizona.

2. Why is it so valuable for scientists to find animals that have been preserved in ice?
   Scientists can gather information they don't usually have access to.

3. Name two types of animals that have been found in the La Brea Tar Pits.
   Answers will vary.

4. How do insects or small animals become preserved in amber?
   They become caught in the sap of certain trees and cannot free themselves.

5. Why is the work of paleontologists important?
   They bring us closer to understanding the history of the natural world.

6. On the lines below, write a summary of paragraph 5.
   Animals caught in organic material are often well preserved.

7. What is one way that plants and animals trapped in amber are similar to those trapped in ice?
   Possible answer: Parts of the animals that usually decompose are preserved.

Circle the word that best completes each sentence.

8. The soft parts of a plant or an animal usually ___decompose___.
   harden (decompose) uncover

9. In petrified wood, the soft tissues have been ___replaced___ by minerals.
   determined trapped (replaced)

Study Skills

Use the pronunciation key on the inside back cover of this book to write the words that match these pronunciations.

1. /fō′ tə graf′/ photograph
2. /krē′ vis/ crevice
3. /bē nēth′/ beneath
4. /ser′ tən/ certain
5. /fā məs/ famous

125

Page 127

Vocabulary Skills

Write the words from the passage that have the meanings below.

1. to give or help bring about
   contribute

2. understanding of others' feelings
   sympathetic

3. the state of being poor; having little wealth
   poverty

4. uncertain or doubtful
   hesitant

In each row, circle the word that does not belong.

5. collect collector (discovery) collection
6. recognize (society) accept acknowledge
7. (remember) rare uncommon unusual

Reading Skills

1. Check the words that describe Mary Anning.
   _✓_ determined   _✓_ scientific
   _✓_ intelligent   ___ suspicious
   ___ outgoing

2. Check the word that best describes what type of selection this is.
   ___ fiction
   ___ legend
   _✓_ biography

3. Check the sentence that best states the main idea of the selection.
   ___ Mary Anning's father died while she was still a child, and she and her brother helped support the family.
   _✓_ Mary Anning was a fossil hunter from the 1800s whose contributions are still recognized today.
   ___ Mary Anning lived near the cliffs at Lyme Regis in Great Britain.

4. Who bought the fossils that Mary and her brother found?
   local collectors and tourists

Study Skills

Use the time line below to answer the questions that follow.

Mary Anning born — Mr. Anning died — Mary discovered Plesiosaur skeleton — Mary discovered Pterodactyl skeleton — Mary died
1800 1810 1820 1830 1840 1850

1. In what year did Mr. Anning die?
   1810

2. What happened in 1828?
   Mary discovered a pterodactyl skeleton.

3. How many years passed between Mary's discovery of the Plesiosaur and the Pterodactyl?

127

Page 129

Vocabulary Skills

Check the meaning of the underlined word in each sentence.

1. Jamila shifted her bike into second gear.
   ___ equipment used for a specific activity
   _✓_ a mechanism that affects speed in a car or bicycle

2. Jamila wanted to train to ride in the fundraiser.
   _✓_ to practice and get into shape
   ___ a string of railroad cars

Compound words are divided into syllables between the two words that make the compound. For example, play/ground. Divide the words below into syllables using a slash (/).

3. s k a t e/b o a r d
4. b i r t h/d a y
5. g r a n d/p a r/e n t
6. f u n d/r a i s/e r
7. a f/t e r/n o o n
8. f l o w/e r/b e d

Reading Skills

1. Check the phrase that best describes the author's purpose.
   _✓_ to entertain
   ___ to instruct
   ___ to explain

2. What problem does Jamila have at the beginning of the story?
   She doesn't have enough money to buy the bike she wants to train for a fundraiser.

3. How does Tyler help her solve the problem?
   He suggests that she can earn money by doing chores for her parents.

4. Why does Mrs. Johnson like Tyler's idea?
   Answers will vary.

Write **F** before the sentences that are facts. Write **O** before the sentences that are opinions.

5. __F__ Jamila wants to buy a new bike.
6. __F__ Jamila helps her mom weed the garden.
7. __O__ Tyler is a creative thinker.
8. __F__ Tyler hopes that Jamila and her mother will make cookies.
9. __O__ Jamila's parents should buy the bike for her.

Study Skills

Use the information below to answer the questions that follow.

Chores	Time Spent
Paint garage door	2 hours
Wrap presents	1 hour
Weed flowerbeds	1.5 hours
Clean attic	3 hours
Sort recycling	1.5 hours

1. How long did it take Jamila to weed the flowerbeds?
   1.5 hours

2. Which chore took Jamila the longest amount of time?
   cleaning the attic

3. If Jamila earns three dollars an hour, how much money did she make painting the garage door?
   six dollars

129

Answer Key

Page 131

Vocabulary Skills

Write the words from the passage that have the meanings below.

1. a country's form of money
   currency
2. one of the parts into which something is divided
   division
3. the passage of something from person to person or place to place
   circulation
4. copy; reproduce
   duplicate
5. outsmart or be more clever than someone
   outwit

Find an antonym in the selection for each of the words below.

6. new — worn
7. easier — harder
8. invisible — visible
9. dim — bright

Circle the homophone that correctly completes each sentence below.

10. A ___worn___ bill will eventually be replaced. (worn, warn)
11. I received a crisp, ___new___ five-dollar bill from the bank. (knew, new)
12. A nickel is worth five ___cents___. (sense, cents)

Reading Skills

Write **T** before the sentences that are true. Write **F** before the sentences that are false.

1. __F__ On average, coins last about 50 years.
2. __T__ U.S. currency is printed on a special type of paper.
3. __F__ Today, all U.S. currency is printed in Washington, D.C.
4. __F__ Two-dollar bills have not been printed since 1946.
5. __T__ USA appears on the security thread of bills issued today.
6. What is one way in which a five dollar bill and 50-dollar bill are similar?
   Possible answer: They both contain a security thread.
7. What is one way in which they are different?
   Possible answer: the length of time they last
8. Why does advanced technology make it more of a challenge for the government to outwit counterfeiters?
   It is easier for people to make realistic-looking copies of money.
9. What are the seven denominations of bills?
   $1, $2, $5, $10, $20, $50, and $100
10. What is a watermark?
    a security mark that is visible when the bill is held up to bright light

131

Page 133

Vocabulary Skills

Read each word below. Then, write the letter of its synonym on the line beside the word.

1. __b__ watched   a. amazed
2. __d__ jumped   b. observed
3. __a__ surprised   c. buy
4. __c__ purchase   d. amazed

The suffix **-ment** means *the state or condition of being*. For example, *excitement* means *the state or condition of being excited*. Write a word using **ment** to match each definition below. Then, write a sentence using each word.

5. the state or condition of governing
   government
   Answers will vary.
6. the state or condition of placing
   placement
   Answers will vary.
7. the state or condition of being improved
   improvement
   Answers will vary.

Reading Skills

1. The **protagonist** is the main character in a story, or the person the story is mostly about. Who is the protagonist in this story?
   Jamila
2. What is Jamila saving her money to buy?
   a new bike
3. What is one reason that a savings account would be a good idea for Jamila?
   Answers will vary.
4. If Jamila left her money in a savings account for a year, would it earn more or less interest than if she left it there for two years?
   less

Mark each sentence below **F** if it is in first-person point of view and **T** if it is in third-person point of view.

5. __F__ The key to my piggybank doesn't work.
6. __T__ Jamila and her mother went to the bank to open a savings account.
7. __T__ The bank specialist smiled at Jamila.

Study Skills

Use the savings account form to answer the questions.

Savings Account Application		
last name	first name	middle initial
street address		
city	state	zip code
date of birth	parent's or guardian's name	

1. What are the first two pieces of information the application asks for on the third line?
   city and state
2. Whose name, other than your own, do you need to include on the application?
   a parent's or guardian's name
3. What other information should the form ask?
   Answers will vary.

133

Page 135

Vocabulary Skills

Write the words from the passage that have the meanings below.

1. a fun activity done in one's spare time
   hobby
2. putting money to use by buying something that will become more valuable in the future
   investment
3. a specific subject or topic
   theme
4. something that is rare or unusual
   rarity
5. value
   worth

Write a compound word using two words in each sentence.

6. Shells that are found near the sea are
   seashells
7. A small book that contains more than one match is a ___matchbook___.
8. Pots that are used to brew tea are
   teapots
9. A bank that is shaped like a piggy and used to store money is called a
   piggybank

Reading Skills

1. What is a numismatist?
   a coin collector
2. In the United States Mint's 50 State Quarters Program, how many new quarters are released every year?
   5

3. Name two reasons that people like to collect coins.
   Answers will vary.
4. How does the demand for a coin affect its value?
   The greater the demand, the more valuable the coin.
5. Where can you find more information about starting a coin collection?
   at the library or on the Web site of the United States Mint
6. Why do you think that serious collectors handle their valuable coins so carefully?
   so they don't damage them or cause them to become less valuable

Study Skills

United States Mint
50 State Quarters Program

State	Year Minted	# out of 50
Delaware	1999	1
Florida	2004	27
Kentucky	2001	5
Louisiana	2002	18
Missouri	2003	24

1. Which state's quarter was minted in 2002?
   Louisiana
2. In what year was Kentucky's quarter released?
   2001
3. Which state's quarter was the first released in the U.S. Mint's program?
   Delaware

135

Page 137

Vocabulary Skills

Read each sentence below. Then, write the word from the **ight** word family that best completes the sentence.

bright	sights	tonight	slight	right

1. Raj and Malcolm feel that they have made the ___right___ choice.
2. Raj would most like to see the ___sights___ in the Amazon.
3. Malcolm plans to take several books home with him ___tonight___.

Underline the word with a prefix or suffix in each sentence. Then, write the meaning of the word on the line.

4. Charles Darwin was a well-known naturalist from Great Britain.
   someone who studies nature
5. Malcolm suggests that he and Raj reread the assignment.
   read again
6. Malcolm shakes his head in amazement at all the different species of wildlife that live in the Galápagos Islands.
   the act of being amazed

Reading Skills

1. Do you think that Raj and Malcolm would choose to work on another project together in the future? Why or why not?
   Answers will vary.
2. Does this story take place in reality, or is it a fantasy?
   It takes place in reality.

3. What is one way in which the Galápagos Islands and the Amazon are similar?
   Answers will vary.
4. What is one way in which the Galápagos Islands and the Amazon are different?
   Possible answer: The Amazon has the largest rain forest in the world.
5. What does Raj find most interesting about the Amazon?
   Answers will vary.
6. What is the longest river in the world?
   the Nile
7. Check the words that describe Malcolm.
   ✓ enthusiastic   ✓ intelligent
   ___ lonely   ___ rude

Study Skills

1. Number the words below in alphabetical order.
   4 propose
   1 present
   3 proposal
   2 presentation

Check each word that could be found on a dictionary page having the guide words shown in dark print.

2. trestle—triplet
   ___ troll   ✓ trillion   ✓ tributary
3. mole—monsoon
   ✓ money   ___ modern
   ✓ monkey wrench

137

Answer Key

Page 139

Vocabulary Skills

Write the words from the passage that have the meanings below.

1. a light shade of a color
   tint *Par. 2*
2. very bright and strong
   vivid *Par. 2*
3. difference
   variation *Par. 3*
4. sets apart or makes different
   distinguishes *Par. 3*
5. blended or joined together
   fused *Par. 3*

Read each pair of words listed below. If the words are synonyms, write **S** on the line. If the words are antonyms, write **A** on the line.

6. _A_ stiff   flexible
7. _S_ safe   protected
8. _S_ worried   concerned
9. _A_ temporary   permanent

Fill in the blanks below with the possessive form of the word in parentheses.

10. Scientists are not sure why the
    botos' skin is pink. (botos)
11. The pink dolphin's nose is long and thin. (dolphin)
12. Botos can become tangled in
    fishermen's nets. (fishermen)

Reading Skills

1. Check the best summary for paragraph 5.
   ___ Myths and legends surround the pink dolphin.
   _✓_ Conservation groups have reason to be worried about pink dolphins.
   ___ Rivers where botos live are becoming more polluted.

Write **F** before the sentences that are facts. Write **O** before the sentences that are opinions.

2. _F_ More than 20 species of dolphins exist.
3. _O_ Dolphins tend to have friendly faces.
4. _F_ Botos do not develop their pink coloring until they are adults.
5. _O_ Because of their unusual coloring, botos are the most beautiful species of dolphin.
6. _O_ More should be done to help protect botos.
7. Name two threats to the safety of botos.
   Possible answers: fishermen's nets and pollution

Study Skills

Next to each topic below, write the letter you would use to find more information in an encyclopedia.

1. _D_ pink dolphins
2. _R_ rain forests
3. _A_ the Amazon River
4. _S_ South American rivers
5. _E_ endangered species

139

Page 141

Vocabulary Skills

Write the words from the passage that have the meanings below.

1. unable to be harmed
   invincible *Par. 1*
2. a large area of land
   landmass *Par. 3*
3. not originally from a particular place
   nonnative *Par. 4*
4. protect
   defend *Par. 6*

In each row, circle the word that does not belong.

5. damp   moist (dry) wet
6. cats (tortoises) rats goats
7. (destroy) save   protect   conserve

Reading Skills

1. Check the phrase that best describes the author's purpose.
   _✓_ to inform
   ___ to entertain
   ___ to instruct

Circle the word that best completes each sentence.

2. The eggs of the Galápagos tortoise are
   threatened by other animals.
   protected (threatened) ignored
3. Conservationists release the young tortoises when they can defend themselves.
   breed   feed (release)

4. The Galápagos Islands are located in a
   remote area.
   (remote) urban   new

Read the descriptions below. Write **S** next to the phrase if it describes the saddle-backed tortoise. Write **D** if it describes the domed tortoise.

5. _S_ lives on hotter, drier islands
6. _S_ has longer legs and neck
7. _D_ has a rounder shell
8. _D_ lives on wetter, cooler islands
9. Why did the crews of whaling ships capture the giant tortoises?
   so they could have fresh meat during long voyages at sea
10. What is the biggest threat to the survival of the Galápagos tortoise today?
    predators that eat the eggs and young tortoises

Study Skills

Write the name of the reference source you could use to answer each question below.

atlas	dictionary
encyclopedia	thesaurus

1. How are the different species of turtles similar and different?
   encyclopedia
2. How is the word *Galápagos* pronounced?
   dictionary
3. What is a synonym for *defend*?
   thesaurus
4. What country, other than Ecuador, are the Galápagos Islands closest to?
   atlas

141

Page 143

Vocabulary Skills

Write the words from the story that have the meanings below.

1. to express in another language
   translate *Par. 1*
2. imitated
   mimicked *Par. 3*
3. took hold of; grasped
   clasped *Par. 6*
4. said to be better than it really is
   overrated *Par. 13*

Compound words are divided into syllables between the two words that make the compound. For example, *play/ground*. Divide the words below into syllables using a slash (/).

5. b a c k / s e a t
6. s o m e / h o w
7. r e a r / v i e w
8. y o u r / s e l v e s

Reading Skills

1. What problem do the four cousins have at the beginning of the story?
   They do not speak the same language and they have to find a way to communicate.
2. How do they solve their problem?
   They act things out.
3. Why does David tell his dad that "language is way overrated"?
   He is excited that they have found other ways to communicate.

4. What does Elena try to explain to Luis about her skills as a runner?
   She tries to tell him that she is not a fast runner but she can run for long distances.
5. Why didn't Mrs. Rodriguez translate for the cousins?
   She said they would have to figure out a way to make themselves understood sooner or later.
6. Number the events below to show the order in which they happened.
   _4_ Luis gives Elena the thumbs-up sign.
   _1_ David asks his cousins if they play baseball.
   _5_ Mr. Rodriguez sets the table for dinner.
   _3_ Elena tells Luis that she is a runner, too.
   _2_ Mrs. Rodriguez decides not to translate.

Read the descriptions below. Write **E** next to the phrase if it describes Elena. Write **D** if it describes David. Write **B** if it describes both David and Elena.

7. _B_ don't speak much Spanish
8. _E_ is a good runner
9. _E_ says Luis is a fast runner

Study Skills

Use the pronunciation key on the inside back cover of this book to write the words that match these pronunciations.

1. /kə myū′ ni kāt′/ communicate
2. /kuz′ inz/ cousins
3. /stā shən/ station
4. /bē sīd′/ beside

143

Page 145

Vocabulary Skills

Write the words from the passage that have the meanings below.

1. to send from one place to another
   transmit *Par. 1*
2. created
   devised *Par. 3*
3. sudden progress
   breakthrough *Par. 4*
4. able to be used in many ways
   versatile *Par. 5*
5. something that gets in the way
   interference *Par. 6*
6. a shortened way to communicate something
   shorthand *Par. 6*

Read each word below. Then, write the letter of its antonym on the line beside the word.

7. _c_ transmit   a. different
8. _d_ weak   b. professional
9. _a_ common   c. receive
10. _b_ amateur   d. strong

The suffix **-ous** means *full of* or *having*. For example, *humorous* means *full of humor*. Write a word using **ous** to match each definition below. Then, write a sentence using each word.

11. full of joy joyous
    Answers will vary.
12. full of poison poisonous
    Answers will vary.

Reading Skills

Write **F** before the sentences that are facts. Write **O** before the sentences that are opinions.

1. _F_ Messages can be sent in Morse code using sound, light, and radio signals.
2. _F_ Morse code allows people who speak different languages to communicate.
3. _O_ More people should learn to use Morse code today.
4. _F_ On May 24, 1844, Morse and Vail sent their first long-distance message.
5. _O_ Morse code is a simple system to learn.
6. On the lines below, write the words *come see* in Morse code using the information from the selection.
   _·_·_ ___ ··· __·

Study Skills

Write the part of a book you would use to find the information to answer each question below.

table of contents	glossary
index	

1. On what page can you find information about Samuel Morse?
   index
2. What part of speech is the word *telegraph*?
   glossary
3. Which chapter explains how Morse code was invented?
   table of contents

145

Spectrum Reading Grade 5

Answer Key

169

Answer Key

Page 147

Vocabulary Skills

Write the words from the passage that have the meanings below.

1. guessed; calculated roughly
   estimated Par. 1

2. first in order of importance
   primary Par. 1

3. varieties of a language that change based on the group or part of the country
   dialects Par. 2

4. large areas
   regions Par. 3

5. saying out loud
   uttering Par. 4

6. What do the abbreviations *ASL* and *BSL* stand for?
   American Sign Language and British Sign Language

Write the idiom from paragraph 2 on the line next to its meaning.

7. do something quickly fly through the motions

Write S if the possessive word is singular. Write P if it is plural.

8. __S__ the girl's signs
9. __S__ the deaf community's identity
10. __P__ the dialects' differences

Reading Skills

1. What is fingerspelling?
   using the signs for individual letters to spell words

2. What are the four basic hand forms of ASL?
   hand shape, hand location, hand movement, and hand orientation

3. Why do some hearing people know and use sign language?
   so they can communicate with friends or family members who are deaf

4. Why do you think that sign language might be part of the cultural identity of being deaf?
   Possible answer: It is a skill that they share that not many other people have.

5. Why are ASL and BSL viewed as two separate languages?
   They contain as many differences as British English and American English do.

Write T before the sentences that are true. Write F before the sentences that are false.

6. __F__ Only deaf people use sign language.
7. __T__ Fingerspelling is slower than using other signs.
8. __F__ There is only one dialect of ASL.
9. __T__ Some signs may translate to an entire phrase or sentence.
10. __F__ About two million people in North America use ASL.

Study Skills

Use the key below to read the sentence in sign language. Then, write the sentence on the line.

1. I saw Will.

147

Page 149

Vocabulary Skills

Write the words from the story that have the meanings below.

1. unhappily; with discouragement
   gloomily Par. 1

2. not stiff or crisp
   limp Par. 2

3. vows or pledges to do something
   resolutions Par. 2

4. with strong positive feelings
   enthusiastically Par. 5

5. Find the pair of homophones in paragraph 1, and write them on the lines below.
   one   won

Find a homophone in the story for each word below.

6. duct   ducked Par. 3
7. our   hour Par. 4

Read each pair of words listed below. If the words are synonyms, write S on the line. If the words are antonyms, write A on the line.

9. __A__ empty   full
10. __S__ fantastic   wonderful
11. __S__ tossed   threw
12. __A__ won   lost

Reading Skills

1. Who is Casey?
   Nate's sister

2. Why do you think Nate wants to give skiing another try?
   because his family enjoys it; because he hasn't gone on a family ski trip in years

3. What bad habit does Sierra resolve to break?
   biting her nails

4. Check the words that describe Sierra.
   _✓_ supportive
   ___ timid
   _✓_ competitive
   _✓_ kind
   ___ nervous

5. **Hyperbole** is an exaggerated statement that is used to make a point. Find the hyperbole in paragraph 6, and write it on the line below.
   Casey always has a list a mile long.

Study Skills

Use the pie graph below to answer the questions that follow.

1. Which resolution was the most popular?
   get in shape

2. What percentage of people chose *learn a new skill*?
   13%

3. Which resolution received 32% of the votes?
   break a bad habit

149

Page 151

Vocabulary Skills

Write the words from the passage that have the meanings below.

1. good-bye
   farewell Par. 1

2. the length of a circle from one side to the other
   diameter Par. 3

3. approaching; next
   upcoming Par. 4

4. condition of being lucky and successful
   prosperity Par. 5

5. bad luck
   misfortunes Par. 5

Read each word or phrase below. Then, write the letter of its abbreviation in the space beside it.

6. __b__ post-meridian   **a.** Jan.
7. __e__ feet   **b.** P.M.
8. __a__ January   **c.** NY
9. __c__ New York   **d.** Dec.
10. __d__ December   **e.** ft.

Reading Skills

1. Check the line beside the word that best describes what type of selection this is.
   ___ fiction
   _✓_ informational
   ___ folktale

2. How do people celebrate New Year's Eve in Times Square?
   by watching the ball drop

3. Name two foods that people traditionally eat on New Year's Day.
   Possible answers: black-eyed peas, ham, cabbage, grapes, doughnuts, soba noodles, seafood, dumplings

4. Why does the Chinese New Year fall on a different day than the American New Year?
   It is based on the lunar calendar, not the Julian calendar.

Circle the word that best completes each sentence.

5. New Year's customs and traditions vary from country to country.
   (vary) decline exist

6. The foods people eat in celebration of the New Year often _symbolize_ their wishes for the coming year.
   cancel explain (symbolize)

7. Many people see the beginning of a new year as a time to make a _fresh_ start.
   special (fresh) careful

Study Skills

Join Us for a New Year's Eve Party!
When: December 31, 8:00 P.M.
Where: The DeJohns' House
        1548 Nicholson Ave.
Who: Bring your family, bring your friends!
We will provide snacks, noisemakers, and party hats.

1. Will the hosts provide food?
   They will provide snacks.

2. At which address will the party be held?
   1548 Nicholson Ave.

3. What time will the party begin?
   8:00 P.M.

151

Notes

Notes

Notes